EUCHOLOGY.

EUCHOLOGY

A MANUAL OF PRAYERS

OF THE

HOLY ORTHODOX CHURCH

DÓNE INTO ENGLISH

BY

G. V. SHANN.

AMS PRESS
NEW YORK

Reprinted from the edition of 1891, Kidderminster
First AMS EDITION published 1969
Manufactured in the United States of America

Library of Congress Catalogue Card Number: 75-82260

AMS PRESS, INC.
New York, N. Y. 10003

TO

THE VERY REVEREND,

THE ARCHPRIEST

EUGENE SMIRNOFF,

CHAPLAIN TO

THE IMPERIAL RUSSIAN EMBASSY

IN LONDON,

THIS EUCHOLOGY

IS GRATEFULLY INSCRIBED

BY THE TRANSLATOR.

PREFACE.

IT is purposed in the following pages to give the English Reader a brief but complete synopsis of the Daily Divine Worship of the Orthodox Church.

Much of that here given I have printed previously, in one form or another, at different periods and under various circumstances. In 1877 I issued privately a version of the All-Night-Vigil, and of the First, Third, and Sixth Hour Offices. In like manner in 1879 I brought out a small work, entitled Manual of Prayers, which contained the Devotions before and after Holy Communion, together with the Troparia &c. for the whole year, and sundry other matter.

And from time to time I have contributed to the pages of the *Orthodox Catholic Review* renderings of the Passion of the Lord, of the Easter Matins, and of the greater part of the Daily Office.

These intermittent and scattered labours are now collected, with additions, into one whole, and arranged in lucid order, with a few explanatory notes. Note 5 indicates the sources from which I have drawn in compiling the work, but it is fitting that I should especially mention how greatly I am indebted to Rajewsky's *Euchologion* for the admirable arrangement of the Daily Office, and to Neale's *Introduction* and Littledale's *Offices* for many very accurate renderings of the original.

Had the limits of the work permitted, I could have wished to have given the secret prayers of the Liturgies, notwithstanding that Neale's incomparable

translations of these are readily acces-
sible, and that the scope of this book
is principally that of a *Vade mecum*
for the laity; but I have had to content
myself with giving only the audible
parts, inserting in their proper places
in the Order of the Service the variable
Hymns &c. for Sundays and Week
Days and for the principal of the
Greater Festivals.

Now that the work is in type in its
present form I find here and there, owing
to the fact that the translations have
been made at intervals, some slightly
varying renderings of one and the same
original. For these, if they are faults,
and for any errors into which I may
have inadvertently fallen, I entreat the
forbearance of the Reader, trusting
only that the end purposed has been
attained, and that the endeavour to
make more widely known our Church's
ancient Worship may prove of some

small service towards furthering the union of all the Churches, for which we daily pray.

G. V. SHANN.

Hurcott Road, Kidderminster,
Epiphany, 1891.

NOTES.

NOTE I. ON THE ARRANGEMENT OF THE CHURCH, AND ON THE RITUAL.

An Orthodox Church is divided into three parts, namely, 1. The Sanctuary, for the Clergy. 2. The Nave, for the Faithful. 3. The Porch, for the Catechumens and the Penitents.

The Sanctuary, towards the east, is separated from the Nave, above which it is raised by steps, by a solid screen, called the Iconostas (*lit.* image-stand), pierced by three doorways, which are furnished with doors opening inwards, the centre ones being double, and called the Royal Gates. These latter are not solid throughout, but at the upper part are formed of open wood or metal work, and behind them hangs a curtain or veil, which is drawn and withdrawn as the ritual requires.

In the middle of the Sanctuary stands the Altar, vested, first, with a linen covering, and, over this, with one of rich brocade.

Behind the Altar stands a representation of the Crucifixion, and before this a taper or lamp stand with seven branches. A Ciborium stands upon the Altar, and, at all times, a Book of the Gospels and a Cross lie upon it. When the Ciborium contains the holy Sacrament, reserved for the communion of the sick or the absent, or for the Liturgy of the Pre-sanctified, a suspended lamp burns before it. At the Celebration of the Liturgy, a small cloth, containing Relics, called the Antimins, is spread upon the Altar, and upon this are placed the sacred vessels with their coverings or veils.

In the north of the Sanctuary is the Chapel of the Prothesis, where stands the Table of Oblations, also richly vested, upon which the sacred Gifts are prepared with significant rites before the beginning of the Liturgy. In the south of the Sanctuary is the Vestry. This and the Chapel of the Prothesis communicate with the Nave by the doors already mentioned as being in the Iconostas on either side of the Royal Gates.

The raised floor of the Sanctuary projects westward beyond the Iconostas into the Nave, and forms the part called the Soleas, where the Choir stands, and in the middle of which is the Ambo, where the Deacon says the Ectenias and reads the Gospel.

The Iconostas is adorned with representations of the Redeemer and of the Saints. In a panel on the right hand or south side of the Royal Gates there is always a representation of the Lord, and in a panel on the opposite side, one of the Mother of God. The most ancient examples of Iconostases are divided into three tiers. In the first and lowest of these are the representations of the Redeemer and of the Mother of God disposed as before mentioned, and in other panels those of the Saint to whom the Church is dedicated, of the Forerunner, of S. Nicolas, and of the Angels. In the second tier are depicted the Company of the holy Apostles, and in their midst an image of the Lord, with the Virgin and John the Baptist. In the third and highest tier appear the Company of holy Prophets, and in their midst an image of the Tokens of the Mother of God. Above the centre of the Iconostas is fixed a Cross, either standing alone, or flanked by representations of the Virgin and of John the Divine. On the Royal Gates are depicted the Annunciation and the holy Evangelists, and above them, the Last Supper, and on the north and south doors, the holy Archdeacons, or the holy Archangels.

The Porch in the ancient Church, was reserved for the Catechumens and the Penitents, but now is used for other purposes; for example, for Litanies in the Vigils of Great Festivals, for Prayers for the Departed, and for Baptisms; and in the Monasteries it is furnished with a table for Icons.

At the Service time the Priest and Deacon put on tunicles over their ordinary cassocks, and maniples upon their wrists. The Priest puts the Epitrachelion about his neck, and the Deacon the Orarion upon his left shoulder. The Priests' Epitrachelion is a broad strip of brocade hanging down before him, and is the token of his sacerdotal office. He puts on moreover a vestment or cope, called the Phelonion. The Deacon's Orarion is a long narrow scarf, hanging from his shoulder back and front, and is the emblem of his serving office. He holds the fore end of this in his fingers when saying the Ectenias, and binds the whole about his shoulders in the form of a cross during the time of the Communion. The Readers also are vested in tunicles.

The attitude at worship is standing. This is in accordance with a decree of the First Ecumenical Synod of Nicæa. Kneelings and prostrations are also practised, in the Great Fasts and at the Diptychs as directed by the rubric, and at other times according to individual choice. The worshippers make the

sign of the Cross on entering and leaving
the Church, at the more solemn moments
of the Service, and as devotion prompts.
This is done by joining the thumb and first
two fingers of the right hand, and touching
therewith, first, the forehead, next, the breast,
then, the right shoulder, and lastly, the left.

The normal position of the Priest is on
the west side of the Altar, facing the east,
and at the Celebration of the Liturgy the
details of the Consecration and of the Frac-
tion of the Host are not visible to the Congregation.

The holy Sacrament is consecrated in
leavened bread, and, in the preparation of
the holy Gifts at the Table of Oblations,
wine and water are poured into the Chalice.

In blessing the people, the Priest turns
towards them, and at all times gives the
blessing with the sign of the Cross.

Much incense is offered during Divine
Worship, the Sanctuary and the whole
Church being perfumed at the beginning of
the Service, and again and again repeatedly
at the more solemn acts of the Celebration,
such as the Introits, the Reading of the
Gospel, and after the Consecration.

Lamps and tapers burn about the Altar
and before the Icons and Shrines, and on
certain occasions, for example, at the Easter

Matins and during the reading of the Gospels of the Passion on Good Friday, all the worshippers hold lighted candles.

The Hymns &c. are sung, without instrumental accompaniment, in 8 Tones based upon the ancient classical modes, namely, the Dorian, Phrygian, Lydian, and Jonian for Tones 1 to 4, and the minors of these for Tones 5 to 8.

The Offices are usually recited at full length only in the Monasteries, but in the Parish Churches, with the exception of the Liturgy, with much abbreviation.

NOTE 2. ON THE BOOKS CONTAINING THE DIVINE SERVICE.

These may be classed under three heads, namely, 1. Those for the use of the Laity. 2. Those for the use of the Readers and the Choir. 3. Those for the use of the Clergy.

1. The principal Book for the use of the Laity is the *Molitvoslov* or *Euchology,* which is published both in large and small editions, and contains extracts, more or less complete, from the various other Service Books suitable to the needs of the Laity in their own homes or when assisting at the public worship of the Church. It is upon the scope of this Book that the present volume is based.

2. The Books for the use of the Readers
and the Choir are, the *Chasoslov* or *Horo-
logy*, the *Psalter*, the *Irmologion*, the *Octoëchos*, the *Menea*, the *Lenten Triodion*, and
the *Ferial Triodion* or *Pentecostarion*. The
Chasoslov contains the Daily Offices of
Vespers, Compline, Nocturns, Matins, and
Hours, with some of the more frequently
used Commemorations, such, for example,
as the Troparia for Sundays and Week
Days, and other matter. The *Psalter*, in
its smaller edition, contains the Psalms of
David divided into the 20 Kathisms, the
Magnifyings with selected verses for Festivals,
the 9 Scriptural Odes, and the Diptychs. In
its larger edition, it contains moreover all
that is found in the *Chasoslov*, together with
many other devotions, such as the Prayers
before and after Holy Communion, a Service for Sunday and one for every other
day of the Week, &c. The *Irmologion* contains those parts of the Service that are
usually sung by the Choir, and notably the
Irmi of the Canons, whence its name. The
Octoëchos, the *Menea*, and the *Triodia* are
Books containing exclusively ecclesiastical
compositions, namely, the Canons, Stichera,
Troparia &c. that make up the Commemorations for the whole year. They are used
concurrently. The *Octoëchos*, or Book of

b

8 Tones, contains Commemorations for 8 weeks:
on Mondays, of the Angels; on Tuesdays, of
the Forerunner; on Wednesdays, of the
Mother of God; on Thursdays, of the Apostles
and of S. Nicolas; on Fridays, of the Cross;
on Saturdays, of All Saints and of the
Departed; and on Sundays, of the Resurrection.
The rule is to begin this Book on the Monday following the Sunday of All Saints, which
is the First Sunday after Pentecost, and in
this week the Canons &c. in Tone 1 are
sung, in the next week those in Tone 2,
and so on, and when 8 weeks have elapsed
Tone 1 is sung again, this order, with a few
exceptions, being repeated throughout the
year. The *Menea* contains the Canons &c.
for the whole year according to the days of
the month. It is published in two forms,
1. As a work of 12 volumes, one for every
month. 2. As a work of 2 volumes, one
containing the Canons &c. for the Greater
Festivals, and the other, those common for
the Saints. The *Lenten Triodion* contains
the penitential Commemorations from the
Sunday of the Publican and Pharisee, which
is the Sunday preceding that of Septua-
gesima, until Easter Eve; and the *Ferial
Triodion*, the joyful ones from Easter Day
until the Sunday of All Saints.

    3. The Books for the use of the Clergy

are the *Sloujébnik* and the *Trébnik*. The
Sloujébnik (*lit.* Service Book) contains the
Prayers, audible and secret, of the Priest and
Deacon at Vespers, Matins, and the Liturgies. The *Trébnik* (*lit.* Ritual) contains, in
its smaller form, the rest of the Sacraments
affecting the Laity other than the Eucharist,
and, in addition, the Churching of Women,
the Visitation and Communion of the Sick,
the Burial of the Dead, the Santification of
Water on the Day of the Epiphany, and other
matter; and, in its larger form, besides the
fore-mentioned, the Ordinal, the Professing of
Monks, the Consecration of Churches, &c.

There are moreover the Book of the
Gospels and the Book of the Epistles, which,
in the public worship, are used, the former
by the Deacon, and the latter by the Reader.

NOTE 3. ON SOME UNTRANSLATABLE TERMS.

Acathist. A term applied to certain hymns
during the singing of which sitting is pro-
hibited.

Condakion. A term the origin of which
is uncertain. It is itself a verse which ex-
presses briefly the purport of the whole
Commemoration of any given Festival or
occasion. Its proper place in ecclesiastical
composition is after the Sixth Ode in a
Canon, and it is usually followed by another

b*

verse called *Icos*, a word corresponding with
the anglicized italian word, *Stanza*.

Ectenia. A term applied to the Suffrages,
because of their *protracted* character.

Exapostilarion. A verse preceding the
Psalms of Praise at Matins, sung by one of
the clergy who is *sent out* of his place into
the middle of the Church to sing it.

Hypacoë. A term implying that the verse
bearing its name should be *listened to* with
particular attention.

Irmos. A verse that is the rhythmical
model of others that follow it. Every Ode
in a Canon is preceded by such a verse,
which may, or may not, form an integral
part of the particular theme of the Ode.
See the Canon for Easter where the *Irmi*
do, and the Canon for Holy Communion
where they do not form such parts of their
respective Odes. The *Irmi* in a Canon are
the verses usually sung, while those that
follow them may be read, or even omitted.

Katavasia. A verse sung at the conclusion
of an Ode, frequently the Irmos of that
Ode, when the Choirs *descend* from their
places in the stalls into the middle of the
Church to sing it.

Kathism. A term applied to certain lections and chants, principally of the Psalter,
during which the people may *sit*.

Prokimenon. A verse preceding (*lit.* lying before) the Lections from the holy Scriptures.

Stichera. A series of *verses*, usually ecclesiastically composed ones.

Troparion. A verse that is composed (*lit.* turns) upon a rhythmical model. It has however come to have a wider meaning, and, like Condakion (q. v.), or, together with this, serves briefly to commemorate any given occasion.

These terms are all of Greek origin, and are also used in Slavonic without translation.

NOTE 4. EXPLANATION OF RUBRICS ETC.

A. The Prefatory Psalm. Page 2.

The Office of Vespers is always begun with this Psalm for the reason that it recounts the wonders of Creation, and is therefore a fitting beginning for the complete performance of a day's Divine Worship, which, commencing with Vespers, concludes with the celebration of Liturgy, in which the great act of Redemption is shewn forth.

B. The First Antiphon of the Psalter. Page 4.

This is an abbreviation of the 1st Stasis of the 1st Kathism of the Psalter. Vide Chap. XXVII.

C. The "Lord, I have cried". Page 5.

This is the proper Vesper Psalm. Its selection is obvious from the expression of the second verse, "Let my prayer be set forth before thee as incense, the lifting up of my hands as the evening sacrifice". Other appropriate Psalms recording prophetically the descent of the Redeemer into hades on the evening of the day after his Passion are subjoined. With the verses of these Psalms are interspersed proper verses (Stichera) commemorative of the occasion. It is however only in the Monasteries that the Psalms and Stichera are recited and sung at length. In the Parish Churches it is customary to sing only the first two verses of the "Lord I have cried", and to add two Stichera, with *Glory. Both now,* between these. Vide the selections for the Sundays of Palms and Pentecost at pages 272 and 411. In the Service for a Sunday in Tone 6, and in the Penitential Service to the Lord (Chapters XVII and XVIII) a fuller number of Stichera is given; and for Holy and Great Saturday, at page 362, the special Stichera for that day are conjoined with those on the Resurrection, thus illustrating the manner in which the *Lenten Triodion* is used concurrently with the *Octoëchos.* It may here be remarked that the Stichera for Sundays in Tones 1 and 2 are found respectively at pages 362—4 and 400—402, thus supplying, in this work, commemorations of the Resurrection in three of the Eight Tones in which these Stichera are sung with the "Lord, I have cried".

D. The Evening Hymn to the Son of God. Page 8.

This is the proper Vesper Hymn of the Church. It is designated throughout this work, "The Tranquil Light", and is said to be the composition of the Martyr Athenogenes, A. D. 296.

E. The Prokimenon. Page 9.

This, as explained at page XXI, is a verse preceding Lections from the Scriptures. Here, though the singing of the Prokimenon is retained, the Lections, excepting on the Eves of Great Festivals, have fallen into disuse. When used their number varies, but it is generally three; for example, those for the Eves of the Sundays of Palms and Pentecost are respectively,

Of Palms.	Of Pentecost.
1. Gen. XLIX. 1, 2, 8—12.	1. Num. XI. 16, 17, 24—29.
2. Soph. III. 14—19.	2. Joel II. 23—32.
3. Zach. IX. 9—15.	3. Ezek. XXXVI. 24—28.

On Easter Eve there are no less than fifteen Lections. Vide page 365, et seq.

F. The Stichera according to the day. Page 13.

These are verses in which the occasion of the day is further commemorated. In the Monasteries the singing of them on the Eve of a Great Festival is preceded by a procession of the Priest, Deacon and Choir, carrying burning tapers, into the Porch, where a Litany is sung, and is followed by a rite performed in the Nave, called, The Benediction of the Loaves. This rite is described in detail by Dr. Neale in his "Introduction".

G. The "Many mercies". Page 24.

The abbreviated form here given is that used in the Parish Churches. The "Many mercies" is sung on Sundays when the "Blessed are they that are undefiled". (Kathism 17) is not appointed to be read (Vide the Table on pages 478 and 479), and also on the Festivals printed in the Kalendar in capitals and italics.

H. The Gradual. Page 27.

This is the 1st Antiphon of the Graduals in Tone 4. The Graduals are common to all the Tones. For those in Tone 6 vide page 185.

I. The Canon. Page 33.

A brief indication of the composition of this is given in a foot note, but it may be well to remark that the Canon is, as the name implies, the ruling feature of all Commemorations. Every day throughout the year is provided with one or more, though, excepting in the Monasteries, they are not recited in full, their Irmi and Condakia, or even the Condakia alone, sufficing for their whole.

J. The Psalms of Praise. Page 36.

To the singing of the verses of these with the conjoined Stichera the same remarks apply as to the "Lord, I have cried".

K. The Great Canon of S. Andrew of Crete. Page 62.

For the Irmi of this vide page 267, et seq.

L. Antiphons etc. Chap. XV.

Antiphons, Introits, Prokimena, Irmi of Odes IX, Communion Hymns, &c. not given in this Chap. will be found in Chap. XXIV.

M. Diptychs. Chap. XXVI.

This, though found in the Psalter, is rather a private than a public devotion. It may however be very fittingly used by a Christian on any occasion as opportunity serves.

N. The Kalendar. Chap. XXIX.

The arrangement of the Commemorations varies slightly in different Service Books, and even in different editions of the same Book. The arrangement here given is taken from an edition of the *Molitvoslov* published at Kiev in the reign of the Empress Elizabeth.

NOTE 5. LIST OF BOOKS CONSULTED IN COMPILING THIS WORK.

Ἀπόστολος. — ἐν Βενετίᾳ, 1866.

The Holy Bible. — English authorized version.

The Holy Bible. — Translated from the Latin Vulgate. — London.

The Book of Common Prayer of the Church of England.

Св. Евангеліе. — Москва, изд. 1885 и 1889.

Εὐχολόγιον τὸ μέγα. — ἐν Βενετίᾳ, 1862.

Euchologion der orthodox-catholischen Kirche, von M. Rajewsky. — Wien, 1861—62.

A History of the Holy Eastern Church, General Introduction, by Dr. J. M. Neale. — London, 1850.

Ирмологъ. — Москва, 1877.

The Divine and Sacred Liturgies of our Fathers among the Saints, John Chrysostom and Basil the Great, by J. N. W. B. Robertson. — London, 1886.

The Divine Liturgy of our Father among the Saints, John Chrysostom. — London, 1866.

The Divine Liturgies of our holy Fathers, John the Goldenmouthed (S. Chrysostom) and Basil the Great. — London, 1865.

Die göttlichen Liturgieen unserer heiligen Väter, Johannes Chrysostomos, Basilios des Grossen, und Gregorios Dialogos, von Alexios Maltzew. — Berlin, 1890.

Manuel de Prières à l'usage des Chrétiens de l'église orthodoxe catholique d'Orient, par J. Wassilieff. — Paris 1862.

Manuscript translations of the All-Night Vigil, the Office for Holy Communion, the Passion

of the Lord, the Easter Matins, and many
of the Troparia and Condakia for various
occasions, by the late Reverend Basil
Popoff, Chaplain to the Imperial Russian
Embassy in London, circa 1875.

Молитвословъ. — Санктпетербургъ, 1879.
    — Кіевъ, circa 1760.

Сокращенный Молитвословъ. — Санктпетербургъ, 1873.

The New Testament. — Revised English
version. — Oxford, 1881.

Новый Завѣтъ. — Кіевъ, 1880.

Сокращенный Обиходъ Нотнаго Пѣнія. —
Москва, 1863.

Office for the Lord's Day, as prescribed by
the Orthodox Greek Church. — London, 1880.

Offices from the Service Books of the Holy
Eastern Church, by Dr. R. F. Littledale.
— London, 1863.

Ὀκτώηχος. — ἐν Βενετίᾳ, 1865.

The Oriental Church Magazine. — The
Nocturnal Service. — New-York, 1879.

Ἡ Παλαιὰ Διαθήκη κατὰ τοὺς Ἑβδομή-
κοντα. — Londini.

Псалтирь малая. — Кіевъ, circa 1817.

The Rites and Ceremonies of the Greek Church
in Russia, by Dr. J. G. King. — London, 1772.

The Septuagint Version of the Old Testament
in English, by Sir Lancelot Charles Lee
Brenton, Bart. — London, 1844.

Служебникъ. — Санктпетербургъ, 1867.

Σύνοψις ἱερά. — ἐν Κωνσταντινουπόλει, 1877.

Тріодь постная. — Москва, 1745.

Кратное Ученіе о святомъ храмѣ, свя-
щенно-церковно-служителяхъ, богослу-
женіи и богослужебныхъ книгахъ пра-
вославной Русской Церкви. — Санктпетербургъ, 1863.

Часословъ. — Санктпетербургъ, 1867.

Ὡρολόγιον τὸ μέγα. — ἐν Βενετίᾳ, 1868.

———◄►———

ERRATA.

Page 4, line 2, *for* siek, *read* sick.

„ 8, „ 14, *for* plenteons, *read* plenteous.

„ 12, „ 29, *for* he, *read* be.

„ 22, „ 26, *for* desolute, *read* desolate.

„ 31, „ 22, *for* And repeateth, *read And repeateth.*

„ 43, „ 12, *for* occassion, read *occasion.*

„ 47, „ 18, *for* Thee, *read* Thou.

„ 48, „ 7, *for* became, *read* become.

„ „ „ 8, *omit the word,* whom.

„ 55, „ 11, *for Vīde, read Vide.*

„ 65, „ 25, *for* come, *read* came.

„ 91, „ 25, *for* strenghtened, *read* strength-ened.

„ 103, „ 15, *for* o, *read* on.

„ 115, „ 24, *for* God-head, *read* Godhead.

„ 132, „ 15, *after the word, substituted, add the words, on Week Days.*

„ 134, „ 6, *for* be, *read* he.

„ 145, „ 12, *for* hand-maiden, *read* handmaid-en.

„ 148, „ 16, *for* hand-maid, *read* handmaid.

„ 208, „ 19, *for* ceas—, *read* cease—.

„ 216, „ 10, *for* salvaton, *read* salvation.

„ 242, „ 17, *for* jugdment, *read* judgment.

„ 322, „ 8, *for* aquaintance, *read* acquaint-ance.

„ 349, lines 20 and 21, *for* hy, *read* by.

„ 355, line 20, *for* annointed, *read* anointed.

„ 380, „ 2, *for wax, read* wax.

„ 466, „ 1, *for* fcr, *read* for.

There are a few other trifling obvious errors, principally in the punctuation, owing to the distance from the press at which the proofs were corrected.

CONTENTS.

I was glad when they said
unto me, We will go into the
house of the Lord.

Psalm 121 (122).

I. THE ALL-NIGHT VIGIL

AS HELD ON THE EVE OF A FESTIVAL WHEN
THE GREAT VESPERS AND THE GREAT MATINS
ARE CONJOINED.

———⊷◦⊶———

THE GREAT VESPERS.

*When the time for the Service is come the
Warden lighteth the lamps and tapers, and
the Priest and Deacon put on their vestments.
And the Priest taketh the censer, and, accompanied by the Deacon bearing a lighted taper,
he censeth the Altar.*

And the Deacon beginneth,

RISE! Master, give the blessing.
The Priest saith,
GLORY to the holy, consubstantial,
life-giving and undivided Trinity, always,
now and ever, and to ages of ages.

And the Choir answereth, Amen.

Then saith the Priest,

O COME, let us worship God our King.

O come, let us worship and fall down before Christ God, our King.

O come, let us worship and fall down before Christ himself, our God and King.

And then he censeth the whole Church and the Congregation. And the Choir singeth the Prefatory .Psalm, namely, Psalm 103 (104), *which is usually abbreviated as followeth,*

BLESS the Lord, O my soul: blessed art thou, O Lord.

O Lord my God, thou art very great: blessed art thou, O Lord.

Thou art clothed with honour and majesty: blessed art thou, O Lord.

Above the hills the waters stand: marvellous are thy works, O Lord.

Between the hills the waters flow: marvellous are thy works, O Lord.

In wisdom hast thou made them all: Creator of all things, glory to thee.

Glory to the Father, and to the Son, and to the Holy Ghost. Creator of all things, glory to thee.

Both now, and ever, and to ages of ages. Amen. Creator of all things, glory to thee.

Then followeth the Ectenia of Peace.

Deacon. In peace let us pray to the Lord.

Choir. Lord, have mercy. *And so after the succeeding petitions.*

Deacon. For the peace that is from above, and for the salvation of our souls, let us pray to the Lord.

For the peace of the whole world, the good estate of the holy Churches of God. and for the union of them all, let us pray to the Lord.

For this holy Church, and for them that with faith, piety and fear of God enter into it, let us pray to the Lord.

For the most holy governing Synod (*or, For our Metropolitan N., as so subject*), for the honourable Presbytery, the Diaconate in Christ, for all the clergy and the laity, let us pray to the Lord.

Here follow petitions for the Sovereign and the other members of the Reigning House, mentioning them by name.

To aid them in battle and to put down under their feet every enemy and adversary, let us pray to the Lord.

For this city (*or, if it is a Monastery,* For this holy Habitation), for every city and country, and for the faithful dwelling in them, let us pray to the Lord.

For healthiness of weather, plentifulness of the fruits of the earth and for peaceful times, let us pray to the Lord.

For them that are at sea, for travellers, for the sick, for them that are in bonds and captivity, and for their salvation, let us pray to the Lord.

For our deliverance from all affliction, passion and want, let us pray to the Lord.

Help us, save us, have mercy on us, and keep us, O God, by thy grace.

Commemorating our most holy, most pure, most blessed glorious Lady, the God-bearing ever-virgin Mary, together with all the Saints, let us commend ourselves, and one another, and all our life to Christ our God.

Choir. To thee, O Lord. *Exclamation.*

Priest. For to thee are due all glory, honour and worship, to the Father, and to the Son, and to the Holy Ghost, now and ever, and to ages of ages. *Choir.* Amen.

Then is sung the First Antiphon of the Psalter on this wise:

BLESSED is the man that walketh not in the counsel of the ungodly.

The way of the ungodly shall perish.

Serve the Lord with fear, and rejoice before him with trembling.

Blessed are they that put their trust in him.

Arise, O Lord: save me, O my God.

Thy blessing is upon thy people.

Glory. Both now.

And after every verse, Alleluia, *thrice. Then,*
Alleluia, alleluia, alleluia, glory to thee,
O God, *thrice.*

Then followeth the Little Ectenia.

Deacon. Again and again in peace let us
pray to the Lord.

Choir. Lord, have mercy.

Deacon. Help us, save us, have mercy on
us, and keep us, O God, by thy grace.

Choir. Lord, have mercy.

Deacon. Commemorating our most holy,
most pure, most blessed glorious Lady, the
God-bearing ever-virgin Mary, together with
all the Saints, let us commend ourselves, and
one another, and all our life to Christ our
God.

Choir. To thee, O Lord. *Exclamation.*

Priest. For thine is the strength and thine
is the kingdom, the power and the glory, of
the Father, and of the Son, and of the Holy
Ghost, now and ever, and to ages of ages.

Choir. Amen. *And singeth the* Lord, I
have cried *in the proper Tone.*

LORD, I HAVE CRIED.

LORD, I have cried unto thee, hear me.
Hear me, O Lord.
Lord, I have cried unto thee, hear

me: attend to the voice of my prayer when I cry unto thee.

Hear me, O Lord.

Let my prayer be set forth before thee as incense, the lifting up of my hands as the evening sacrifice.

Hear me, O Lord.

The ensuing verses are usually read.

Set a watch, O Lord, before my mouth, and a door of defence about my lips.

Incline not my heart to evil words to make excuses for sins.

With men that work transgression, and I will not unite with their chosen ones.

The righteous shall chasten me in mercy and reprove me, but let not the oil of the sinner anoint my head.

For my prayer also is still by their good-will: their judges have been swallowed up in stony places.

They shall hear my words, for they have been strong: as a clod of earth is crushed upon the earth, their bones have been scattered beside hades.

For mine eyes look unto thee, O Lord: O Lord, in thee is my trust, O cast not out my soul.

Keep me from the snare which they have laid for me, and from the traps of the wicked doers.

Sinners shall fall into their own net together: I am as one alone until I pass away.

I have cried unto the Lòrd with my voice, with my voice unto the Lord did I make my prayer.

I will pour out my prayer before him, I will declare before him mine affliction.

When my spirit went forth from me, then thou knewest my paths.

In the way wherein I walked they hid a snare for me.

I looked on my right hand and beheld, and there was none that knew me.

Refuge failed me, and there was no one caring for my soul.

I have cried unto thee, O Lord: I have said, Thou art my trust, my portion in the land of the living.

Attend unto my prayer, for I am brought low exceedingly.

Deliver me from them that persecute me, for they are stronger than I.

Here beginneth the singing of the Stichera, if there are 10 *appointed.*

Bring my soul out of prison, that I may give thanks unto thy name.

The righteous wait for me until thou reward me.   *Here, if* 8.

Out of the depths have I cried unto thee O Lord, O Lord, hear my voice.

O let thine ears be attentive unto the voice of my prayer.

Here, if 6.

If thou, O Lord, shouldest mark transgression, O Lord, who should stand? But with thee there is propitiation.

For thy name's sake have I waited for thee, O Lord: my soul hath waited for thy word, my soul hath trusted in the Lord.

Here, if 4.

From the morning watch until night, from the morning watch let Israel trust in the Lord.

For with the Lord is mercy, and with him is plenteons redemption, and he shall redeem Israel from all his transgressions.

Praise the Lord, all ye nations, praise him, all ye peoples.

For his mercy is confirmed upon us, and the truth of the Lord remaineth for ever.

Glory. Both now.

When the singing of the Stichera is ended the Deacon saith with a loud voice,

Wisdom! Stand up!

And the Introit is made. And the Choir singeth the Evening Hymn to the Son of God.

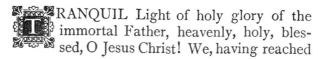RANQUIL Light of holy glory of the immortal Father, heavenly, holy, blessed, O Jesus Christ! We, having reached

the setting sun, seeing the evening light, sing Father, Son, and Holy Spirit, God. Worthy art thou at all times to be sung with reverent voices, Son of God, Life-giver. Wherefore the world doth glorify thee.

This being ended, the Deacon saith, Let us attend. *Priest.* Peace to all. *Choir.* And to thy spirit. *Deacon.* Wisdom! Let us attend. *Reader.* Prokimenon!

Here followeth the Prokimenon.

On Saturday Evening. The Lord is king: he hath put on glorious apparel.

Verse. The Lord hath put on might and hath girded himself.

On Sunday Evening. Behold now bless the Lord, all ye servants of the Lord.

Verse. Ye that stand in the house of the Lord, in the courts of the house of our God.

On Monday Evening. The Lord will hear me when I call upon him.

Verse. Hear me when I call, O God of my righteousness.

On Tuesday Evening. Thy mercy, O Lord, shall follow me all the days of my life.

Verse. The Lord is my shepherd, therefore shall I lack nothing: he shall feed me in a green pasture.

On Wednesday Evening. Save me, O God, for thy name's sake, and avenge me in thy strength.

Verse. Hear my prayer, O God, hearken unto the words of my mouth.

On Thursday Evening. My help is from the Lord, who hath made heaven and earth.

Verse. I have lifted up mine eyes to the hills, whence cometh my help.

On Friday Evening. God is my defence, the God of my mercy shall prevent me.

Verse. Deliver me from mine enemies, O God, defend me from them that rise up against me.

After the Prokimenon are read the Lections from the Old Testament, if any are appointed.

Then followeth the Great Ectenia.

Deacon. Let us all say with our whole soul, and with our whole mind let us say,

Choir. Lord, have mercy.

Deacon. O Lord almighty, God of our fathers, we pray thee, hear and have mercy.

Choir. Lord, have mercy.

Deacon. Have mercy on us, O God, according to thy great mercy, we pray thee, hear and have mercy.

Choir. Lord, have mercy, *thrice. And so after the succeeding petitions, those immediately following being for the Sovereign and the other members of the Reigning House, mentioning them by name.*

Again let us pray for the most holy Governing Synod (*If subject to a Metropolitan,* Again let us pray for our Metropolitan *N.*), and for all our brotherhood in Christ.

Again let us pray for all their Christ-loving army.

Again let us pray for the blessed and ever memorable founders of this holy (Church, *or*) Habitation, and for all our right-believing fathers and brethren that have fallen asleep before us(that rest here and in every other place).

Again let us pray for mercy, life, peace, health, salvation, protection, forgiveness and remission of sins for the servants of God, the brethren of this holy Habitation. (*Or*, the servants of God here present and praying unto thee).

Again let us pray for them that bring forth fruit and do good works in this holy and all venerable Church, serving and singing in it, and for all the people standing about, expecting from thee great and rich mercy.

Exclamation.

Priest. For a merciful and man-loving God thou art, and we ascribe glory to thee, to the Father, and to the Son, and to the Holy Ghost, now and ever, and to ages of ages.

Choir. Amen.

Then is read the following Prayer.

VOUCHSAFE, O Lord, to keep us this evening without sin. Blessed art thou, O Lord God of our fathers, and blessed and hallowed is thy name to ages. Amen. O Lord, let thy mercy lighten upon us, like as we have put our trust in thee. Blessed art thou, O Lord: O teach me thy statutes. Blessed art thou, O Master: make me to understand thy statutes. Blessed art thou, O Holy One: enlighten me with thy statutes. O Lord, thy mercy endureth for ever: despise not thou the works of thine own hands. To thee is due praise, to thee is due a hymn, to thee is due glory, Father, Son, and Holy Ghost, now and ever, and to ages of ages. Amen.

Then the Ectenia of Supplication.

Deacon. Let us accomplish our evening prayer to the Lord. *Choir.* Lord, have mercy.

Deacon. Help us, save us, have mercy on us and keep us, O God, by thy grace.

Choir. Lord, have mercy.

Deacon. That the whole evening may be perfect, holy, peaceful and sinless, let us ask of the Lord. *Choir.* Vouchsafe, O Lord. *And so after the succeeding petitions.*

Deacon. An Angel of peace, a faithful guide, a guardian of our souls and bodies, let us ask of the Lord.

Pardon and remission of our sins and of our transgressions, let us ask of the Lord.

What is good and profitable for our souls, and peace for the world, let us ask of the Lord.

That the remaining time of our life may he spent in peace and repentance, let us ask of the Lord.

A Christian end to our life, without pain and shame, peaceful, and a good confession before the terrible judgment-seat of Christ let us ask.

Commemorating our most holy, most pure, most blessed glorious Lady, the God-bearing ever-virgin Mary, together with all the Saints, let us commend ourselves and one another, and all our life to Christ our God.

Choir. To thee, O Lord. *Exclamation.*

Priest. For a good and man-loving God thou art, and we ascribe glory to thee, to the Father, and to the Son, and to the Holy Ghost, now and ever, and to ages of ages. *Choir.* Amen.

Priest. Peace to all. *Choir.* And to thy spirit.

Deacon. Let us bow our heads to the Lord. *Choir.* To thee, O Lord. *Exclamation.*

Priest. Blessed and glorified be the might of thy kingdom, of the Father, and of the Son, and of the Holy Ghost, now and ever, and to ages of ages.

Choir. Amen. *And singeth the Stichera according to the day.*

Then is read the Prayer of S. Simeon.

LORD, now lettest thou thy servant depart in peace according to thy word. For mine eyes have seen thy salvation, which thou hast prepared before the face of all people, to be a light to lighten the gentiles and to be the glory of thy people Israel. *Then,*

HOLY God, Holy Mighty One, Holy Immortal One, have mercy upon us, *thrice.*
Glory. Both now.

O MOST Holy Trinity, have mercy upon us. O Lord, cleanse our sins. O Master, forgive our transgressions. Visit us, O Holy One, and heal our infirmities, for thy name's sake. Lord, have mercy, *thrice.*

Glory. Both now.

OUR Father, which art in heaven. Hallowed be thy name. Thy kingdom come. Thy will be done on earth, as it is in heaven. Give us this day our daily bread. And forgive us our trespasses, as we forgive them that trespass against us. And lead us not into temptation. But deliver us from evil.

Priest. For thine is the kingdom, the power and the glory, of the Father, and of the Son, and of the Holy Ghost, now and ever, and to ages of ages.

Choir. Amen. *And continueth,*

HAIL! Virgin Mother of God. O Mary, full of grace, the Lord is with thee. Blessed art thou among women, and blessed is the fruit of thy womb; for thou hast borne the Saviour of our souls.

Otherwise the proper Troparion of the Day is sung.

They sing also,

BLESSED be the name of the Lord from henceforth, and to all ages, *thrice.*

Then is read Psalm 33 (34).

I WILL bless the Lord at all times, his praise shall continually be in my mouth. My soul shall make her boast in the Lord, the humble shall hear thereof and be glad. O magnify the Lord with me, and let us exalt his name together. I sought the Lord, and he heard me, and delivered me from all my fears. Ye came unto him and were enlightened, and your faces were not ashamed. This poor man cried, and the Lord heard him, and saved him out of all his afflictions. The Angel of the Lord shall encamp round about them that fear him, and shall deliver them. O taste and see that the Lord is good: blessed is the man that trusteth in him. O fear the Lord, all ye his saints, for there is no want to them that fear him. The rich do lack and suffer hunger, but they that seek the Lord shall not want any good thing.

Priest. The blessing of the Lord, by his own divine grace and love to man, be upon you always, now and ever, and to ages of ages.

Choir. Amen.

And now immediately followeth the Great Matins, the Reader beginning forthwith to read the Six Psalms.

THE GREAT MATINS.

THE SIX PSALMS.

G LORY to God in the highest, and on earth peace, goodwill towards men, *thrice.*

O Lord, open thou my lips, and my mouth shall shew forth thy praise, *twice.*

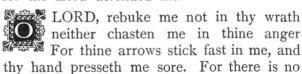 ORD, why are they that afflict me multiplied? many are they that rise up against me. Many one there be that say of my soul, There is no salvation for him in his God. But thou, O Lord, art my defender, my glory and the lifter up of my head. I cried unto the Lord with my voice, and he heard me out of his holy hill. I laid me down and slept: I rose up again, for the Lord defended me. I will not be afraid for ten thousands of people that have set themselves against me round about. Arise, O Lord, save me, O my God. For thou hast smitten all that without cause are mine enemies, thou hast broken the teeth of sinners. Salvation belongeth unto the Lord, and thy blessing is upon thy people.

I laid me down and slept: I rose up again, for the Lord defended me.

LORD, rebuke me not in thy wrath neither chasten me in thine anger For thine arrows stick fast in me, and thy hand presseth me sore. For there is no

health in my flesh because of thine anger,
neither is there any rest in my bones by
reason of my sins. For my transgressions
have gone over my head, as a heavy burden
they are heavy upon me. My wounds have
become noisome and corrupt because of my
foolishness. I am wretched and bowed down
continually, I go mourning all the day long.
For my loins are filled with illusions, and
there is no health in my flesh. I have been
wrought evil and humbled exceedingly, I have
cried bitterly, because of the groaning of my
heart. Lord, all my desire is before thee,
and my groaning is not hidden from thee.
My heart is troubled, my strength hath failed me, and the light of mine eyes, it also
is gone from me. My friends and my neighbours drew near and stood against me, and
my nearest of kin stood afar off. And they
that sought my soul used violence, and they
that sought my hurt spake vanities and imagined deceits all the day long. But I, as a
deaf man, heard not, and I was as a dumb
man that openeth not his mouth. And I
became as a man that heareth not, and in
whose mouth are no reproofs. For in thee,
O Lord, have I trusted, thou wilt hear me,
O Lord my God. For I said, Lest at any
time mine enemies rejoice against me, and
when my feet slipped they spake great things

against me. For I am ready for scourges, and my grief is continually before me. For I will confess my transgression, and be sorry for my sin. But mine enemies live and are mightier than I, and they that hate me wrongfully are multiplied. They that render me evil for good slandered me, because I followed goodness. Forsake me not, O Lord, my God, be not thou far from me. Attend unto my help, O Lord of my salvation.

Forsake me not, O Lord my God, be not thou far from me. Attend unto my help, O Lord of my salvation.

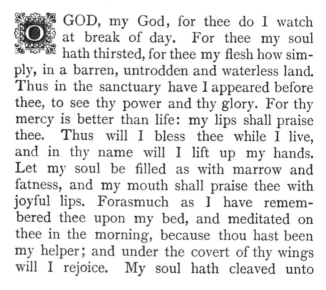 GOD, my God, for thee do I watch at break of day. For thee my soul hath thirsted, for thee my flesh how simply, in a barren, untrodden and waterless land. Thus in the sanctuary have I appeared before thee, to see thy power and thy glory. For thy mercy is better than life: my lips shall praise thee. Thus will I bless thee while I live, and in thy name will I lift up my hands. Let my soul be filled as with marrow and fatness, and my mouth shall praise thee with joyful lips. Forasmuch as I have remembered thee upon my bed, and meditated on thee in the morning, because thou hast been my helper; and under the covert of thy wings will I rejoice. My soul hath cleaved unto

thee, and thy right hand hath upholden me. But they that vainly sought after my soul, they shall go into the lowest parts of the earth. They shall be delivered up to the hand of the sword, they shall be portions for foxes. But the king shall rejoice in God: every one that sweareth by him shall be commended, for the mouth of them that speak unjustly shall be stopped.

I have meditated on thee in the morning, because thou hast been my helper, and under the covert of thy wings will I rejoice. My soul hath cleaved unto thee, and thy right hand hath upholden me.

Glory. Both now. Alleluia, alleluia, alleluia, glory to thee, O God, *thrice.* Lord, have mercy, *thrice. Glory. Both now.*

O LORD God of my salvation, I have cried day and night before thee. O let my prayer come in before thee, incline thine ear to my petition. For my soul is full of trouble, and my life draweth nigh to hades. I am counted among them that go down to the pit: I am as a man without help, free among the dead. Like the slain sleeping in the grave, whom thou rememberest no more, and they are cut away from thy hand. They laid me in the lowest pit, in darkness and in the shadow of death. Thy

2*

wrath hath pressed heavily upon me, and all thy waves thou hast brought in upon me. Thou hast put mine acquaintance far from me, they have made me an abomination to themselves. I was delivered up and came not forth, mine eyes were dimmed through poverty. I cried unto thee, O Lord, all the day long, I stretched forth my hands unto thee. Wilt thou work wonders for the dead? or shall physicians raise them up, and they confess thee? Shall any one declare thy mercy in the grave, and thy truth in destruction? Shall thy wonders be known in the darkness, and thy righteousness in the land of forgetfulness? But unto thee have I cried, O Lord, and in the morning shall my prayer come before thee. Wherefore, O Lord, dost thou reject my soul, and turn away thy face from me? I am poor and in troubles from my youth up, and having been exalted, I have been brought low and into despair. Thine anger hath passed over me, and thy terrors have disquieted me. They came round about me like water, all the day they beset me together. Friend and neighbour hast thou put far from me, and mine acquaintance from my misery.

O Lord God of my salvation, I have cried day and night before thee. Let my prayer come in before thee, incline thine ear to my petition.

BLESS the Lord, O my soul, and all that is within me bless his holy name. Bless the Lord, O my soul, and forget not all his benefits. Who forgiveth all thy transgressions, who healeth all thy diseases. Who redeemeth thy life from corruption, who crowneth thee with mercy and compassion. Who satisfieth thy desire with good things, so that thy youth is renewed as an eagle's. The Lord executeth mercy and judgment for all that suffer wrong. He made known his ways unto Moses, his will unto the children of Israel. The Lord is compassionate and merciful, longsuffering and of many mercies. He will not always be angry, neither will he be wrathful for ever. He hath not dealt with us after our transgressions, nor rewarded us according to our sins. For according to the height of heaven above the earth, so hath the Lord confirmed his mercy upon them that fear him. As far as the east is from the west, so far hath he removed our transgressions from us. As a father hath compassion upon his sons, so hath the Lord compassion upon them that fear him. For he knoweth our frame, he remembereth that we are but dust. As for man, his days are as grass, as a flower of the field so shall he flourish. For the spirit passeth through in him, and he is not, and shall know his place no more. But the mercy of the Lord is from ages and unto ages upon them that fear him. And his righteousness upon sons' sons, to them that keep his testament, and remember his commandments to do them. The Lord hath prepared his throne in heaven, and his kingdom ruleth over all. Bless the Lord, all ye his Angels, mighty in strength, that fulfil his word, hearkening unto the voice of his orders. Bless the Lord, all ye his Hosts, ye Ministers of his that do his will. Bless the Lord, all ye his works, in every place of his dominion. Bless the Lord, O my soul.

In every place of his dominion, bless the Lord, O my soul.

O LORD, hear my prayer, give ear unto my supplication in thy truth, hear me in thy righteousness. And enter not into judgment with thy servant, for in thy sight shall none living be justified. For the enemy hath persecuted my soul, he hath smitten my life down to the ground. He hath made me to dwell in dark places as them that have been long dead, and my spirit is vexed within me, my heart within me is desolate. I remember the days of old, I meditate on all thy doings, I muse on the works of thy hands. I stretch forth my hands unto thee, my soul gaspeth unto thee as a thirsty land Hear me, O Lord, and that soon, for my spirit waxeth faint. Hide not thy face from me, lest I be like unto them that go down into the pit. O let me hear thy mercy betimes in the morning, for in thee is my trust. Make known unto me, O Lord, the way wherein I should walk, for I have lifted up my soul unto thee, Deliver me from mine enemies, O Lord, for I fly unto thee to hide me. Teach me to do thy will, for thou art my God. Thy good Spirit shall lead me into the land of righteousness: thou shalt quicken me, O Lord, for thy name's sake. In thy righteousness thou shalt bring my soul out of affliction, and in thy mercy thou shalt cut off mine enemies, and shalt destroy all them that afflict my soul, for I am thy servant.

Hear me, O Lord, in thy righteousness, and enter not into judgment with thy servant, *twice.* Thy good Spirit shall lead me into the land of righteousness.

Glory. Both now.

Alleluia, alleluia, alleluia, glory to thee, O God, *thrice.*

Then followeth the Ectenia of Peace, as in the Vespers. Vide page 2.

Then saith the Reader,

THE Lord is God, and hath appeared unto us. Blessed be he that cometh in the name of the Lord.

The Choir repeateth the same, likewise also after every one of the following verses.

Verse. O give thanks unto the Lord, because he is good, because his mercy endureth for ever.

Verse. They compassed me about, yea, they compassed me about, but in the name of the Lord will I destroy them.

Verse. I shall not die, but live, and declare the works of the Lord.

Verse. The stone which the builders refused is become the head-stone of the corner. This is the Lord's doing, and it is wonderful in our eyes.

Then are sung the Troparia proper to the day. And, Lord, have mercy, *thrice. Glory.*

Reader. Both now. And beginneth to read the Kathisms of the Psalter.

After the Kathisms, the Little Ectenia, with the Exclamation, For thou art a good and man-loving God, and to thee we ascribe glory, to the Father, and to the Son, and to the Holy Ghost, now and ever, and to ages of ages. *Choir.* Amen. *And singeth the* Many mercies, *that is, Psalms* 134 (135) *and* 135 (136), *usually on this wise:*

PRAISE ye the name of the Lord, alleluia. Praise him, all ye servants of the Lord, alleluia.

Blessed be the Lord out of Sion, who dwelleth in Jerusalem, alleluia.

O give thanks unto the Lord, because he is good, alleluia, alleluia: because his mercy endureth for ever, alleluia.

O give thanks unto the God of heaven, alleluia, alleluia: because his mercy endureth for ever, alleluia.

And on the Sundays of Meat Fare and of Cheese Fare they add the following verses from Psalm 136 (137).

BY the waters of Babylon we sat down and wept, when we remembered thee, O Sion, alleluia.

Blessed shall he be that taketh thy children and dasheth them against the stones, alleluia.

Here on Festivals of the Lord, or of the Mother of God, or of the Saints, is sung the Magnifying with the appointed verses.

But on Sundays they sing the following Troparia in Tone 5.

Refrain. Blessed art thou, O Lord: O teach me thy statutes.

THE assembly of Angels were amazed seeing thee numbered among the dead, thee, O Saviour, that didst destroy the might of death, that didst raise Adam together with thyself, and deliver us all from hades.

Why, O ye disciples, do ye mingle the myrrh with pitying tears? said the radiant Angel at the grave to the myrrh-bearing women. Behold ye the grave, and be glad, for the Saviour is risen from the tomb.

Very early in the morning the myrrh-bearing women came to thy tomb lamenting, but the Angel stood before them and said, The time of wailing is past, weep not, but go and tell the Resurrection to the Apostles.

The myrrh-bearing women, coming with myrrh to thy tomb, O Saviour, wept, but an Angel spake unto them and said, Why think ye that the Living is among the dead? For, as God, he is risen from the tomb. *Glory.*

Let us worship the Father, and the Son, and the Holy Ghost, the Holy Trinity in One Substance, crying with the Seraphim, Holy, holy, holy art thou, O Lord. *Both now.*

Thou, O Virgin, didst bring forth the Giver of life, hast delivered Adam from sin, and given joy to Eve instead of sorrow; for he that was incarnate from thee, being God and man, hath restored to life them that had fallen from it.

Alleluia, alleluia, alleluia, glory to thee, O God, *thrice.*

After the Magnifying, or the foregoing Troparia, followeth the Little Ectenia, with the Exclamation, For blessed is thy name and glorified is thy kingdom, Father, Son, and Holy Ghost, now and ever, and to ages of ages. *Choir.* Amen. *And singeth the Gradual. That for Festivals is,*

FROM my youth up many passions have afflicted me, but thou, my Saviour, thyself deliver me and save me.

They that hate Sion shall be confounded by the Lord, like grass by fire so shall they be withered.

Glory. Both now.

Every soul is quickened by the Holy Ghost, and by his purity is elevated, and is mystically enlightened by the Trinal Unity.

Then saith the Deacon, Let us attend. Wisdom!

Reader. Prokimenon. *And readeth the appointed verse from one of the Psalms.*

And the Choir repeateth the same thrice.

Deacon. Let us pray to the Lord.

Choir. Lord, have mercy.

Priest. For holy art thou, our God, and thou restest in the holy places, and to thee we ascribe glory, to the Father, and to the Son, and to the Holy Ghost, now and ever, and to ages of ages. *Choir.* Amen.

Deacon. Let every thing that hath breath praise the Lord.

The Choir repeateth the same.

Deacon. O praise God in his holy places, praise him in the firmament of his power.

Choir. Let every thing that hath breath praise the Lord.

Deacon. Let every thing that hath breath.

Choir. Praise the Lord.

Deacon. And let us pray to the Lord God that he would make us worthy to hear the holy Gospel.

Choir. Lord, have mercy, *thrice.*

Deacon. Wisdom! Stand up! Let us hear the holy Gospel.

Priest. Peace to all.

Choir. And to thy spirit.

Priest. The reading from the holy Gospel according to *N.*

Choir. Glory to thee, Lord, glory to thee.

The Priest readeth the Gospel.

At its conclusion the Choir again singeth,
Glory to thee, Lord, glory to thee.

Here the order of the Service is somewhat varied according to the day.

A. *On Sundays after the* Glory to thee, Lord, glory to thee, *they sing,*

HAVING seen the Resurrection of Christ, we adore the holy Lord Jesus, who alone is without sin. Thy Cross, O Master, we worship, and sing and glorify thy holy Resurrection; for thou art our God, we know none other beside thee, we call upon thy name. O come, all ye faithful, let us adore Christ's holy Resurrection; for, by the Cross great joy is come into all the world. Therefore, ever blessing the Lord, we sing his Resurrection; for, enduring crucifixion, death by death he overthrew.

Then is read Psalm 50 (51).

HAVE mercy upon me, O God, according to thy great mercy, and according to the multitude of thy compassions, cleanse my transgression. Wash me throughly from my transgression, and cleanse me from my sin. For I know my transgression, and my sin is continually before me. Against thee only have I sinned, and done evil in thy sight, that thou mightest be justified in thy words and mightest overcome when thou art judged. Behold, I was shapen in transgressions, and in sins did my mother conceive me. Behold, thou hast loved truth, thou hast manifested to me the secret and hidden things of thy wisdom. Thou shalt sprinkle me with hyssop, and I shall be clean: thou shalt wash me, and I shall be made whiter than snow. Thou shalt make me to hear of joy and gladness, and the bones which thou hast broken shall rejoice. Turn thy face from my sins, and cleanse all my transgressions. Create in me a clean heart, O God, and renew a right spirit within me.

Cast me not away from thy presence, and take not thy holy Spirit from me. Restore unto me the joy of thy salvation, and stablish me with thy free Spirit. I will teach thy ways unto transgressors, and the wicked shall be converted unto thee. Deliver me from blood-guiltiness, O God, thou that art the God of my salvation, and my tongue shall sing of thy righteousness. Thou shalt open my lips, O Lord, and my mouth shall shew forth thy praise. For if thou hadst desired sacrifice, I would have given it, but thou delightest not in burnt offerings. Sacrifice to God is a broken spirit, a broken and contrite heart God will not despise. Be gracious, O Lord, in thy good pleasure unto Sion, and let the walls of Jerusalem be built. Then shalt thou be well pleased with the sacrifice of righteousness, with the oblations and holocausts. Then shall they offer young bullocks upon thine altar.

After this the Choir singeth, Glory.

Through the prayers of the Apostles, O Merciful One, cleanse the multitude of our transgressions.

Both now.

Through the prayers of the Mother of God, O Merciful One, cleanse the multitude of our transgressions.

Have mercy upon me, O God, after thy

great goodness : according to the multitude of thy mercies cleanse mine offences.

Jesus hath risen from the grave, as he foretold, granting us eternal life and great mercy.

B. *On the Festivals of the Lord, after the Gospel and the* Glory to thee, Lord . . . *Psalm 50 (51) is read, and the Choir singeth, Glory, and the Verse for the Festival, for example,* All things to-day are filled with joy, Christ is born of the Virgin, *or,* is baptized in Jordan, *according to the day. Both now. And repeateth the Verse,* All things to-day .... *continuing,* Have mercy upon me, O God, after . . . . *and the appointed Sticheron or Hypacoë of the Festival.*

C. *On the Festivals of the Mother of God, or of the Saints, after Psalm 50 (51), Glory.* Through the prayers of the Mother of God, (*or,* of thy Martyr, *or,* of thy Saint, *N.*), O Merciful One, cleanse the multitude of our transgressions. *Both now.* And repeateth *the Verse, continuing,* Have mercy upon . . . *and the appointed Sticheron or Hypacoë.*

D. *On the Sunday of the Publican, and thence until the Fifth Sunday of the Great Fast, after the Hymn,* Having seen the Resurrection . . . . *and the reading of Psalm 50 (51), they sing,*

Glory. Open thou, O Life-giver, the gates of repentance to me, for my soul longeth for thy holy temple, though its own bodily temple is wholly defiled, but thou, in thy bounty, cleanse it according to thy loving-kindness.

Both now.

O Mother of God, lead me into the path of salvation, for I have hardened my soul by shameful sins, and I have spent all my life in sloth. Save me then by thy prayers from all impurity.

Have mercy upon me, O God, after thy great goodness : according to the multitude of thy mercies cleanse mine offences.

When I, accursed, meditate on the number of evils I have wrought, I tremble for the terrible day of judgement. Still, trusting in the mercy of thy loving-kindness, I cry to thee as David, Have mercy upon me, O God, according to thy great mercy.

And now the Deacon saith the following Prayer.

GOD, save thy people and bless thine inheritance, visit the world with thy mercy and bounties, exalt the horn of Orthodox Christians, and send down upon us thy rich mercies, through the prayers of our most holy Lady, the God-bearing ever-virgin Mary, through the might of the honourable and life-giving Cross, through the intercessions of the honourable, immaterial, heavenly Hosts, of the honourable glorious Prophet, Forerunner and Baptist John, of the glorious and all-praised Apostles, of our Fathers among the Saints, great Hierarchs and ecumenical Teachers, Basil the Great, Gregory the Divine and John Chrysostom, of our Father among the Saints, Nicolas, Archbishop of Myra in Lycia, the Wonder-worker, of the Russian Wonderworkers, Peter, Alexis, Jonas, and Philip, of the glorious and victorious Martyrs, of our venerable and God-bearing Fathers, of the holy and righteous Progenitors of God, Joakim and Anna, and of all the Saints, we beseech thee, O most merciful Lord, hearken unto us sinners praying unto thee, and have mercy upon us.

Choir. Lord, have mercy, *twelve times.*

Priest. Through the mercy, and bounties, and loving-kindness of thine only-begotten Son, with whom thou art blessed, together with thy most holy, and good, and life-creating Spirit, now and ever, and to ages of ages.

Choir. Amen. *And beginneth to sing the Canon.* *

---

*) CANON: — An ecclesiastical composition, commemorative of the occasion, based upon the Nine

After the Third Ode of this occurreth the Little Ectenia, with the Exclamation, For thou art our God, and to thee we ascribe glory, to the Father, and to the Son, and to the Holy Ghost, now and ever, and to ages of ages.

Choir. Amen. *And singeth the Kathisma, or the Hypacoë.*

After the Sixth Ode, the Little Ectenia, with the Exclamation, For thou art the King of peace and the Saviour of our souls, and to thee we ascribe glory, to the Father, and to the Son, and to the Holy Ghost, now and ever, and to ages of ages.

Choir. Amen. *And singeth the Condakion and the Icos.*

At the close of the Eighth Ode, the Reader exclaimeth, Let us bless the Lord, the Father, the Son, and the Holy Ghost. *And we answer,* Let us praise, let us bless, let us

---

Scriptural Odes, namely, I. The Song of Moses in Exodus. *Chap. XV. 1—19.* II. The Song of Moses in Deuteronomy. *Chap. XXXII. 1—43. (This Ode is proper for Lent only).* III. The Prayer of Anna. *1. Kings. II. 1—10.* IV. The Prayer of Abbacum. *Chap. III. 2 ad fin.* V. The Prayer of Esaias. *Chap. XXVI. 9—20.* VI. The Prayer of Jonas. *Chap. II. 2—9.* VII. The Prayer of the Three Children. *Daniel III.* VIII. The Song of the same. *(Benedicite.)* IX. The Song of Zacharias. *(Benedictus),* preceded by that of the Virgin. *(Magnificat.)*

worship the Lord, singing unto him and setting him up for ever. *And we sing the Katavasia, that is, the Irmos of the Eighth Ode.*

Then saith the Deacon with a loud voice,

Let us magnify in hymns the Mother of God and the Mother of Light.

And the Choir singeth,

MY soul doth magnify the Lord, and my spirit hath rejoiced in God my Saviour.

For he hath regarded the lowliness of his handmaiden; for, behold, from henceforth, all generations shall call me blessed.

For he that is mighty hath magnified me, and holy is his name, and his mercy is on them that fear him from generation to generation.

He hath shewed strength with his arm, he hath scattered the proud in the imaginations of their hearts.

He hath put down the mighty from their seats, and he hath exalted the lowly : he hath filled the hungry with good things, and the rich he hath sent empty away.

He, remembering his mercy, hath holpen his servant Israel, as he promised to our forefathers, to Abraham and to his seed for ever.

3*

And after every verse is added,

THE more honourable than the Cherubim, and incomparably more glorious than the Seraphim, who didst bear without corruption God the Word, thee, verily the Mother of God, we magnify.

And they sing the Ninth Ode.

Then the Little Ectenia, with the Exclamation, For all the Hosts of heaven praise thee, and to thee we ascribe glory, to the Father, and to the Son, and to the Holy Ghost, now and ever, and to ages of ages. *Choir.* Amen.

Deacon. Holy is the Lord our God.

The Choir repeateth the same.

Deacon. For holy is the Lord our God.

Choir. Holy is the Lord our God.

Deacon. Above all nations is our God.

Choir. Holy is the Lord our God.

And singeth the Exapostilarion of the Festival.

Then they sing the Psalms of Praise, namely, Psalms 148, 149 *and* 150.

LET every thing that hath breath praise the Lord.

Praise the Lord from the heavens, praise him in the highest.

To thee is due a hymn, O God.

Praise him, all ye his Angels: praise him, all ye his Hosts.

To thee is due a hymn, O God.

The ensuing verses are usually read.

Praise him, O sun and moon, praise him, all ye stars and light.

Praise him, ye heaven of heavens, and ye waters that are above the heavens.

Let them praise the name of the Lord; for he spake and they were made, he commanded and they were created.

He hath founded them to ages, and to ages of ages: he hath made a decree, and it shall not pass away.

Praise the Lord from the earth, ye dragons and all deeps.

Fire, hail, snow and ice, stormy winds that fulfil his word.

Mountains and all hills, fruitful trees and all cedars.

Beasts and all cattle, creeping things and feathered fowls.

Kings of the earth and all peoples, princes and all judges of the earth.

Young men and maidens, let the old with the young praise the name of the Lord, for his name only is exalted.

His confession is above earth and heaven, and he shall exalt the horn of his people.

A hymn to all his saints, to the children of Israel, a people that draw nigh to him.

O sing unto the Lord a new song: his praise is in the Church of his saints.

Let Israel rejoice in him that made him, and let the children of Sion he joyful in their King.

Let them praise his name in the choir, let them sing praises unto him with timbrel and psaltery.

For the Lord hath pleasure in his people, and will exalt the meek unto salvation.

The saints shalt exult in glory, and shall rejoice upon their beds.

The high praises of God shall be in their mouths, and a two-edged sword in their hands;

To execute vengeance upon the nations, and chastisement upon the peoples;

To bind their kings with chains, and their nobles with links of iron:

To do unto them the judgment written, This glory shall be for all his saints.

Here beginneth the singing of the Stichera.

O praise God in his saints, praise him in the firmament of his power.

Praise him for his mighty acts, praise him according to the greatness of his majesty.

Praise him with the sound of the trumpet, praise him with psaltery and harp.

Praise him with timbrel and choir, praise him with stringed instruments and organ.

Praise him with well-tuned cymbals, praise him with loud cymbals. Let everything that hath breath praise the Lord.

Glory. Both now.
And the following Verse to the Virgin.

MOST blessed art thou, Virgin Mother of God, for by him that was incarnate of thee hades hath been led captive, Adam hath been recalled, the curse hath been made void, Eve hath been set free, death hath died and we have been made alive. Wherefore praising thee we cry, Blessed art thou, O Christ our God, who so willed it, glory to thee.

This Verse is sung on Sundays only. On other days they sing the proper appointed Verse.

Then saith the Priest, Glory to thee who hast shewed light unto us.

And the Choir singeth the Great Doxology.

GLORY to God in the highest, and on earth peace, goodwill to men. We hymn thee, we bless thee, we worship thee, we glorify thee, we give thanks to thee for thy great glory, O Lord, King of heaven, God the Father almighty, O Lord, only-begotten Son, Jesu Christ, and O Holy Ghost. O Lord God, Lamb of God, Son of the Father, thou that takest away the sins of the world, have mercy upon us. Thou that

takest away the sins of the world, accept
our prayer. Thou that sittest on the right
hand of the Father, have mercy upon us.
For thou only art holy, thou only art Lord,
O Jesu Christ, to the glory of God the Father.
Amen.

Every day will I bless thee, and praise thy
name to ages, and to ages of ages.

Vouchsafe, O Lord, to keep us this day
without sin. Blessed art thou, O Lord God
of our fathers, and praised and glorified is
thy name to ages. Amen.

O Lord, let thy mercy lighten upon us,
like as we do put our trust in thee.

Blessed art thou, O Lord, O teach me
thy statutes, *thrice.*

Lord, thou hast been our refuge from
generation to generation. I have said,
O Lord, have mercy upon me, heal my soul,
for I have sinned against thee.

Lord, I flee unto thee. Teach me to
do thy will, for thou art my God. For in
thee is the fountain of life, in thy light shall
we see light. O continue forth thy loving
mercy to them that know thee.

Holy God, Holy Mighty One, Holy Immortal One, have mercy upon us, *thrice.*

Glory. Both now.

Holy Immortal One, have mercy upon us.

And, in a louder tone,

Holy God. Holy Mighty One, Holy Immortal One, have mercy upon us.

Then the proper Troparion of the Day.

Sunday Troparia. In Tones 1, 3, 5 & 7.

TO-DAY is salvation come unto the world. Let us sing unto him that arose from the grave, the Author of our life; for, having vanquished death by death, he hath given victory unto us and many blessings.

But in Tones 2, 4, 6 & 8.

O LORD, thou didst arise from the grave and burst the bonds of hades; thou didst destroy the sentence of death and deliver all from the snares of the enemy; thou didst appear to thine Apostles and send them forth to preach, and, through them, hast granted thy peace to the world, O thou most Merciful One.

Here followeth the Great Ectenia.

Have mercy on us, O God . . . . *Vide page* 10.

Then that of Supplication.

Let us accomplish our morning prayer to . . . . *Vide page* 12.

Exclamation.

Priest. For thou art the God of mercies and bounties, and that lovest mankind, and to thee we ascribe glory, to the Father, and to the Son, and to the Holy Ghost, now and ever, and to ages of ages.

Choir. Amen.

Priest. Peace to all.

Choir. And to thy spirit.

Deacon. Let us bow our heads to the Lord. *Choir.* To thee, O Lord.

Exclamation.

Priest. For it is thine to pity and to save us, O our God, and to thee we ascribe glory, to the Father, and to the Son, and to the Holy Ghost, now and ever, and to ages of ages. *Choir.* Amen.

Deacon. Wisdom! *Choir.* Give the blessing.

Priest. Blessed be Christ our God, always, now and ever, and to ages of ages.

Choir. Amen. *And continueth*, Stablish, O God, our pious (Emperor, *or* King, *or* Queen, *or* Prince *N.*), and the orthodox faith of all Orthodox Christians to ages of ages.

Priest. Save us, O most holy Mother of God.

Choir. The more honourable than the Cherubim . . . .

Priest. Glory to thee, O Christ, our God, our Hope, glory to thee.

Choir. *Glory.* *Both now.* Lord, have mercy, *thrice.* Give the blessing.

Priest. (He that arose from the dead, *or*, that ascended with glory into the heavens, and sat down at the right hand of our God and Father, *or*, that sent down from heaven the most Holy Spirit in the likeness of fiery tongues upon his holy Disciples and Apostles, *or*, that was transfigured in glory on mount Tabor before his holy Disciples and Apostles, *or*, that was born in a cave and laid in a manger for our salvation, *or*, that vouchsafed to be circumcised in the flesh on the eighth day for our salvation, *or*, that vouchsafed to be baptized by John in Jordan for our salvation, *or*, that vouchsafed to sit on the foal of an ass for our salvation, *according to the occassion of the Festival*), Christ our true God, through the prayers of his most pure Mother, of the holy, glorious and all-praised Apostles, of the holy *N.*, whose memory we this day celebrate, and of all the Saints, have mercy upon us, and save us; for he is good, and the Lover of men.

Choir. Lord have mercy, *thrice. And singeth the* Many Years *for the Reigning House.*

Here followeth the First Hour.

II. THE GREAT VESPERS

AS SAID ON THE EVE OF A FESTIVAL WHEN A
VIGIL IS NOT HELD.

*At the conclusion of the Ninth Hour the
Priest saith,*

BLESSED be our God, always, now and ever, and to ages of ages.

Reader. Amen. O come, let us worship God, our King.

O come, let us worship and fall down before Christ God, our King.

O come, let us worship and fall down before Christ himself, our God and King.

And the Prefatory Psalm, the Ectenia and the rest follow, as in the Great Vespers at page 2.

After the Troparion of the Day, the Deacon saith, Wisdom! *Choir.* Give the blessing.

Priest. Blessed be Christ our God . . . .
As at the conclusion of the Great Matins.

Then shall be read the Little Compline.

III. THE NOCTURNS ON SUNDAYS.

The Priest beginneth, Blessed be our God . . . .

Reader. Amen. Glory to thee, our God, glory to thee.

HEAVENLY King, O Paraclete, the Spirit of truth, that art every where present and that fillest all things, that art the Treasury of blessings and the Giver of life; come, and make thine abode in us, and cleanse us from every defilement, and save our souls, O Blessed One.

HOLY God, Holy Mighty One, Holy Immortal One, have mercy upon us, *thrice*.

Glory to the Father, and to the Son, and to the Holy Ghost, both now and ever, and to ages of ages. Amen.

O MOST Holy Trinity, have mercy upon us. O Lord, cleanse our sins. O Master, forgive our transgressions. Visit us, O Holy One, and heal our infirmities, for thy name's sake.

Lord, have mercy, *thrice*. *Glory. Both now.*

OUR Father, which art in heaven, Hallowed be thy name. Thy kingdom come. Thy will be done on earth, as it is in heaven. Give us this day our daily bread. And forgive us our trespasses, as we forgive them them that trespass against us. And lead us not into temptation. But deliver us from evil.

Priest. For thine is the kingdom, and the power, and the glory, of the Father, and of the Son, and of the Holy Ghost, now and ever, and to ages of ages.

Reader. Amen. Lord, have mercy, *twelve times. Glory. Both now.*

O come, let us worship God, our King.

O come, let us worship and fall down before Christ God, our King.

O come, let us worship and fall down before Christ himself, our God and King.

Then Psalm 50 (51). *Vide page* 29.

After this shall be sung the Canon to the Holy Trinity according to the Tone.

At the conclusion of the Canon follow these verses of Gregory of Sinai.

IT is very meet to praise the super-divine Trinity, the unbeginning Father and Creator of all things, and the co-unbeginning Word, who was unspeakably begotten of the Father before all time, and the Holy Ghost proceeding from the Father from eternity.

It is very meet to glorify thee, O God the Word, before whom the Cherubim fear and tremble, and whom the heavenly Hosts glorify. Let us glorify with fear Christ the Life-giver, who rose the third day from the dead.

Let us all, with divine songs becoming unto God, sing the Father, and the Son, and the Divine Spirit, the tri-personal Might, the one Kingdom and Lordship.

Thee that all the earth-born sing and heavenly Powers glorify, by all things art faithfully worshipped, O Unity in essence and tri-personal.

O sovereign Lord of Cherubim and incomparable divine King of Seraphim, O undivided Trinity in Unity, thou divinely ruling Essence, we magnify thee.

I worship the unbeginning Father and God, and the co-unbeginning Word, with the Spirit. The undivided Oneness, the united Essence, the tri-numbered Unity, let us honour with songs.

Let thy radiant splendour illuminate me,

O my God, tri-personal Maker of all things, and make me the dwelling-place of thine unapproachable glory, thou that art light, and light-bearing, and unchangeable.

Him before whom the Cherubim fear and tremble, and angel Hosts glorify, of the Virgin unspeakably became incarnate, even Christ the Life-giver, whom with fear let us glorify.

Trisagion. O most holy Trinity. Our Father. *The Hypacoë of the Tone.* Lord, have mercy, *forty times. Glory. Both now.* The more honourable . . . . In the name of the Lord, father, give the blessing.

Priest. God be merciful unto us, and bless us, and shine the light of his countenance upon us, and have mercy upon us.

Reader. Amen. *And saith the following Prayer.*

OMNIPOTENT and quickening and light-originating holy Trinity, who, by thy goodness alone, hast from nothing produced all creatures visible and invisible, and providest for them and dost keep them, and among other thine unspeakable bounties to mankind dost grant us, even until death, repentance on account of our carnal weakness; leave thou not us to die condemned in our evil deeds, neither to be the scorn of the author of evil, of the envious one, of the destroying one. Thou seest, O Bountiful One, on the one hand his snares and enmity against us, and on the other our passions, weakness and forgetfulness. But we pray thee that thy merciful grace may be granted unto us, who offend thee every day and hour by transgressing thy holy and life-giving commandments. And pardon and forgive us all wherein we have sinned during our past life, and until the present hour, in deed and word and intention. And grant that we may finish the remaining time of our life in repentance and contrition, and in obedience to thy holy precepts. If, captivated by pleasure, we have sinned in divers manners, or, deceived by wicked desires, useless and harmful, we have been overcome; if, excited by anger and foolish passion, we have injured our brother; if we have bound ourselves by our tongue in inevitable, injurious and strong snares; if, by any of our senses or by all, willingly or unwillingly, knowingly or unknowingly, by surprise or habit, we have foolishly transgressed; if, by evil and vain imaginations, we have defiled our conscience, and if in any other manner, by evil chance or custom, we have sinned; do thou pardon and forgive us, O most Compassionate, most Good and most Merciful One, and grant us future watchfulness and strength to do according

4

to thy good and acceptable and perfect will.
Let nightly and dark evil deeds be changed to
shining repentance, and so, walking honestly
as in the day, may we, though unworthy, be
found clean before thee, O Lover of mankind,
and praise and magnify thee for ever. Amen.

Here followeth the Dismissal.

Priest. Glory to thee, O Christ, our God,
our Hope, glory to thee.

Reader. *Glory.* *Both now.* Lord, have
mercy, *thrice.* Give the blessing.

Priest. Christ our true God, through the
prayers of his all-pure Mother, of the holy,
glorious and all-praised Apostles, of Saint
N., whose memory we this day celebrate, and
of all the Saints, have mercy upon us and save
us, for he is good and the Lover of men.

Reader. Amen.

Priest. Bless me, holy fathers and brethren,
and pardon me, a sinner, wherein I have
sinned, in words, deeds, thoughts, and with
all my senses.

People. God pardon thee, holy father.

Priest. Let us pray for our God-fearing
and God-protected Sovereign (Emperor, *or,*
King, *or,* Queen, *or,* Prince) *N.*

Choir. Lord, have mercy. *And so after
the succeeding petitions.*

Priest. For (the most holy Governing
Synod and for) our Bishop *N.*

For the prosperity and strength of the Christ-loving army.

For our father (*the Abbot of the Monastery*) *N.*, and for all our brotherhood in Christ.

For them that hate us, and them that love us.

For them that are beneficent and minister unto us.

For them that have bidden us, unworthy ones, to pray for them.

For the deliverance of captives.

For our absent fathers and brethren.

For them that are at sea.

For them that lie in sickness.

Let us also pray for plentifulness of the fruits of the earth.

And for every Orthodox Christian soul.

Let us bless pious kings.

Orthodox bishops.

The founders of this holy Monastery.

Our parents, and teachers, and all our before-departed fathers and brethren, that lie here, and the Orthodox everywhere. And let us say for them, Lord, have mercy.

Choir. Lord, have mercy, *thrice.*

Priest. Through the prayers of our holy Fathers, O Lord Jesus Christ our God, have mercy upon us.

Choir. Amen.

IV. THE GREAT MATINS

AS SAID ON A FESTIVAL WHEN A VIGIL IS NOT HELD.

At the conclusion of Nocturns the Priest beginneth,

Blessed be our God . . . .

Reader. Amen. O come, let us worship ... *thrice. Psalms* 19 (20) *and* 20 (21). *Glory. Both now. Trisagion.* O most holy Trinity. Our Father. *And the following Troparia.*

 LORD, save thy people and bless thine inheritance, granting victory to our God-fearing Sovereign (Emperor, *or*, King, *or*, Queen, *or*, Prince) *N.*, over enemies, and preserving thine estate by thy Cross.

Glory.

Thou that wast of thine own will raised on the Cross, bestow thy bounties on the new estate called by thy name, O Christ our God. Rejoice in thy strength our God-fearing Sovereign (Emperor, *or*, King, *or*, Queen, *or*, Prince) *N.*, granting *him* victory over *his* enemies; for *he* hath thine assistance, a shield of peace, a trophy that cannot be overcome. *Both now.*

Refuge terrible in strength, and that cannot be put to confusion, Mother of God, good and all-praised; confirm the estate of the Orthodox. Preserve our God-fearing Sovereign (Emperor, *or*, King, *or*, Queen, *or*, Prince) *N.*, whom thou hast chosen to rule, and give *him* the victory from heaven; for thou, the blessed one, didst bring forth God.

Priest. Have mercy upon us, O God, according to thy great mercy, we pray thee, hear and have mercy.

Choir. Lord, have mercy, *thrice. And so after the succeeding petitions.*

Priest. Again let us pray for our God-fearing and God-protected Sovereign (Emperor, *or*, King, *or*, Queen, *or*, Prince, *according to the country*) *N.*

Again let us pray for (the most holy Governing Synod, *or*, our Metropolitan, *or*, Archbishop) our Bishop *N.*

Again let us pray for all our brotherhood in Christ.   *Exclamation.*

For a merciful and man-loving God thou art, and we ascribe glory unto thee, Father,

Son, and Holy Ghost, now and ever, and to ages of ages.

Choir. Amen. *And continueth,*

In the name of the Lord, father, give the blessing.

Priest. Glory to the holy, consubstantial, life-giving and undivided Trinity, always, now and ever, and to ages of ages.

Reader. Amen. *And beginneth the Six Psalms, saying,*

Glory to God in the highest . . . . *thrice.*

O Lord, open thou my lips . . . . *twice.*

And the rest of the Great Matins. Vide page 16, *et seq.*

V. THE LITTLE DAILY VESPERS.

At the conclusion of the Ninth Hour the Priest saith,

Blessed be our God . . . .

Reader. Amen. O come, let us worship . . . . *thrice. And Psalm* 103 (104).

Then followeth the Ectenia of Peace. Vide page 2. *After this the proper Kathism of the Psalter. Then the* Lord, I have cried, *with the Stichera of the day. These being ended, the Reader saith the* Tranquil Light, *and the proper Prokimenon is sung. Vide page* 9. *Then immediately, without Ectenia preceding, the Prayer,* Vouchsafe, O Lord, to keep us this evening . . . .

Then the Ectenia, Let us accomplish our evening prayer . . . . *Vide page* 12.

After this are sung the proper Stichera of the Day. And the Reader then readeth the

Prayer of S. Simeon, Trisagion, &c. After the Our Father *followeth the Troparion of the Day.*

Then is said the Great Ectenia, Have mercy upon us, O God . . . . *Vide page* 10.

After the Ectenia the Dismissal is given, as at the close of the Great Matins. Vide page 42.

Then is read the following Prayer of Basil the Great.

BLESSED art thou, O Lord almighty, who hast lit up the day with the sun's light and brightened the night with shining stars, who hast granted unto us to pass the length of the day and to reach the limits of night. Hearken unto our prayer, and to that of all thy people, and forgive us all our voluntary and involuntary sins. Accept our evening prayers, and send down the riches of thy mercies and bounties upon thine estate. Guard us, as with a wall, by thy holy Angels. Arm us with the armour of righteousness. Preserve us by thy truth. Save us by thy power. Deliver us from all misfortune, and from all malice of the enemy. Grant that this present evening, with the coming night, as well as all the days of our life, may be perfect, holy, peaceful and sinless, and free from temptations

and imaginings of evil, through the prayers
of the holy Mother of God and of all the
Saints who from ages have found favour
before thee.

NOTE I. *In the Fasts, and on Days of
Remembrance for the Departed, the second part
of the Vespers is somewhat varied, thus,*

After the Tranquil Light, *instead of the
Prokimenon the following Verses are substituted.*

On Monday. Alleluia, alleluia, alleluia.

Verse I. O Lord, rebuke me not in thine
anger, neither chasten me in thy fury. Alleluia.

Verse 2. And to ages of ages. Alleluia.

On Tuesday and Thursday. Alleluia,
alleluia, alleluia.

Verse I. Worship the Lord our God, and
adore his footstool, for he is holy. Alleluia.

Verse 2. And to ages of ages. Alleluia.

On Wednesday. Alleluia, alleluia, alleluia.

Verse I. Their sound is gone out into all
lands, and their words to the end of the
world. Alleluia.

Verse 2. And to ages of ages. Alleluia.

On Friday and Saturday Alleluia *is never
sung.*

After the Alleluia, *the Reader saith,*

Vouchsafe, O Lord, to keep us this
evening . . . .

Then followeth the Ectenia, Let us accomplish our evening prayer . . . . *Vide page* 12.

After this the Stichera, with which the following verses are said.

UNTO thee have I lifted up mine eyes, O thou that dwellest in heaven. Behold, as the eyes of a servant are towards the hand of his master and the eyes of a maidservant are towards the hand of her mistress, so our eyes are towards the Lord our God until he have mercy upon us.

Have mercy upon us, O Lord, have mercy upon us; for we have been greatly filled with contempt. Our souls have been exceedingly filled with the reproach of the rich and the contempt of the proud.

Then the Prayer of S. Simeon. Trisagion. O most holy Trinity. Our Father. *And the following Troparia are sung.*

HAIL! Virgin Mother of God. O Mary, full of grace, the Lord is with thee. Blessed art thou among women, and blessed is the fruit of thy womb; for thou hast borne the Saviour of our souls.

O Baptist of Christ, remember us all, that we may be saved from our iniquity; for to thee hath been given grace to pray for us.

Glory.

Pray for us, ye holy Apostles, aud all ye

Saints, that we may be saved from danger and sorrow; for in you we have warm advocates before our Saviour.

Both now.

To thy protection we betake ourselves, O Mother of God. Despise not our prayers in our necessities, but save us from dangers, thou all-pure, all-blessed one.

Reader. Lord, have mercy, *forty times.*

Glory. Both now. The more honourable...

In the name of the Lord, father, give the blessing.

Priest. Blessed be Christ our God, always, now and ever, and to ages of ages.

Reader. Amen. O heavenly King, stablish our faithful Sovereign, confirm the faith, quiet the heathen, give peace to the world, place our departed fathers and brethren in the tabernacles of the just, and accept us sorrowers and penitents; for thou art good and the Lover of men.

Then we all bow down lowly to the earth three times, while the Priest prayeth

The Prayer of S Ephrem the Syrian.

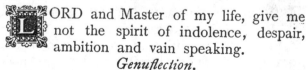

ORD and Master of my life, give me not the spirit of indolence, despair, ambition and vain speaking.

Genuflection.

But rather the spirit of chastity, humble-

mindedness, patience and love do thou grant
unto me, thy servant.

Genuflection.

Yea, O Lord King, let me see my own
faults, and let me not judge my brother; for
thou art blessed to ages of ages.   Amen.

Genuflection.

*Now all bow, but not so lowly, twelve times,
and every time say,*

O God, cleanse me, a sinner.

Then again the entire Prayer,

Lord and Master of my life . . . . *And one
lowly Genuflection.*

Then followeth, Trisagion. O most holy
Trinity. Our Father. Lord, have mercy,
*twelve times. And the Dismissal as at Noc-
turns. Vide page* 50.

And the Prayer of S. Basil, as at page 56,
is read.

NOTE 2. *So endeth the Vespers in the ordinary Fasts, but in the Great Quadragesima,
after the* Our Father *and* Lord, have mercy,
twelve times, the following Prayer is read,

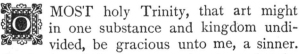 MOST holy Trinity, that art might
in one substance and kingdom undi-
vided, be gracious unto me, a sinner.
Confirm and instruct my heart, and take
from me all my defilement. Illuminate my
thoughts, that I may ever praise, sing and

worship, and say, One holy, one Lord Jesus Christ to the glory of God the Father. Amen.

BLESSED be the name of the Lord, from henceforth and to all ages, *thrice. Glory. Both now.*

Then Psalms 33 (34) *and* 144 (145). *And in conclusion.*

IT is very meet to bless thee, the holy Virgin, the ever blessed, the entirely spotless, and Mother of our God. The more honourable than the Cherubim, and incomparably more glorious than the Seraphim, who didst bear without corruption God the Word, thee, verily the Mother of God, we magnify.

And the Dismissal and the Prayer of S. Basil as before indicated.

And now in the Great Fasts shall be read the Great, but in ordinary times, the Little Compline.

VI. THE GREAT COMPLINE.

The beginning is as at Nocturns on Sundays. Vide page 45.

In the First Week of the Great Quadragesima, after, O come, let us worship ....
thrice. Psalm 50 (51). *And immediately shall follow the Great Canon of S. Andrew of Crete.*

On other days, after, O come, let us worship . . . . *thrice.*

Psalms 4, 6 & 12 (13). *Glory. Both now.* Alleluia, *&c.*

Psalms 24 (25), 30 (31) & 90 (91). *Glory. Both now.* Alleluia, *&c.*

Then shall be sung antiphonally.

GOD is with us. Let the nations know and be discomfited.

For God is with us. *These words are repeated after every verse.*

Hear ye, even to the ends of the earth.

Though ye were strong ye were made weak.

And if again ye shall strengthen yourselves, again ye shall be discomfited.

And if ye take counsel and devise it, the Lord shall scatter it.

And the word which ye shall speak, it shall not stand with you.

And we will not be afraid of your terror, neither will we be troubled.

But we will hallow the Lord our God, and he shall be our fear.

And if I trust in him, he will be to my sanctification.

And I will trust in him, and I shall be saved by him.

Behold me, and the children that God hath given me.

The people that walked in darkness have seen a great light.

To us that dwell in a far country and in the shadow of death light is sprung up.

For unto us a Child is born, unto us a Son is given.

And the government shall be upon his shoulder.

And there shall be no end of his peace.

And his name shall be called the Angel of the Great Counsel,

The wonderful Counsellor,

The mighty God, the Potentate, the Prince of peace,

The Father of the world to come.

God is with us. Let the nations know and be discomfited.

Glory to the Father, and to the Son, and to the Holy Ghost.

God is with us. Let the nations know and be discomfited.

Both now, and ever, and to ages of ages. Amen.

God is with us. Let the nations know and be discomfited.

Likewise the following Troparia.

I HAVE passed through the day and I thank thee, O Lord, and I pray that the evening and the night may be sinless. Grant me this, O Redeemer, and save me.

Glory. I have come through the day and I praise thee, O Master, and I pray that the evening and the night may be void of offence. Grant me this, O Redeemer, and save me.

Both now. I have finished the day and I sing to thee, O Holy One, and I pray that the evening and the night may be guileless. Grant me this, O Redeemer, and save me.

Then they sing,

THE bodiless powers of Cherubim praise thee with loudest songs. The six-winged living Seraphim extol thee with ceaseless voices. And all the hosts of Angels sing thrice-holy hymns to thee. For thou, O Father, wast from everlasting, and with thee is thine unbeginning Son, and from thee cometh the living Spirit, and the Oneness of the Trinity is shewn. Most holy Virgin Mother of God, ye witnesses and servants of the Word, ye choirs of Prophets and of Martyrs who have found eternal life, pray earnestly for us, for we are all in need, that evil beset us not, so we may sing the Angels' hymn, O holy, holy, holy, thrice-holy Lord, save us, and have mercy on us. Amen.

And now shall be said the Confession of the Faith.

BELIEVE in one God, the Father almighty, Maker of heaven and earth, and of all things visible and invisible. And in one Lord Jesus Christ, the only-begotten Son of God, who was begotten of the Father before all ages, Light of Light, very God of very God, begotten, not made, consubstantial with the Father, by whom all things were made; Who for us men, and for our salvation, come down from the heavens, and was incarnate of the Holy Ghost and the Virgin Mary, and was made man; And was crucified also for us under Pontius Pilate, and suffered and was buried; And rose again

5

the third day according to the Scriptures;
And ascended into the heavens, and sitteth
at the right hand of the Father; And shall
come again with glory to judge both the
quick and the dead, of whose kingdom there
shall be no end. And in the Holy Ghost,
the Lord, the Giver of life, who proceedeth
from the Father, who with the Father and
the Son is together worshipped and glorified,
who spake by the Prophets. In one, holy,
catholic, and apostolic Church. I acknowledge one Baptism for the remission of sins.
I look for the Resurrection of the dead,
And the life in the ages to come. Amen.

After the Confession of Faith, these Verses

O MOST holy Lady, Mother of God, pray
for us sinners.

All ye heavenly hosts of holy Angels and
Archangels, pray for us sinners.

Ye holy and glorious Apostles, Prophets
and Martyrs, and all ye Saints, pray for us,
sinners,

Ye our venerable and God-bearing Fathers,
Pastors and Teachers of the world, pray for
us sinners.

O thou invincible, incomprehensible and
divine might of the honourable and life-giving Cross, forsake us not sinners.

O God, cleanse us sinners.

O God, cleanse us sinners, and have mercy upon us.

Then, Trisagion. O most holy Trinity. Our Father. *And the Troparion of the Festival.*

But if not a Festival, the following.

On Monday and Wednesday Evenings.

LIGHTEN mine eyes, O Christ my God, lest I sleep the sleep of death, lest mine enemy say, I have prevailed against him.

Glory.

O God, be the defender of my soul, for I walk in the midst of many snares. Deliver me from these and save me, O good Lover of mankind.

Both now.

As we have not daring on account of our many sins, do thou, O Virgin Mother of God, pray him that was born of thee. For thy maternal prayer availeth much to gain the clemency of the Lord. Despise not, O most pure one, the prayers of sinners, for he that vouchsafed to suffer for us is merciful and powerful to save.

But on Tuesday and Thursday Evenings.

LORD, thou knowest the watchfulness of mine invisible enemies, and thou who madest me seest the weakness of my flesh.

5*

Therefore into thine hands do I commit my spirit. Keep me under the shadow of the wings of thy goodness, lest I sleep the sleep of death. Enlighten the eyes of my mind with thy divine words, and in due time awaken me to praise thee, O good Lover of mankind.

Verse. Look upon me and have mercy upon me, O Lord my God.

How fearful shall thy judgment be, O Lord, when Angels stand around and men be there, when the books be opened and our actions shewn, and our intentions tried. What then shall be my sentence, for I was born in sin? Who shall quench the flame for me? Who shall make my darkness light, if thou, O Lord, the Lover of mankind, do not have mercy on me?

Glory.

Give to me tears, O God, as once thou gavest to the sinful woman, and let me wash thy feet therewith, thy feet that saved me from the path of sin. And let me cleanse my life with penitence, and so bring thee fragrant myrrh. And let me hear thy sacred words, Go thou in peace, thy faith hath made thee whole.

Both now.

O Mother of God, I have an unashamed trust in thee and shall be saved. I have

thine help, most pure one, and have no fear.
I shall chase mine enemies and subdue them,
with thy protection for my armour. And
asking for thy mighty help I say, Save me,
O Lady, by thy prayers, and rouse me from
darkly sleep to praise thee, through the might
of God the Son, who took his flesh from
thee.

Lord, have mercy, *forty times.* *Glory.*
Both now. The more honourable . . . . In
the name of the Lord, father, give the
blessing.

Priest. Through the prayers of our holy
Fathers, O Lord Jesus Christ our God, have
mercy upon us.

Reader. Amen.

Prayer of Basil the Great.

LORD, O Lord, who savest us from
every arrow that flieth by day, save
us from every danger that lurketh in
darkness. Accept the lifting up of our hands
as an evening sacrifice. Let us pass through
the watches of the night without defilement
and without temptation, and deliver us from
restlessness and fear of the devil. Let the
repentance of our souls and the examination
of our intentions in the light of thy terrible
and righteous judgment be pleasing before
thee. Penetrate our flesh with fear of thee,

and mortify our earthly members, so that in our sleep we may be enlightened with the vision of thy judgment. Remove far from us every unseemly imagination and every harmful lust. And rouse us at the hour of prayer, strengthened in faith and advanced in thy commandments. Through the satisfaction and goodness of thine only-begotten Son, with whom, and with thy most holy, and good, and life-creating Spirit, thou art blessed, now and ever, and to ages of ages. Amen.

Then forthwith, O come, let us worship.... *thrice.*

Psalms 50 (51) *and* 101 (102).

And the Prayer of Manasses, King of Juda.

 LORD almighty, God of our fathers, Abraham, Isaac and Jacob, and of their righteous seed; who hast made heaven and earth, with all the ornament thereof; who hast bound the sea by the word of thy commandment; who hast shut up the deep, and sealed it by thy terrible and glorious name; whom all men fear, and tremble before thy power; for the majesty of thy glory cannot be borne, and thine angry threatening toward sinners is importable; but thy merciful promise is unmeasurable and unsearchable; for thou art the most high

Lord, of great compassion, long-suffering, very merciful, and repentest of the evils of men. Thou, O Lord, according to thy great goodness, hast promised repentance and forgiveness to them that have sinned against thee; and of thine infinite mercies hast appointed repentance unto sinners, that they may be saved. Thou therefore, O Lord, that art the God of the just, hast not appointed repentance to the just, as to Abraham, and Isaac, and Jacob, which have not sinned against thee; but thou hast appointed repentance unto me that am a sinner; for I have sinned above the number of the sands of the sea. My transgressions, O Lord, are multiplied; my transgressions are multiplied, and I am not worthy to behold and see the height of heaven for the multitude of mine iniquities. I am bowed down with many iron bands, that I cannot lift up mine head, neither have any release; for I have provoked thy wrath, and done evil before thee; I did not thy will, neither kept I thy commandments; I have set up abominations, and have multiplied offences. Now therefore I bow the knee of mine heart, beseeching thee of grace. I have sinned, O Lord, I have sinned, and I acknowledge mine iniquities. Wherefore, I humbly beseech thee, forgive me, O Lord, forgive me, and destroy me not

with mine iniquities. Be not angry with me
for ever, by reserving evil for me; neither
condemn me into the lower parts of the
earth. For thou art the God, even the God
of them that repent; and in me thou wilt
shew all thy goodness; for thou wilt save
me, that am unworthy, according to thy great
mercy. Therefore I will praise thee for ever
all the days of my life. For all the powers
of the heavens do praise thee, and thine is
the glory to ages of ages. Amen.

Trisagion, &c. After, Our Father, *the
following Troparia.*

HAVE mercy upon us, O Lord, have mercy
upon us; for knowing not what to say,
we sinners offer this to thee, our Master,
this one prayer, Have mercy upon us.

Glory.

O Lord, have mercy upon us, for we have
put our trust in thee. Be not very angry
with us and remember not our transgressions;
but look down upon us now as ever mercifully, and deliver us from our enemies. For
thou art our God, and we are thy people:
all of us are the work of thy hands, and
we call upon thy name.

Both now.

O blessed Mother of God, open unto us
the gates of mercy, that, trusting in thee, we

perish not, but be delivered from evils by thee, for thou art the salvation of the Christian race.

Lord, have mercy, *forty times.* *Glory.* *Both now.* The more honourable . . . . In the name of the Lord, father, give the blessing.

Priest. Through the prayers of our holy Fathers, O Lord Jesus Christ our God, have mercy upon us. *Reader.* Amen.

Prayer.

ASTER, God, Father almighty; Lord, only-begotten Son, Jesus Christ, and Holy Ghost, one God-head, one Might! be gracious unto me, a sinner; and, by ways thou knowest, save me, thine unworthy servant; for thou art blessed to ages of ages. Amen.

Then again, O come, let us worship . . . . *thrice. Psalms* 69 (70) *and* 142 (143). *And the Doxology.*

LORY to God in the highest, and on earth peace, goodwill towards men. We hymn thee, we bless thee, we worship thee, we glorify thee, we give thanks to thee for thy great glory, O Lord, King of heaven, God the Father almighty, O Lord, only-begotten Son, Jesu Christ, and O Holy

Ghost. O Lord God, Lamb of God, Son of the Father, thou that takest away the sins of the world, have mercy upon us; thou that takest away the sins of the world, accept our prayer; thou that sittest on the right hand of the Father, have mercy upon us. For thou only art holy, thou only art Lord, O Jesu Christ, to the glory of God the Father. Amen.

Every evening will I bless thee, and praise thy name to ages, and to ages of ages.

Lord, thou hast been our refuge from generation to generation. I have said, O Lord, have mercy upon me, heal my soul, for I have sinned against thee. Lord, I flee unto thee, teach me to do thy will, for thou art my God. For in thee is the fountain of life, in thy light shall we see light. O continue forth thy loving-mercy to them that know thee.

Vouchsafe, O Lord, to keep us this evening without sin. Blessed art thou, O Lord, God of our fathers, and praised and glorified is thy name to ages. Amen.

O Lord, let thy mercy lighten upon us, like as we do put our trust in thee. Blessed art thou, O Lord, O teach me thy statutes. Blessed art thou, O Master, make me to understand thy statutes. Blessed art thou, O Holy One, enlighten me with thy statutes.

O Lord, thy mercy endureth for ever, despise not thou the works of thine own hands. To thee is due praise, to thee is due a hymn, to thee is due glory, Father, Son, and Holy Ghost, now and ever, and to ages of ages. Amen.

Then is sung the Canon of the Day.

At its conclusion, Trisagion, &c. Our Father. *And the following Verses are sung antiphonally.*

O LORD of hosts, be thou with us, for we have no other help but thee in sorrows. O Lord of hosts have mercy on us, *twice.*

Praise God in his Saints, praise him in the firmament of his power. O Lord of hosts, be thou with us.

Praise him for his mighty acts, praise him according to the greatness of his majesty. O Lord of hosts, be thou with us.

Praise him with the sound of the trumpet, praise him with psaltery and harp. O Lord of hosts, be thou with us.

Praise him with timbrel and choir, praise him with stringed instruments and organ. O Lord of hosts, be thou with us.

Praise him with well-tuned cymbals, praise him with loud cymbals. Let everything that hath breath praise the Lord. O Lord of hosts, be thou with us.

Praise God in his Saints. O Lord of hosts, be thou with us.

Praise him in the firmament of his power. O Lord of hosts, be thou with us.

Glory. O Lord, if we had not thy Saints to pray for us, and thy goodness so merciful to us, how could we dare, O Saviour, to sing to thee, whom Angels unceasingly glorify? O thou that knowest the hearts, spare our souls.

Both now. O Mother of God, to thee do I approach on account of the great multitude of my transgressions, desiring salvation. Visit thou my ailing soul, and beseech thy Son and our God to grant me remission of the evil I have wrought, for thou art the blessed one.

O most holy Mother of God, forsake me not during the course of my life, give me not over to the intercession of man, but thyself protect and have mercy upon me.

All my trust do I place in thee, O Mother of God, keep me under thy protection.

Reader. Lord, have mercy, *forty times.*

And this Prayer.

THOU that in all times and at every hour, in heaven and upon earth, art worshipped and glorified, Christ God, long-suffering, most merciful and of great tenderness, who lovest the righteous and art merciful to sinners, who hast called all men to salvation by the promise of future blessings; do thou, O Lord, accept our prayers at this hour, and guide our life in thy commandments. Sanctify our souls, make chaste our bodies, govern our thoughts, purify our intentions, and deliver us from every affliction and pain, and from all evil. Surround us by thy holy Angels, that, preserved and guided by their hosts, we may come to the unity of the faith, and to the knowledge of thine inaccessible glory; for blessed art thou to ages of ages. Amen.

Lord, have mercy, *thrice. Glory. Both now.* The more honourable than the Cherubim .... In the name of the Lord, father, give the blessing.

Priest. God be merciful unto us, and bless us, and shine the light of his countenance upon us, and have mercy upon us.

Then the Prayer of S. Ephrem, with the Genuflections. Vide page 59.

After this the Reader saith Trisagion, &c. After the Our Father *followeth* Lord, have mercy, *twelve times, and this Prayer to the Mother of God.*

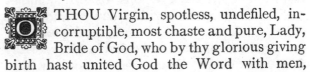 THOU Virgin, spotless, undefiled, incorruptible, most chaste and pure, Lady, Bride of God, who by thy glorious giving birth hast united God the Word with men,

and linked our apostate nature with heavenly
things; who art the one hope of the hopeless, the helper of the oppressed, the ready
protection of them that flee unto thee, and
the refuge of all Christians; despise not me,
a defiled sinner, who, by my impious thoughts,
words and deeds, have made myself an unprofitable servant, and, by reason of my
sloth, am become a slave of sensual life.
But thou, O Mother of the man-loving God,
have mercy and compassion upon me, a
sinner and a prodigal. Accept this my
prayer offered unto thee by unhallowed lips,
and using thy maternal influence with thy
Son, our Lord and Master, beseech him to
open unto me the loving tenderness of his
grace, and, despising my numberless transgressions, to bring me to repentance, and
make me a zealous doer of his commandments. Be ever present with me, as the merciful, compassionate, good and loving helper
and advocate in this present life, turning
aside the assaults of enemies and guiding
me unto salvation. And at the hour of my
death preserve my miserable soul, and drive
far from it all dark visions of evil demons.
Deliver me on the terrible day of judgment
from everlasting punishment, and make me
an inheritor of the unspeakable glory of thy
Son, our God. Grant me to obtain this,

O most holy Lady and Mother of God through thine intercession and protection, by the grace and loving-kindness of thine only-begotten Son, our Lord, God, and Saviour, Jesus Christ, to whom with his Father everlasting, and the most holy, and good, and life-creating Spirit, is due all honour, glory and worship, now and ever, and to ages of ages. Amen.

Prayer to the Lord Jesus Christ.

AND grant unto us, O Master, now retiring to sleep, repose of body and soul, and keep us from the dark sleep of sin, and from every dark and nightly lust. Subdue our unruly passions, and quench the fiery darts of the evil one that are treacherously thrown against us. Quell the commotions of our flesh, and lull our earthly and sinful thoughts to sleep. And give unto us, O God, a watchful mind, pure thoughts, a temperate heart, and quiet sleep free from every illusion of Satan. And rouse us at the hour of prayer confirmed in thy commandments, and with the remembrance of thy judgment strong within us. And make us worthy to sing thy nocturnal song, and to bless and glorify thy most honourable and majestic name, of the Father, and of

the Son, and of the Holy Ghost, now and
ever, and to ages of ages. Amen.

O most glorious, ever-virgin Mother of
Christ our God, bring our prayers to thy
Son and our God, that, for thy sake, he
may save our souls.

The Father is my trust, the Son is my
refuge, the Holy Ghost is my protection.
O holy Trinity, glory to thee.

Glory. Both now.

Lord, have mercy, thrice.   Give the
blessing.

Priest. O Lord Jesus Christ our God, for
the sake of the prayers of thy most holy
Mother, and of all the Saints, have mercy
upon us, for thou art good and the Lover
of men.

Reader. Amen. And the Absolution and
Ectenia follow, as at Nocturns. Vide page 50.

Then all depart, and say this Prayer.

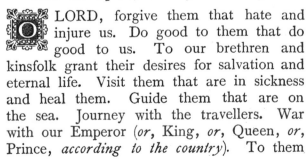 LORD, forgive them that hate and
injure us. Do good to them that do
good to us.   To our brethren and
kinsfolk grant their desires for salvation and
eternal life. Visit them that are in sickness
and heal them. Guide them that are on
the sea. Journey with the travellers. War
with our Emperor (or, King, or, Queen, or,
Prince, according to the country). To them

that minister and are beneficent unto us
grant forgiveness of sins. According to thy
great mercy, have mercy upon them that
have desired us, unworthy ones, to pray for
them. Remember, O Lord, our fathers and
brethren that have fallen asleep before us,
and give them rest where the light of thy
countenance shineth. Remember, O Lord,
our brethren that are in captivity, and deliver them from all their bonds. Remember,
O Lord, them that bring forth fruit and do
good works in thy holy Churches, and grant
them their desires for salvation and eternal
life. Remember us also, O Lord, thine
humble, sinful and unworthy servants; and
enlighten our minds with the light of thy
knowledge, and guide us in the way of thy
commandments. Through the prayers of our
most holy Lady, the God-bearing ever-virgin
Mary, and of all thy Saints; for thou art
blessed to ages of ages. Amen.

VII. THE LITTLE COMPLINE.

The beginning is as at Nocturns on Sundays. Vide page 45.
After O come, let us worship .... *thrice,*
Psalm 50 (51).
Have mercy upon me, O God .... *Vide page* 29.

Psalm 69 (70).

GOD, come to mine assistance : O Lord, make haste to help me. Let them be ashamed and confounded that seek after my soul. Let them be turned backward and put to confusion that wish me evil. Let them be turned back instantly and put to shame that cry over me, There, there. But let all that seek thee, O God, rejoice and be glad in thee. And let them that love thy salvation say alway, The Lord be magnified. But I am poor and in misery : O God, help me. Thou art my helper and my redeemer: O Lord, make no long tarrying.

Psalm 142 (143).

O Lord, hear my prayer .... *Vide page* 22.

Then the Doxology, as in the Great Compline. Vide page 73.

The Confession of Faith. Vide page 65.

It is very meet to bless thee .... *Vide page* 61.

Trisagion, &c. After Our Father, *the Condakion of the Day. Or they say the following,*

O GOD of our Fathers, who ever dealest with us according to thy clemency; remove not thy mercy from us, but, by their intercessions, direct our life in peace.

Thy Church, clad in beautiful raiment with the blood of thy Martyrs in all the world, as with purple and fine linen, through them crieth unto thee, O Christ our God, Send down thy bounties upon thy people, give peace to thine estate, and great mercy to our souls. *Glory.*

O Christ, rest the souls of thy servants with the Saints, where there is no sickness, nor sadness, nor sighing, but life without ending. *Both now.*

Through the prayers, O Lord, of all the Saints, and of the Mother of God, grant us

6*

thy peace, and have mercy upon us; for thou alone art merciful.

On Friday Evening they substitute as followeth,

APOSTLES, Martyrs, Prophets, Divines, Venerables and Just, who have wrought a good work, have kept the faith, and have daring with the Saviour; we entreat you, O ye blessed ones, to pray for the salvation of our souls.   *Glory.*

O Christ, rest the souls .... *As before written. Both now.*

To thee, O Lord, the Author of creation, the world bringeth the God-bearing Martyrs as the first-fruits of nature. At their intercessions, through the Mother of God, preserve, O most Merciful One, thy Church and thine estate in perfect peace.

Lord, have mercy, *forty times.*

The Prayer. Thou that at all times .... *Vide page* 76.

Lord, have mercy, *thrice.* The more honourable .... Give the blessing. *And the Priest having given this, the Prayer to the Mother of God followeth, and the rest, as in the Great Compline.*

———+·–()–·+———

VIII. THE DAILY NOCTURNS.

The beginning is the same as in the Sunday Nocturns until the end of Psalm 50 (51). Then followeth the 17th Kathism of the Psalter on every day but Saturday, and on Saturday the 9th Kathism.

After the Kathism is said the Confession of Faith. Then, Trisagion, &c. After Our Father, *the following Troparia, except on Saturday.*

BEHOLD the Bridegroom cometh in the middle of the night, and blessed is that servant whom he shall find watching, but unworthy he whom he shall find careless. Beware then, my soul, lest thou be weighed down by sleep, lest thou be given over to death and be shut out from the kingdom; but awake, crying, Holy, holy, holy art thou, O God. Through the Mother of God, have mercy upon us. *Glory.*

While meditating, O my soul, upon that fearful day, keep watch, lighting thy lamp and feeding it with oil; for thou knowest not when the voice shall come that crieth, Behold the Bridegroom. Beware then, my soul, lest thou slumber, lest thou remain knocking without, like the five virgins. But persevere in watchfulness, that thou mayest meet Christ with rich oil, and that he may open to thee the divine bridechamber of his glory.   *Both now.*

O God-bearing Virgin, that art an untaken wall, a fortress of salvation, to thee we pray, Destroy the counsel of adversaries, turn the grief of thy people into joy, protect thy city, war with our Emperor (*or*, King, *or*, Queen, *or*, Prince) *N.*, intercede for the peace of the world. For thou, O Mother of God, art our hope.

And on Saturday they say,

O UNCREATED Nature, Author of all things, open our lips to declare thy praise and cry, Holy, holy, holy art thou, O God. Through the Mother of God, have mercy upon us.

Glory.

Imitating upon earth the Hosts above, to thee, O Blessed One, we offer the triumphal hymn, Holy, holy, holy art thou, O God.

Through the Mother of God, have mercy upon us.

Both now.

Thou hast aroused me from my bed and from sleep, O Lord. And now enlighten my mind and heart, and open my lips to sing to thee, O holy Trinity, Holy, holy, holy art thou, O God. Throngh the Mother of God, have mercy upon us.

Lord, have mercy, *forty times.*

The Prayer. Thou that in all times . . . . *Vide page* 76.

Lord, have mercy, *thrice. Glory. Both now.* The more honourable. Give the blessing. *This the Priest giveth.* [*And in the Fasts the Prayer of S. Ephrem is said here, with the Genuflections.*]

And now shall be said the following Prayers.

First Prayer.

Master, God, Father almighty . . . . *Vide pape* 73.

Second Prayer. [*Said only from September 22 until Palm Sunday.*]

LORD almighty, God of hosts and of all flesh, who dwellest on high and lookest down on the humble, who searchest the hearts and reins, and foreseest

clearly things hidden unto men, Light without beginning and everlasting, with whom is
no variableness nor the shadow of turning;
thyself, O immortal King, accept the prayers
which, trusting in the multitude of thy
mercies, we dare to offer unto thee with our
impure lips. And forgive us the offences
which we have committed in deeds, words
and thoughts, knowingly and unknowingly.
Cleanse us from every defilement of the flesh
and spirit; and grant that we may, with
watchful heart and sober mind, pass through
all the night of our present life, awaiting
the coming of the bright and appointed day
of thine only-begotten Son, our Lord, God
and Saviour, Jesus Christ, in the which he
shall come with glory to judge all men and
render to every one according to his works,
so that, neither lapsing nor slothful, but
watchful and doing, we may be found prepared, and may enter into the joy and divine
mansion of his glory, where unceasing is the
voice of the feasting, and unspeakable the
bliss of them that behold the infinite goodness of thy countenance. For thou art the
true Light, which enlighteneth and sanctifieth
all things, and all creation singeth thee to
ages of ages. Amen.

Third Prayer.

E bless thee, O God most high and Lord of mercy, who ever doest amongst us great and unsearchable, glorious and terrible things, of which there is no number, and who grantest unto us sleep to rest our weakness and to relieve the labour of our toiling flesh. We give thee thanks that thou hast not destroyed us in our transgressions, but, in thy wonted love to man, hast raised us lying in despair to glorify thy power. Therefore we pray thee of thine unmeasurable goodness to enlighten our thoughts and our eyes, and to raise our minds from the heavy sleep of sloth. Open our lips and fill them with thy praise, that we may continually sing and give thanks unto thee, O God, the unbeginning Father, who in all things and by all things, together with thine only-begotten Son, and thy most holy, and good, and life-creating Spirit, art glorified, now and ever, and to ages of ages. Amen.

Second and concluding Prayer for Saturdays.

WILL magnify thee exceedingly, O Lord, because thou hast regarded my lowliness and hast not delivered me up into the hands of mine enemies, but hast

saved my soul out of necessities. And now,
O Master, let thy hand cover me and thy
mercy come upon me, for my soul is troubled
and afflicted concerning its departure from
this mine accursed and defiled body, lest
the evil counsel of the adversary meet and
hinder it in the darkness because of the
sins I have knowingly and unknowingly
committed in this life. Be merciful unto
me, O Master, and let it not behold the
dark vision of evil demons, but let thy bright
and shining Angels receive it. Give glory to
thy holy name, and by thy power lead me
to thy divine judgment-seat. When I am
judged let not the hand of the prince of
this world seize and drag me, a sinner, into
the abyss of hades; but stand thou near
me, and be unto me a Saviour and a Redeemer. For these bodily sufferings are joy
unto thy servants. Have mercy, O Lord,
upon my soul which is defiled with the
passions of this life, and receive it purified
through repentance and thanksgiving; for
thou art blessed to ages of ages. Amen.

After the Prayers, O come, let us worship . . . . *thrice. Psalms* 120 (121) *and* 133
(134). *Glory. Both now.*

Trisagion, &c. After Our Father, *the
following Troparia in Tone* 2.

REMEMBER thy servants, O Lord, for thou art good, and forgive them their sins during life; for there is none sinless save thee, who art able to give rest unto the departed.

Thou, the Creator, that in the depth of wisdom dost appoint all things in loving-kindness unto men, and dost grant unto them needful things; give rest, O Lord, unto the souls of thy servants; for in thee, our Maker, Author and God, they have put their trust.

Glory.

O Christ, rest the souls of thy servants with the Saints, where there is no sickness, nor sadness, nor sighing, but life without ending.

Both now.

All generations bless thee, O God-bearing Virgin; for in thee the Uncontainable, even Christ our God, vouchsafed to be contained. And we are also blessed who have thee for our mediatress; for day and night thou prayest for us, and the sceptres of the kingdom are strenghtened by thy prayers. Therefore, praising thee, we cry, Hail! full of grace, the Lord is with thee.

Lord, have mercy, *twelve times.*

And this Prayer.

REMEMBER, O Lord, our fathers and brethren who sleep in hope of resurrection to eternal life, and all who have departed in piety and faith. And forgive them all their sins, voluntary and involuntary, which by deed, word, or intention, they have committed. And place them in shining, tranquil and refreshing places, whence are driven away all sickness, sadness and sighing, and where the light of thy countenance shineth and rejoiceth all thy Saints for ever. Grant unto them and unto us thy kingdom, and the communion of thine unspeakable and eternal blessings, and the enjoyment of thine endless and blissful life. For thou art the Resurrection, and the Life, and the Repose of thy sleeping servants, O Christ our God, and to thee we ascribe glory, with thine unbeginning Father, and thy most holy, and good, and life-creating Spirit, now and ever, and to ages of ages. Amen.

O MOST glorious ever-virgin Mother of Christ our God, bring our prayers to thy Son and our God, that, for thy sake, he may save our souls.

The Father is my trust, the Son is my

refuge, the Holy Ghost is my protection. O holy Trinity, glory to thee.

Glory. Both now. Lord, have mercy, *thrice.* Give the blessing.

And the Priest giveth this, saying, Christ our true God . . . . *And the rest, as at the conclusion of the Sunday Nocturns. Vide page* 50.

IX. THE DAILY MATINS.

—◦—

The beginning and first part is as in the Matins for a Festival when no Vigil is held. Vide page 52. *The variations take place after the Six Psalms and the Ectenia of Peace. On ordinary days after the Ectenia they sing,* The Lord is God .... *and the Troparia of the Day. But in the Fasts and the Days of Remembrance for the Departed they sing* Alleluia, *with which, either by the Reader or the Deacon, the following verses are read.*

Verse 1. In the night season my soul keepeth watch unto thee, O God, for thine ordinances are light upon the earth.

Verse 2. Learn righteousness, O ye that dwell upon the earth.

Verse 3. Anger shall fall upon the people that have not corrected themselves.

Verse 4. Render evil unto them, O Lord, render evil unto them, even unto the proud ones of the earth.

After the Alleluia, *instead of the Troparia are sung the following Songs to the Trinity.*

I. In the Week in which Tone 1 *is sung.*

B Y thoughtful immaterial mind raised into bodily forms of bodiless Hosts, and receiving illumination through singing the thrice-holy song to the tri-personal Deity, let us like the Cherubim cry to the one God, Holy, holy, holy art thou, our God . . . .

Conclusion of the verse. On Monday. Through the intercession of thy bodiless ones have mercy upon us.

On Tuesday. Through the prayers of thy Forerunner have mercy upon us.

On Wednesday and Friday. Through the might of thy Cross keep us, O Lord.

On Thursday. Through the prayers of thy holy Apostles, and of Nicolas the Divine, have mercy upon us.

On this wise, according to the Day of the Week, is sung the conclusion of the first verse of the Songs to the Trinity in all the Tones.
Glory.

With all the heavenly Hosts let us like the Cherubim cry to him that dwelleth on

high, offering thrice-holy praise, Holy, holy, holy art thou, our God.   Through the prayers of thy Saints have mercy upon us.
Both now.

On rising from sleep we fall down before thee, O Blessed One, and sing the angelic hymn to thee, O Mighty One, Holy, holy, holy art thou, our God.   Through the Mother of God have mercy upon us.

II.   In the Week in which Tone 2 is sung.

IMITATING upon earth the Hosts above, we offer unto thee, O Blessed One, the song of victory, Holy, holy, holy art thou, our God . . . . *Glory.*

O uncreated Nature, Creator of all things, open our lips that we may proclaim thy praise, crying, Holy, holy, holy art thou, our God.   Through the prayers of thy Saints have mercy upon us. *Both now.*

Thou hast aroused me from my bed and from sleep, O Lord.   And now enlighten my mind and heart, and open my lips to sing thee, O holy Trinity.   Holy, holy, holy art thou, our God.   Through the Mother of God have mercy upon us.

III.   In the Week in which Tone 3 is sung.

O CONSUBSTANTIAL   and   undivided Trinity,   tri-personal   and   co-eternal Unity, to thee, O God, we cry the angelic hymn, Holy, holy, holy art thou, our God . . . *Glory.*

The unbeginning Father and the also unbeginning Son, and the eternal Spirit, daring like the Cherubim to glorify, we say, Holy, holy, holy art thou, our God. Through the prayers of thy Saints have mercy upon us.

Both now.

Suddenly the Judge shall come, and the deeds of every one shall be revealed, but at midnight we will cry in fear, Holy, holy, holy art thou, our God. Through the Mother of God, have mercy upon us.

IV. In the Week in which Tone 4 is sung.

DARING to offer the hymn of thy spiritual Ministers, we mortals say, Holy, holy, holy art thou, our God . . . . *Glory.*

Like the hosts of Angels in heaven, yet standing in fear as men upon the earth, a victorious hymn we offer unto thee, O Blessed One, Holy, holy, holy art thou our God. Through the prayers of thy Saints have mercy upon us. *Both now.*

Thine unbeginning Father, and thee, O Christ our God, and thy most holy Spirit, daring like the Cherubim to glorify, we say, Holy, holy, holy art thou, our God. Through the Mother of God have mercy upon us.

V. In the Week in which Tone 5 is sung.

IT is the time of song and the hour of prayer, and fervently we cry to the one God, Holy, holy, holy art thou, our God. . . .

Glory.

Daring to represent thy spiritual Hosts, O unbeginning Trinity, with unworthy lips we cry, Holy, holy, holy art thou, our God. Through the prayers of thy Saints have mercy upon us.

Both now.

Thou that wast contained within the Virgin's womb and wast not separated from the bosom of the Father, accept us, O Christ our God, crying with the Angels unto thee, Holy, holy, holy art thou, our God. Through the Mother of God have mercy upon us.

VI. In the Week in which Tone 6 is sung.

BEFORE thee stand the Cherubim fearful and the Seraphim with awe, offering with resounding voice the hymn thrice-holy, with whom we sinners also cry, Holy, holy, holy art thou, our God . . . . *Glory.*

With bodiless mouth the six-winged ones chant with resounding songs the hymn thrice-holy to thee, our God, and we upon earth with unworthy lips offer thee praise, saying, Holy, holy, holy art thou, our God.

Through the prayers of thy Saints have mercy upon as. *Both now.*

Let us glorify the Godhead of Tri-unity in uncommingled Oneness, and sing the Angels' song, Holy, holy, holy art thou, our God. Through the Mother of God have mercy upon us.

VII. In the Week in which Tone 7 is sung.

THOU that in highest might art sung by Cherubim, and in divine glory worshipped by Angels, accept us who upon earth with unworthy lips offer thee praise, and say, Holy, holy, holy art thou, our God . . . .
Glory.

As putteth away sloth and sleep our soul, so let us while praising shew amendment to the Judge, and cry in fear, Holy, holy, holy art thou, our God. Through the prayers of thy Saints have mercy upon us. *Both now.*

Ascribing the thrice-holy praise of the Seraphim to the Trinity in Unity, let us cry in fear, Holy, holy, holy art thou, our God. Through the Mother of God have mercy upon us.

VIII. In the Week in which Tone 8 is sung.

HAVING our hearts in heaven, we imitate the angelic Hosts, and fall down in fear before the Judge, uttering the victorious

7*

praise, Holy, holy, holy art thou, our
God . . . .

Glory.

Not daring to look on thee, the flying Cherubim with acclamation cry the divine song of
thrice-holy sound, with whom we also say, Holy,
holy, holy art thou, our God. Through the
prayers of thy Saints have mercy upon us.

Both now.

Cast down because of the multitude of
our offences, and not daring to look unto
thy heavenly height, bowing down our souls
and bodies, with the Angels we cry to thee
the hymn, Holy, holy, holy art thou, our
God. Through the Mother of God have
mercy upon us.

*After the proper Song to the Trinity shall
follow the reading of the Kathisms of the
Psalter with the Kathismal Hymns in their
order, and thereafter shall be immediately
said Psalm* 50 (51). *Then the Prayer*, O God,
save thy people and bless . . . . *Vide page* 32.
*And after this they shall begin to sing the
proper Canon for the Day.*

*After the Eighth Ode usually followeth the
Canticle of the Mother of God*, My soul doth
magnify the Lord . . . . *with the Refrain*,
The more honourable . . . . *as in the Great
Matins. Vide page* 35.

After the Ninth Ode shall not follow the Little Ectenia, but immediately shall be sung, It is very meet . . . . *Vide page* 61.

And in the Great Quadragesima they shall then sing the Lucern of the proper Tone on this wise,

The Verse is sung thrice, the first time with the addition, where occur the brackets, of,

On Monday, Through the intercession of thy bodiless ones,

On Tuesday, Through the prayers of thy Forerunner,

On Wednesday and Friday, Through the might of thy Cross,

On Thursday, Through the prayers of thy holy Apostles, and of Nicolas the Divine,

The second time, always with the addition of, Through the prayers of thy Saints,

And the third time, always with the addition of, Through the prayers of the Mother of God,

And, Glory, precedeth the first repetition, and, Both now, the second.

Lucerns.

I. In the Week in which Tone I *is sung.*

O Lord, from whom shineth forth light, cleanse my soul from every sin, [. . . .], and save me.

II. In the Week in which Tone 2 is sung.

O Christ our God, send forth thine eternal light, and enlighten the secret eyes of my heart, [. . . .], and save me.

III. In the Week in which Tone 3 is sung.

O Christ our God, send forth thy light, and enlighten my heart, [. . . .], and save me.

IV. In the Week in which Tone 4 is sung.

Thou that shinest light unto all the world, cleanse my darkened soul from every sin, [. . . .], and save me.

V. In the Week in which Tone 5 is sung.

O light-giving Lord, send forth thy light, and enlighten my heart, [. . . .], and save me.

VI. In the Week in which Tone 6 is sung.

[. . . .], send unto our souls thine eternal light.

VII. In the Week in which Tone 7 is sung.

Inspire me, O Lord, to sing thy praise and to do thy will, [. . . .], and save me.

VIII. In the Week in which Tone 8 is sung.

O Christ, who art thyself the Light, enlighten me, [. . . .], and save me.

When however it is not a Fast, the following Exapostilaria shall be sung instead of the Lucern.

On Monday. Thou that dost deck the heaven with stars, and by thine Angels dost enlighten all the earth, Creator of all things, save them that sing thy praise.

Glory. Both now.

The delight of the Angels, the joy of the afflicted, and the refuge of Christians art thou, O Virgin Mother of the Lord. Help us, and deliver us from eternal torment.

On Tuesday. Let us with one accord extol the Precursor and Baptist of the Saviour, the Prophet of prophets, the growth of the wilderness, John, the son of Elizabeth.

Glory. Both now.

The delight of the Angels. *As o Monday.*

On Wednesday and Friday. The Cross is the watcher of all the world, the Cross is the adornment of the Church, the Cross is the might of kings, the Cross is the strength of the faithful, the Cross is the glory of Angels, and the wound of demons. *Glory. Both now.*

Standing by the Cross, she that without seed brought thee forth, lamenting cried, Alas! my sweetest Child, how fadest thou away before mine eyes, how art thou numbered with the dead?

On Thursday. Apostles of the Saviour, ye have gone through all the world and preached Christ's holy incarnation of the

Virgin, have turned the folk from error and enlightened them, and taught all men the worship of the holy Trinity. *Glory.*

Let us with one accord extol that great chief-shepherd and high-priest, Nicolas, Bishop of the Myrians; for he saved many men who were to die unjustly, and in a dream with Ablabius to the king appeared annulling the unjust sentence. *Both now.*

O most pure Mary, golden censer that became the tabernacle of the undivided Trinity; in thee the Father was well pleased, in thee the Son abode, and the Holy Spirit, overshadowing thee, declared thee, Maiden, Mother of God.

On Saturday. Thou that as God hast power over quick and dead, and by thy Saints enlightenest all the earth, Author of all things, save them that sing thy praise.

Glory. Both now.

O Mother of God, we make our boast in thee, and have thee as a mediatress with God. Stretch forth thy matchless hand, and overcome our foes: send to thy servants help from the holy place.

If it be a Minor Holiday, although the Many mercies *be not sung after the Kathisms, and there be no Gospel read, yet from this place shall the rest of this Matins be the same as that indicated in the order of the Great Matins. Vide page* 36, *et seq.*

But if it be a Fast, or an ordinary day, the rest shall be as followeth.

After the Lucern or the Exapostilarion, they shall begin immediately to read the Psalms of Praise, namely, Psalms 148, 149 *and* 150. *Glory. Both now.*

To thee is due glory, O Lord our God, and to thee we ascribe glory, to the Father, and to the Son, and to the Holy Ghost, now and ever, and to ages of ages. Amen. *And the Doxology, as in the Great Compline. Vide page* 73, *substituting* day *for* evening, *where the latter word occurreth.*

After the Doxology shall follow the Ectenia of Supplication. Let us accomplish our morning prayer to the Lord. *Vide page* 12.

Then shall the appointed Stichera for the Day be sung, between which shall be read the following verses.

LET us be filled early with thy mercy, O Lord, so shall we rejoice and be glad all our days. Make us glad for the days in which thou didst afflict us, the years in which we saw evil. And look upon thy servants, and upon thy works, and guide their children.

And let the brightness of the Lord our God be upon us, and prosper thou the work of our hands upon us, yea, prosper thou our handiwork.

Glory. Both now.

After the Stichera, the Reader shall say,

IT is a good thing to give thanks unto the Lord, and to sing to thy name, O Most High, to proclaim thy mercy in the morning and thy truth every night.

Trisagion, &c. After Our Father, *in the fasting time shall follow,*

STANDING in the temple of thy glory, we think that we stand in heaven. O Mother of God, gate of heaven, open to us the gate of thy mercy.

Lord, have mercy, *forty times.*

Glory. Both now. The more honourable than the Cherubim . . . . In the name of the Lord, father, give the blessing.

Priest. Blessed be Christ our God, always, now and ever, and to ages of ages.

Reader. Amen. O heavenly King, stablish our faithful kings, confirm the faith, quiet the nations, give peace to the world, preserve this holy abode, place our departed fathers and brethren in the tabernacles of the just, and accept us, penitent and thanksgiving; for thou art good and the Lover of men.

And the Prayer of S. Ephrem, with the Genuflections. Vide page 59.

Then the First Hour.

But if it is not a fasting time, after the Our Father, *instead of,* Standing in the temple .... *the Troparion of the Day, and straightway shall follow the Great Ectenia,* Have mercy upon us, O God .... *Vide page* 10.

After the Ectenia,

Priest. Wisdom! *Choir.* Give the blessing.

Priest. Blessed be Christ our God, always, now and ever, and to ages of ages.

Choir. Amen. Stablish, O God, our pious Sovereign (Emperor, *or,* King, *or,* Queen, *or,* Prince) *N.,* and the orthodox faith of all Orthodox Christians to ages of ages.

And the First Hour.

X. THE FIRST HOUR,
OR PRIME.

The beginning is as at Nocturns on Sundays. Vide page 45. *Though usually this Service is subjoined to Matins, and is begun immediately with,* O come let us worship.... *thrice.*

Psalms 5, 89 (90) *and* 100 (101).
Glory. Both now. Alleluia, alleluia, alleluia, glory to thee, O God, *thrice.* Lord, have mercy, *thrice. Glory. The Troparion of the Day. Both now.*

WHAT shall we call thee, O full of grace? Heaven? for from thee the Sun of righteousness arose. Paradise? for in thee bloomed the flower of immortality. Virgin? for thou didst remain undefiled. Pure Mother? for in thy holy arms was held the God of all things, even thy Son. Him do thou pray to save our souls. *Then,*

ORDER my steps according to thy word, and let not all transgression have dominion over me.

Deliver me from the wrongful dealings of men, and I will keep thy commandments.

Cause thy face to shine upon thy servant, and teach me thy statutes.

Let my mouth be filled with thy praise, O Lord, that I may sing of thy glory and majesty all the day long.

In the fasting time, or when Alleluia *is sung at Matins instead of* The Lord is God, *the following is said instead of the Troparion of the Day.*

Priest. In the morning hearken unto my voice, my King and my God.

The First Choir repeateth the verse.

Priest. Give ear unto my words, O Lord, understand my cry.

Second Choir. In the morning hearken....

Priest. For unto thee, O Lord, will I pray.

First Choir. In the morning hearken....

Priest. Glory. Reader. Both now. What shall we call thee ....

Then shall they sing antiphonally,
Order my steps ....

Trisagion, &c. After Our Father, *the Condakion of the Day.*

*But in the fasting time, the following Tro-
paria instead of the Condakion.*

On Monday, Tuesday and Thursday.

LET us with heart and lips for ever
   praise the glorious Mother of God, who
is holier than the holy Angels, confessing
her God-bearing, for she verily brought
forth the incarnate God, and she prayeth
without ceasing for our souls.

On Wednesday and Friday. Make haste
to help us, O Christ our God, before we
are enslaved by enemies, who blaspheme thee
and threaten us. Destroy by thy Cross
them that fight against us, that they may
know how much availeth the faith of the
right-believers, through the prayers of the
Mother of God, O only Lover of men.

On Saturday. To thee, O Lord, the
Author of creation, the world bringeth the
God-bearing Martyrs as the first-fruits of
nature. At their intercessions, through the
Mother of God, preserve, O most Merciful
One, thy Church and thine estate in perfect
peace.

Lord, have mercy, *forty times.*

The Prayer. Thou that in all times ....
Vide page 76. Lord, have mercy, *thrice.*
Glory. Both now. The more honourable ....

In the name of the Lord, father, give the blessing.

Priest. God be merciful unto us, and bless us, and shine the light of his countenance upon us, and have mercy upon us.

Reader. Amen. *And saith the closing Prayer. [Here in the Fasts is said the Prayer of S. Ephrem.]*

The closing Prayer.

CHRIST, the true Light which enlighteneth and sanctifieth every man that cometh into the world; let the light of thy countenance be shewed upon us, that in it we may behold the unapproachable light. And make straight our goings to the doing of thy commandments. Through the prayers of thy most pure Mother, and of all the Saints. Amen.

[On Sundays and Festivals the Priest readeth the closing Prayer, and immediately the Choir singeth,

TO thee, O Virgin, the chosen guide, thy servants sing a triumphal song, ascribing thanks to thee for the deliverance from evils, and, since thou hast an invincible might, deliver us, we pray thee, from every ill, that we may cry unto thee, Hail! O unmarried Bride.]

Glory. Both now. Lord, have mercy, *thrice.* Give the blessing.

Priest. Christ our true God, through the prayers of his all-pure Mother, of the holy, glorious and all-praised Apostles, of Saint *N.*, whose memory we this day celebrate, and of all the Saints, have mercy upon us, for he is good and the Lover of men.

Reader. Amen. *Or,* Lord, have mercy, *thrice.*

XI. THE THIRD HOUR,
OR TERCE.

The beginning is as at Nocturns on Sundays.
Vide page 45.
    After O come, let us worship .... *thrice,*
       Psalms 16 (17), 24 (25) *and* 50 (51).
    Glory. Both now. Alleluia .... *thrice.*
Lord, have mercy, *thrice. Glory. The Tro-*
parion of the Day. Both now.

 MOTHER of God, thou art the true vine that budded to us the fruit of life. We beseech thee, O Lady, to pray with the holy Apostles for mercy on our souls.

Blessed be the Lord God, blessed be the Lord day by day. May the God of our salvation further us, even our God, who is the God of salvation.

In the fasting time the following is said instead of the Troparion.

8

Priest. Lord, who didst send down thy most holy Spirit at the third hour upon thine Apostles; take him not from us, O Blessed One, but renew him in us who pray to thee.

The First Choir repeateth the verse.

Priest. Create in me a clean heart, O God, and renew a right spirit within me.

Second Choir. Lord, who didst send down . . . .

Priest. Cast me not away from thy presence, and take not thy holy Spirit from me.

First Choir. Lord, who didst send down . . . .

Priest. Glory. Reader. Both now. O Mother of God, thou art the true vine . . . . *And,* Blessed be the Lord God . . . .

Trisagion, &c. After Our Father, *the Condakion of the Day.*

But in the fasting time, the following,

BLESSED art thou, O Christ our God, who didst make the fishers wise, sending the Holy Ghost on them, and by them didst net all the world. O Lover of men, glory to thee. *Glory.*

A speedy and firm consolation give, O Jesus, to thy servants when our spirits are distressed. Depart not from our souls in affliction, nor stand far off from our minds in trouble, but for ever go before us. Draw nigh unto us, draw nigh, thou that art everywhere present. As thou wast always with thine Apostles, O Compassionate One, be thou with us who long for thee, that, being conjoined with thee, we may hymn and glorify thy most Holy Spirit. *Both now.*

The hope and mediatress and refuge of Christians, the wall that cannot be overthrown, the harbour of the helpless unagitated by storms art thou, O most pure Bearer of God; but, as saving the world by thy ceaseless intercessions, remember us also, O all-celebrated Virgin.

Lord, have mercy, *forty times.*

And the Prayer. Thou that in all times.... *Vide page* 76.

Here in the Fasts is said the Prayer of S. Ephrem.

Closing Prayer of the Third Hour.

MASTER, God, Father almighty, Lord, only-begotten Son, Jesus Christ, and Holy Ghost, one God-head, one Might! be gracious unto me, a sinner; and, by ways thou knowest, save me, thine unworthy servant; for thou art blessed to ages of ages. Amen.

————◦◇◦————

8

XII. THE SIXTH HOUR,
OR SEXT.

O come, let us worship . . . . *thrice.*
Psalms 53 (54), 54 (55) *and* 90 (91).
Glory. Both now. Alleluia . . . . *thrice.*
Lord, have mercy, *thrice. The Troparion
of the Day. Both now.*
As we have not daring . . . . *Vide page* 67.

LET thy compassions soon overtake us,
O Lord, for we have become very
poor. Help us, O God our Saviour,
for the glory of thy name. O Lord,
deliver us and cleanse our sins, for thy
name's sake.

*In the fasting time, instead of the Tro-
parion, the following is said.*

Priest. Thou that at the sixth day and
hour didst nail to the Cross the sin Adam
dared in Paradise; tear asunder also the

handwriting of our offences, O Christ our
God, and save us.

The First Choir repeateth the verse.

Priest. Hearken, O God, unto my prayer,
and despise not my petition.

Second Choir. Thou that at the sixth
day . . . .

Priest. I have cried unto God, and the
Lord heard me.

First Choir. Thou that at the sixth day...

Priest. Glory. Reader. Both now. As
we have not daring . . . . *And,* Let thy
compassions . . . .

Trisagion, &c. After Our Father, *the
Condakion of the Day. Or, in the fasting
time, the following.*

THOU hast perfected salvation in the
midst of the earth, O Christ our God;
thou hast stretched forth thy most pure
hands upon the Cross, gathering together all
the nations to cry unto thee, Glory to thee,
O Lord. *Glory.*

Before thy most pure image we bow down,
entreating forgiveness of our sins, O Christ
our God; for thou wast pleased willingly to
ascend the Cross in thy flesh, that thou
mightest deliver them that thou didst make
from the servitude of the enemy. Therefore we thankfully exclaim to thee, Thou

hast filled all things with joy, O our Saviour, thou that camest to save the world. *Both now.*

Thou that art the fountain of loving-kindness, vouchsafe unto us thy sympathy, O Mother of God. Look down on the people who have sinned, shew unto us thy wonted power; for, trusting in thee, we cry unto thee, Hail! as once did Gabriel the bodiless Chieftain.

Lord, have mercy, *forty times.*

And the Prayer, Thou that in all times.... *Vide page* 76.

In the Fasts, the Prayer of S. Ephrem.

*Closing Prayer of the Sixth Hour.
Of Basil the Great.*

GOD and Lord of hosts, Maker of all creation, who, through the loving-kindness of thine incomparable mercy, didst send thine only-begotten Son, our Lord Jesus Christ, for the salvation of our race, and, through his honourable Cross, hast blotted out the handwriting of our sins, and triumphed over the princes and powers of darkness; thyself, O Lord, accept from us sinners these thankful and prayerful supplications, and deliver us from every dark and deadly sin, and from all visible and invisible enemies that seek our hurt. Penetrate our flesh with the fear of thee, and incline not our hearts to evil words and imaginations, but wound our souls with thy love. Then shall we always look unto thee, and discern thee, who art the unapproachable and everlasting light, and, led thereby, shall ever pay unto thee our vows and thanksgiving, O unbeginning Father, with thine only-begotten Son, and thy most holy, and good, and life-creating Spirit, now and ever, and to ages of ages. Amen.

The Dismissal is as in the First Hour.

XIII. THE NINTH HOUR,
OR NONE.

The beginning is as at Nocturns on Sundays. Vide page 45.
After O come, let us worship . . . . *thrice,
Psalms* 83 (84), 84 (85) *and* 85 (86).
Glory. Both now. Alleluia . . . . *thrice.*
Lord, have mercy, *thrice. Glory. The Troparion of the Day. Both now.*

THOU that for our sakes wast born of the Virgin, and didst, O Blessed One, endure crucifixion, and by death didst spoil death, and, as God, didst shew forth the Resurrection; despise not us whom thine hands did fashion. Shew unto us thy loving-kindness, O Merciful One; accept her that bore thee, the Mother of God, praying for us, and save, O our Saviour, thy despairing people.

O cast us not away at the last for thy name's sake, neither annul thy testament, nor remove thy mercy from us; for the sake of Abraham thy well beloved, and of Isaac thy servant, and Israel thy Saint.

In the fasting time, instead of the Troparion.

Priest. Thou that at the ninth hour didst in thy flesh taste death for us; mortify the lusts of our flesh, O Christ our God, and save us.

The First Choir repeateth the verse.

Priest. Let my prayer come in before thee, O Lord : give me understanding according unto thy word.

Second Choir. Thou that at the ninth hour . . . .

Priest. Let my petition come in before thee, O Lord: deliver me according unto thy word.

First Choir. Thou that at the ninth hour . . . .

Priest. Glory. Reader. Both now. Thou that for our sakes . . . . *And*, O cast us not away . . . .

Trisagion, &c. After Our Father, *the Condakion of the Day. Or, in the fasting time, the following.*

THE thief, seeing the Prince of life hanging upon the Cross, exclaimed, If he who is crucified with us were not incarnate God, the sun would not hide his light, nor would the earth be moved. But, O thou all-enduring Lord, remember me in thy kingdom. *Glory.*

In the midst of two thieves thy Cross appeared a balance of righteousness. On one side it sank to hades through the weight of blasphemy, on the other it rose from iniquity to divine knowledge. O Christ our God, glory to thee. *Both now.*

Thy Mother seeing thee, the Lamb and Shepherd and Saviour of the world, upon the Cross, said with tears, Lo! the world rejoiceth, for it gaineth deliverance; but my heart is broken, for I see thy crucifixion, which for all thou endurest, O my Son and my God.

Lord, have mercy, *forty times.*

And the Prayer, Thou that in all times . . . . *Vide page* 76.

In the Fasts, the Prayer of S. Ephrem.

Closing Prayer of the Ninth Hour. Of Basil the Great.

MASTER, Lord Jesus Christ our God, who art long-patient with our sins, and hast led us even until this present hour, at which thou didst hang upon the life-giving tree, and shew the way into Paradise to the well-intentioned thief, and death by death didst overcome; do thou cleanse us, thy sinful and unworthy servants. For we have sinned and transgressed, and are unworthy to lift up our eyes and look unto the height of heaven, because we have forsaken the way of righteousness and walked according to the desires of our own hearts. But we beseech thee, O Lord, of thine immeasurable goodness to spare us according to the greatness of thy mercy, and to save us for thy holy name's sake, for our days have been consumed in vanity. Deliver us out of the hand of the enemy, and forgive our sins, and slay our fleshly lusts, so that, putting off the old man and putting on the new, we may henceforth live for thee, our Master and Benefactor, and, keeping thy commandments, may gain thine everlasting rest, the dwelling whereof is all gladness. For thou art verily the joy and gladness of them that love thee, O Christ our God, and to thee we ascribe glory, with thine unbeginning Father, and thy most holy, and good, and life-creating Spirit, now and ever, and to ages of ages. Amen.

XIV. THE PRO-LITURGY SERVICE,

CALLED,

THE TYPICA.

———o———

*This Service is said either in the Great
Fasts, when the Hours are conjoined with
the Vespers or with the Liturgy of the Pre-
sanctified, or it is said on ordinary days when
for some reason there is no celebration of
the Liturgy. In the former instance, it serveth
as a transition from the Morning to the Evening Service, and in the latter, it is a Service
in itself instead of the prayers and hymns
of the Liturgy.*

These two uses are indicated as followeth.

A. THE TYPICA IN THE GREAT FASTS.

After the Prayer of the Ninth Hour,
Master, Lord Jesus Christ . . . . *they begin
to sing on this wise,*

The First Choir.

N thy kingdom remember us, O Lord, when thou comest in thy kingdom. Blessed art the poor in spirit, for theirs is the kingdom of heaven. Remember us, O Lord, when thou comest in thy kingdom.

Second Choir. Blessed are they that mourn, for they shall be comforted. Remember us, O Lord . . . . *And so after every verse.*

First Choir. Blessed are the meek, for they shall inherit the earth.

Second Choir. Blessed are they that do hunger and thirst after righteousness, for they shall be filled.

First Choir. Blessed are the merciful, for they shall obtain mercy.

Second Choir. Blessed are the pure in heart, for they shall see God.

First Choir. Blessed are the peace-makers, for they shall be called the children of God.

Second Choir. Blessed are they that are persecuted for righteousness' sake, for theirs is the kingdom of heaven.

First Choir. Blessed are ye when men shall revile you and persecute you, and shall say all manner of evil against you falsely for my sake.

Second Choir. Rejoice, and be exceeding glad, for great is your reward in heaven.

First Choir. Glory. Remember us . . . .

Second Choir. Both now. Remember us....

Chorus. Remember us, O Lord, when thou comest in thy kingdom. Remember us, O Master, when thou comest in thy kingdom. Remember us, O Holy One, when thou comest in thy kingdom.

Reader. The heavenly choir praiseth thee, and saith, Holy, holy, holy Lord Sabaoth, heaven and earth are full of thy glory.

Verse. Ye looked unto him and were enlightened, and your faces were not ashamed.

The heavenly choir . . . . *Glory.*

The choir of holy Angels and Archangels with all the heavenly Hosts praiseth thee, and saith, Holy, holy, holy Lord Sabaoth, heaven and earth are full of thy glory. *Both now.*

Then the Confession of Faith, I believe in one God . . . . *After this,*

O GOD, remit, and pardon, and forgive our sins, whether we did them willingly or not, whether by deeds or words, whether in knowledge or in ignorance, whether by night or day, or if we did them in our thought and purpose, forgive us all, for thou art good and lovest man.

Our Father . . . .

Then the Condakion for the Day. Lord, have mercy, *forty times. Glory. Both now.* In the name of the Lord, father, give the blessing.

Priest. God be merciful unto us, and bless us, and shine the light of his countenance upon us, and have mercy upon us.

And the Prayer of S. Ephrem followeth, and the Reader beginneth immediately the Vespers, saying, O come, let us worship . . . . *Psalm* 103 (104). *And the rest.*

B. THE TYPICA ON ORDINARY DAYS.

At the conclusion of the Sixth Hour, the Reader beginneth,

BLESS the Lord, O my soul. O Lord, thou art blessed. *And Psalm* 102 (103). *Glory. Both now.*

Bless the Lord, O my soul, and all that is within me, bless his holy name. O Lord, thou art blessed.

Then,

Glory. Praise the Lord, O my soul. While I live will I praise the Lord, I will sing praises unto my God while I have being. *And Psalm* 145 (146). *Both now.*

ONLY-BEGOTTEN Son and Word of God, who art immortal, and didst vouchsafe for our salvation to take flesh of the holy Mother of God and ever-virgin Mary, and without mutation didst become man, and wast crucified, Christ our God, and by death didst overcome death, being one of the holy Trinity, and glorified with the Father and the Holy Ghost: O save us.

Then moreover, the Beatitudes, with the following verses.

REMEMBER me, O God my Saviour, when thou comest in thy kingdom, and save me, for thou alone art the Lover of men.

Thou, O Christ, that didst accept the tears of Peter, accept also my repentance, and grant me forgiveness of my sins.

Thou, O Christ, that dost enlighten the heavenly choirs, enlighten also the eyes of my heart.

Thou didst preach repentance unto men, O Baptist and Precursor of the Lord: I pray thee to grant me to repent from my heart.

O Christ, thou wast of thine own accord nailed on the tree, and by thy might hast overcome the arrogance of the proud.

O glorious Apostles, as mysterious rays ye have penetrated the world, and with faith have enlightened the race of men.

Thou, O Lover of men, who hast glorified Prophets, Teachers, Venerables and Just, save our souls by their prayers. *Glory.*

We glorify the Father, and the Son, and

the Holy Ghost, saying, O holy Trinity,
save our souls.

Both now.

All generations call thee blessed, most
pure one, for thou verily didst bring forth
the blessed God.

*Then are read the Epistle and Gospel for
the Day, or, Col.* III. 12—17 *and Mark* VIII. 34
—IX. I.

After the Gospel. Glory. Both now. Remember us, O Lord . . . . The heavenly
choir . . . . *Vide page* 126. *The Confession
of Faith.* O God, remit and pardon . . . .
Our Father. *The Condakion of the Day.*
Lord, have mercy, *twelve times.*

Prayer.

MOST holy Trinity, that art might in
one substance and kingdom undivided,
Fountain of all good; be gracious unto
me, a sinner. Confirm and instruct my heart,
and take from me every defilement. Illuminate my thoughts, that I may always
praise thee, sing and worship thee, and say,
One holy, one Lord Jesus Christ, to the
glory of God the Father. Amen.

BLESSED be the name of the Lord, from
henceforth, and to all ages, *thrice. And
Psalm* 33 (34). *Vide page* 15.

And the Dismissal as in the First Hour.

9

XV. AT THE LITURGIES OF SAINT CHRYSOSTOM AND SAINT BASIL.

The Liturgy of Saint Chrysostom is said on all ordinary occasions, and that of Saint Basil on the Sundays of the Great Quadragesima, excepting Palm Sunday; on Holy Thursday and Holy Saturday; on the Festivals of Christmas and Epiphany, when falling on Sunday or Monday, otherwise on their Eves, and on that of the Saint himself, (Jan. 1). It differeth from the Liturgy of Saint Chrysostom in little but the secret portions, excepting that when said on Holy Thursday and Holy Saturday, and on the Eves of Christmas and Epiphany, it is conjoined with the Vespers, the order of which is followed until the Tranquil Light *and the Prokimena have been sung, and the proper Lections from the Old Testament read, when the order indicated in the ensuing pages is followed, beginning at the place where they sing the Trisagion.*

A. THE LITURGY OF THE CATECHUMENS.

The Deacon beginneth,

MASTER, give the blessing,

The Priest saith,

BLESSED be the kingdom of the Father, and of the Son, and of the Holy Ghost, now and ever, and to ages of ages. *Choir.* Amen.

[*And in the Paschal Season they sing*, Christ is risen from the dead, death by death down doth he tread, and on those within the tombs he bestoweth life. *And the appointed verses.*]

Then the Ectenia of Peace. Vide page 2.

Then they sing the Antiphons.

After the first of these followeth the Little Ectenia, with the Exclamation, For thine is the might, and thine is the kingdom, the power and the glory, of the Father, and of the Son, and of the Holy Ghost, now and ever, and to ages of ages. *The Choir answereth,* Amen. *And singeth the Second Antiphon. This is again followed by the Little Ectenia, but with the Exclamation*, For thou art a merciful and man-loving God, and to

9*

thee we ascribe glory, to the Father, and to the Son, and to the Holy Ghost, now and ever, and to ages of ages. *Choir.* Amen. *And singeth the Third Antiphon.*

On Sundays and Festivals the Antiphons are.

I. Bless the Lord, O my soul. *Psalm* 102 (103).

II. Praise the Lord, O my soul. *Psalm* 145 *(146).* Only-begotten Son . . . .

III. The Beatitudes. Matth. v. 3—12.

As indicated in the Typica. But with the Beatitudes are sung certain verses proper to the day.

The following Antiphons may however be substituted.

I. It is a good thing to give thanks unto the Lord.

It is a good thing to give thanks unto the Lord, and to sing to thy name, O Most High.

To proclaim thy mercy in the morning, and thy truth every night.

For the Lord is righteous, and there is no unrighteousness in him.

Glory. Both now.

And after every verse is added,

Through the prayers of the Mother of God, O Saviour, save us.

II. The Lord reigneth, he is clothed with majesty.

The Lord reigneth, he is clothed with majesty : the Lord is clothed with majesty, and hath girded himself.

For he hath made the whole world so sure that it cannot be moved.

Thy testimonies, O Lord, are exceeding true: holiness becometh thine house, O Lord, for ever.

And after every verse is added,

Through the prayers of thy Saints, O Saviour, save us.

Glory. Both now. Only-begotten Son . . . .

III. O come, let us sing unto the Lord, let us heartily rejoice in God our Saviour.

Let us come before his presence with thanksgiving, and shew ourselves glad in him with psalms.

For the Lord is a great God, and a great King above all the earth.

For in his hands are all the ends of the earth, and the height of the hills is his also.

For the sea is his and he made it, and his hands created the dry land.

And after every verse is added,

O Son of God, who art wonderful in the Saints, save us who sing to thee, Alleluia.

But on the Great Festivals of the Year, to wit, of Palms, Easter, Pentecost, Christmas and Epiphany, there are special Antiphons provided, as follow.

On Palm Sunday.

I. I will love the Lord, because be hath heard the voice of my prayer.

The pains of death came upon me, and the terrors of hades overtook me.

I was in affliction and grief, and I called upon the name of the Lord.

I shall be accepted of the Lord in the land of the living.

Glory. Both now.

And after every verse is added,

Through the prayers of the Mother of God, O Saviour, save us.

II. I believed, therefore have I spoken, but I was brought low exceedingly.

What shall I render unto the Lord for all that he hath done unto me?

I will take the cup of salvation, and call upon the name of the Lord.

I will pay my vows unto the Lord in the presence of all his people.

And after every verse is added,

O Son of God, who didst sit upon an ass's colt, save us who sing to thee, Alleluia.

Glory. Both now. Only-begotten Son . . . .

III. O give thanks unto the Lord, for he is good, because his mercy endureth for ever.

Let the house of Israel say that he is good, because his mercy endureth for ever.

Let the house of Aaron say that he is good, because his mercy endureth for ever.

Let all them that fear the Lord say that he is good, because his mercy endureth for ever.

And after every verse, the Troparion of the Festival.

On Easter Day, and throughout the Bright Week.

I. Make a joyful noise unto God, all the earth.

Sing forth the honour of his name, make his praise glorious.

Say unto God, How terrible art thou in thy works: through the greatness of thy power shall thine enemies submit themselves to thee.

All the earth shall worship thee and sing unto thee, they shall sing to thy name.

Glory. Both now.

And after every verse is added,

Through the prayers of the Mother of God, O Saviour, save us.

II. God be merciful unto us and bless us.

That thy way may be known upon earth, thy saving health among all nations.

Let the people praise thee, O God, let all the people praise thee.

And after every verse is added,

O Son of God, who didst rise from the dead, save us who sing to thee, Alleluia.

Glory. Both now. Only-begotten Son . . . .

III. Let God arise, and let his enemies be scattered, and let them that hate him flee from before him.

As smoke is driven away, so drive them away, as wax melteth at the presence of fire.

So let the sinners perish at the presence of God, but let the righteous rejoice.

This is the day which the Lord hath made, we will rejoice and be exceeding glad therein.

And after every verse, the Troparion, Christ is risen from the dead . . . .

On Pentecost Sunday.

I. The heavens are telling the glory of God, the firmament proclaimeth the work of his hands.

Day unto day uttereth speech, and night unto night sheweth knowledge.

There is no speech nor language where their voices are not heard.

Their sound is gone out into all lands, and their words unto the end of the world.

Glory. Both now.

And after every verse is added,

Through the prayers of the Mother of God, O Saviour, save us.

II. The Lord hear thee in the day of trouble, the name of the God of Jacob defend thee.

Send thee help from the sanctuary, and defend thee out of Sion.

Remember all thy sacrifices, and accept thy burnt offering.

And after every verse is added,

O blessed Paraclete, save us who sing to thee, Alleluia.

Glory. Both now. Only-begotten Son ....

III. The king shall rejoice in thy strength, O Lord, exceeding glad shall he be in thy salvation.

For thou hast given him his heart's desire, and hast not denied him the request of his lips.

For thou shalt prevent him with the blessings of goodness, and shalt set a crown of pure gold upon his head.

He asked life of thee, and thou gavest him long days, even to ages of ages.

And after every verse is added the Troparion of the Festival.

On Christmas Day.

I. I will give thanks unto thee, O Lord, with my whole heart, secretly among the faithful, and in the congregation.

His work is worthy to be praised and had in honour, and his righteousness endureth for ever.

Holy and reverend is his name.

Glory. Both now.

And after every verse is added,

Through the prayers of the Mother of God, O Saviour, save us.

II. Blessed is the man that feareth the Lord: he hath great delight in his commandments.

Riches and plenteousness are in his house. And his righteousness endureth for ever.

And, after every verse,

O Son of God, who wast born of a Virgin, save us who sing to thee, Alleluia.

Glory. Both now. Only-begotten Son ....

III. The Lord said unto my Lord, Sit thou on my right hand until I make thine enemies thy footstool.

The Lord shall send forth the rod of thy power out of Sion : be thou ruler even in the midst among thine enemies.

Thine shall be the dominion in the day of thy power amid the brightness of the Saints.

And after every verse, the Troparion of the Festival.

On the Epiphany.

I. When Israel came out of Egypt, the house of Jacob from among strange people.

The sea saw it and fled, Jordan was driven back.

What ailed thee, O sea, that thou fleddest? and thou Jordan, that thou wast driven back?

Glory. Both now.

And after every verse is added,

Through the prayers of the Mother of God, O Saviour, save us.

II. As Antiphon I on Palm Sunday, but with the Refrain,

O Son of God, who wast baptized by John in Jordan, save us who sing to thee, Alleluia.

III. As Antiphon III on Palm Sunday, but with the Troparion of the present Festival.

When the Choir have finished the singing of the Third Antiphon, the Little Introit with the Gospel is made.

Deacon. Let us pray to the Lord.
Choir. Lord, have mercy.
Priest. Wisdom! Stand up!

And the Choir singeth the Introit.

O COME, let us worship and fall down to Christ. O Son of God, *who art wonderful in the Saints, save us who sing to thee, Alleluia.

It is thus sung on ordinary days, but on Sundays,

*who didst rise from the dead, save us ....

And on Festivals of the Mother of God,

*through the prayers of the Mother of God, save us ....

But on the Great Festivals of the Year, to wit, of Palms, Easter, Pentecost, Christmas and Epiphany, there are special Introits, namely,

On Palm Sunday. Blessed be he that cometh in the name of the Lord. The Lord is God, and hath appeared unto us. O Son of God who didst sit upon an ass's colt, save us who sing to thee, Alleluia.

On Easter Day. Bless ye God in the congregations, the Lord from the fountains of Israel. O Son of God, who didst rise from the dead, save us who sing to thee, Alleluia.

On Pentecost Sunday. Be thou exalted, Lord, in thine own strength, so will we sing and praise thy powerful acts. O blessed Paraclete, save us who sing to thee, Alleluia.

On Christmas Day. Out of the womb before the day-star have I begotten thee. The Lord sware and will not repent, Thou art a priest for ever after the order of Melchisedek. O Son of God, who wast born of a Virgin, save us who sing to thee, Alleluia.

On the Epiphany. Blessed be he that cometh in the name of the Lord. The Lord is God, and hath appeared unto us. O Son of God, who wast baptized by John in Jordan, save us who sing to thee, Alleluia.

And after the Introit are sung the Troparion and Condakion of the Day.

Deacon. Let us pray to the Lord.

Priest. For holy art thou, our God, and to thee we ascribe glory, to the Father, and

to the Son, and to the Holy Ghost, now
and ever,

Deacon. And to ages of ages.
Choir. Amen.

And singeth the Trisagion.

HOLY God, Holy Mighty One, Holy Im-
mortal One, have mercy upon us, *thrice.*
Glory. Both now.
Holy Immortal One, have mercy upon us.

And, with a louder voice,

Holy God, Holy Mighty One, Holy Immortal One, have mercy upon us.

*But on the Festivals of Easter, Pentecost,
Christmas, and Epiphany, as also on the
Saturday of Lazarus, and on Holy Saturday,
they substitute for the foregoing.*

AS many as have been baptized into Christ,
have put on Christ, alleluia, *thrice.*
Glory. Both now.
Have put on Christ, alleluia.

And, in a louder tone,

As many as have been baptized into
Christ, have put on Christ, alleluia.

*And on the Festivals of the Cross, to wit,
on the 14th. day of September and on the
1st. day of August, as also on the Third
Sunday of Lent, they sing,*

THY Cross, O Master, we worship, and glorify thy holy Resurrection, *thrice.*

Glory. Both now.

And glorify thy holy Resurrection.

And, in a louder tone,

Thy Cross, O Master, we worship, and glorify thy holy Resurrection.

At the conclusion of the Trisagion, or of the Hymn sung instead thereof, the Deacon saith, Let us attend.

Priest. Peace to all.

Reader. And to thy spirit.

Deacon. Wisdom!

And the Reader readeth the Prokimenon, i. e., the appointed verse from the Psalms of David, which the Choir repeateth three times.

Prokimena for Sundays.

In Tone I. Let thy mercy, O Lord, come upon us, like as we have put our trust in thee. *Verse.* Rejoice, O ye righteous, in the Lord, for praise becometh the upright.

In Tone II. The Lord is my strength and my song, and is become my salvation. *Verse.* With chastisement thou hast corrected me, O Lord, but hast not delivered me over unto death.

In Tone III. Sing ye unto our God, sing ye, sing ye unto our King, sing ye. *Verse.* O clap your hands together, all ye nations, shout unto God with a voice of gladness.

In Tone IV. How great are thy works, O Lord, in wisdom hast thou made them all. *Verse.* Bless the Lord, O my soul, O Lord my God, thou art very great.

In Tone V. Thou, O Lord, shalt keep us and shalt protect us, from this generation, and for ever. *Verse.* Save me, O Lord, for there is not one holy one left.

In Tone VI. O Lord, save thy people, and bless thine inheritance. *Verse.* Unto thee have I cried, O Lord my God, keep not silence concerning me.

In Tone VII. The Lord will give strength unto his people, the Lord will give his people the blessing of peace. *Verse.* Bring unto the Lord, O ye sons of God, bring unto the Lord glory and might.

In Tone VIII. Make you vows unto the Lord our God, and keep them. *Verse.* In Juda is God known, his name is great in Israel.

Prokimena for Week Days.

On Mondays. (*To the Angels.*) He maketh his Angels spirits, and his Ministers a flame of fire. *Verse.* Bless the Lord, O my soul, O Lord my God, thou art very great.

On Tuesdays. (*To the Forerunner.*) The righteous shall rejoice in the Lord, and put his trust in him. *Verse.* Hearken unto my voice, O God, at whatever time I pray unto thee.

On Wednesdays. (*To the Mother of God.*) My soul doth magnify the Lord, and my spirit hath rejoiced in God my Saviour. *Verse.* Because he hath regarded the lowliness of his hand-maiden; for, behold, from henceforth all generations shall call me blessed.

On Thursdays. (*To the Apostles.*) Their sound is gone out into all lands, and their words unto the end of the world. *Verse.* The heavens are telling the glory of God, the firmament proclaimeth the work of his hands.

On Fridays. (*To the Cross.*) Exalt ye the Lord our God, and worship at his footstool, for he is holy. *Verse.* The Lord reigneth, let the heathen vex themselves.

On Saturdays. (*To All Saints.*) Rejoice in the Lord, and be glad, O ye righteous. *Verse.* Blessed are they whose transgressions are forgiven and whose sins are covered.

Prokimena for the Greater Festivals.

On Palm Sunday. Blessed be he that cometh in the name of the Lord, the Lord is God, and hath appeared unto us. *Verse.* O give thanks unto the Lord, for he is good, because his mercy endureth for ever.

On Easter Day. This is the day which the Lord hath made, we will rejoice and be exceeding glad therein. *Verse.* O give thanks unto the Lord, for he is good, because his mercy endureth for ever.

On Pentecost Sunday. Thy good Spirit shall lead me into the land of righteousness. *Verse.* O Lord, hearken unto my prayer, and despise not my petition.

On Christmas Day. Let all the earth worship thee, and sing to thee, let them sing to thy name, O Most High. *Verse.* Cry aloud unto the Lord, all the earth, sing unto his name, and give glory to his praise.

On the Epiphany. As on Palm Sunday.

And after the Prokimenon the Deacon saith,
Wisdom!

Reader. The Lection from the Epistle of Saint *N.*

Deacon. Let us attend.

The Reader readeth the Epistle. At its close the Priest saith to him, Peace to thee who readest.

Reader. And to thy spirit. *Deacon.* Wisdom!
Choir. Alleluia, alleluia, alleluia.
Priest. Wisdom! Stand up! Let us hear the holy Gospel. Peace to all.
Choir. And to thy spirit.
Deacon. The Lection from the holy Evangelist *N.*
Choir. Glory to thee, Lord, glory to thee.
Priest. Let us attend.

The Deacon readeth the Gospel. At its close the Priest saith to him,

Peace to thee who evangelizest.

Choir. Glory to thee, Lord, glory to thee.

Then followeth the great Ectenia. Vide page 10.

[*After the Exclamation, should there be an Offering for the Departed, the following is added,*

Deacon. Have mercy upon us, O God, according to thy great mercy, we pray thee, hear and have mercy.

Choir. Lord, have mercy, *thrice.*

Deacon. Furthermore let us pray for the repose of the soul of the servant (*or,* handmaid) of God *N.*, and for the forgiveness of all *his* sins, voluntary and involuntary.

Choir. Lord, have mercy, *thrice.*

Deacon. Where the righteous rest, there make *his* soul to rest, O Lord our God.

Choir. Lord, have mercy, *thrice.*

Deacon. That thou wouldest grant *him* the mercy of God, the kingdom of heaven, and forgiveness of *his* sins, we ask from thee, O Christ, our immortal King and God.

Choir. Vouchsafe, O Lord.

Deacon. Let us pray to the Lord.

Exclamation.

Priest. For thou art the Resurrection and the Life, and the Repose of thy sleeping servant (*or*, hand-maid) *N.*, O Christ our God, and to thee the glory we ascribe, with thine unbeginning Father, and thy most holy, and good, and life-creating Spirit, now and ever, and to ages of ages. *Choir.* Amen.]

Then the Ectenia for the Catechumens.

Deacon. Catechumens, pray ye to the Lord.

Choir. Lord, have mercy. *And so after the succeeding petitions.*

Deacon. Let us, the Faithful, pray for the Catechumens.

That the Lord may have mercy upon them.

May teach them the word of truth.

May reveal to them the gospel of right-eousness.

May unite them to his holy, catholic, and apostolic Church.

Save them, have mercy on them, help them, and keep them, O God, by thy grace.

Catechumens, bow your heads to the Lord.

Choir. To thee, O Lord. *Exclamation.*

Priest. That they also, together with us, may glorify thine all-honourable and majestic name, of the Father, and of the Son, and of the Holy Ghost, now and ever, and to ages of ages. *Choir.* Amen.

Deacon. As many as are Catechumens, depart. Ye Catechumens, depart. As many as are Catechumens, depart. Let there be no Catechumens. As many as are of the Faithful,

B. THE LITURGY OF THE FAITHFUL.

GAIN and again in peace, let us pray to the Lord. *Choir.* Lord, have mercy.

Deacon. Help us, save us, have mercy on us, and keep us, O God, by thy grace.

Choir. Lord, have mercy.

Deacon. Wisdom! *Exclamation.*

Priest. For to thee is due all glory, honour, and worship, to the Father . . . .

Choir. Amen.

Deacon. Again and again in peace . . . .

For the peace that is from above . . . .

For the peace of the whole world . . . .

For this holy Church . . . .

For our deliverance from all affliction. . . .

Help us, save us . . . . Wisdom! *Exclamation.*

Priest. That being ever guarded by thy might, we may ascribe glory to thee, to the Father . . . . *Choir.* Amen. *And singeth*

The Cherubic Hymn.

WE, who the Cherubim represent in mystery, and to the life-giving Trinity offer in song the hymn thrice-holy, should now put away all cares of life,

To receive the King of all, invisibly attended by the angelic Orders. Alleluia, alleluia, alleluia.

During the singing of this Hymn, the Procession, called the Great Introit, is made, when the prepared Gifts are carried from the Table of Oblations to the Altar, and the Lord God is desired to remember the Sovereign, and all the members of the Reigning House, the most holy Governing Synod, the Bishop of the Diocese, and all Orthodox Christians in his kingdom, always, now and ever, and to ages of ages.

Now on Holy and Great Thursday they substitute for the foregoing,

OF thy mysterious Supper to-day, O Son of God, accept me as a partaker; for I will not reveal thy Mystery to thine enemies, nor give thee a kiss as Judas, but as the thief I will confess thee, Remember me, O Lord, in thy kingdom.

And on the Great Sabbath they sing,

LET all flesh of man be silent, and let it stand in fear and awe, and think of nothing earthly to itself. For the King of kings and the Lord of lords cometh to be slain, and to be given as food to the faithful. Him do precede the angelic Hosts, with all their Principalities and Powers, the many-eyed Cherubim and the six-winged Seraphim, covering their faces, and singing the song, Alleluia, alleluia, alleluia.

Then followeth the Ectenia of Supplication.

Deacon. Let us accomplish our prayer to the Lord. *Choir.* Lord, have mercy.

Deacon. For the honourable Gifts that have been proposed, let us pray to the Lord.

Choir. Lord, have mercy.

Deacon. For this holy Church, and for them that with faith, piety and fear of God enter into it, let us pray to the Lord.

Choir. Lord, have mercy.

Deacon. For our deliverance from all affliction, passion and want, let us pray to the Lord. *Choir.* Lord, have mercy.

Deacon. Help us, save us . . . . *And the rest of the Ectenia as at page* 12, *concluding with the Exclamation,* Through the compassions of thine only-begotten Son, with whom thou art blessed, together with thy most holy, and good, and life-creating Spirit, now and ever, and to ages of ages. *Choir.* Amen.

Priest. Peace to all. *Choir.* And to thy spirit.

Deacon. Let us love one another, that with one mind we may confess,

Choir. The Father, Son, and Holy Ghost, the Trinity consubstantial and undivided.

Deacon. The doors, the doors! In wisdom let us attend!

And we sing the Confession of the Faith,
I believe in one God . . . .

This being concluded, the Deacon saith,

LET us stand worthily, let us stand with fear, let us attend to offer in peace the holy Oblation.

Choir. The mercy of peace, the sacrifice of praise.

Priest. The grace of our Lord Jesus Christ, and the love of God the Father, and the fellowship of the Holy Ghost be with you all.

Choir. And with thy spirit.

Priest. Lift we up our hearts.

Choir. We lift them up unto the Lord.

Priest. Let us give thanks to the Lord.

Choir. It is meet and right to worship the Father, Son, and Holy Ghost, the Trinity consubstantial and undivided.

Priest. Singing, crying aloud, shouting, and saying the triumphal hymn,

Choir. Holy, holy, holy Lord Sabaoth, heaven and earth are full of thy glory. Hosanna in the highest. Blessed be he that cometh in the name of the Lord. Hosanna in the highest.

Priest. Take, eat, this is my Body, which is broken for you for the remission of sins.

Choir. Amen.

Priest. Drink ye all of this, this is my Blood of the New Testament, which is shed for you and for many for the remission of sins. *Choir.* Amen.

Priest. Thine own of thine own we offer thee in behalf of all, and for all.

Choir. Thee we hymn, thee we bless, to thee we give thanks, O Lord, and pray to thee, our God.

Priest. Especially for our most holy, most pure, most blessed glorious Lady, the God-bearing ever-virgin Mary.

Choir. It is very meet to bless thee, the God-bearing one, the ever-blessed, the entirely spotless, and Mother of our God. The more honourable than the Cherubim, and incomparably more glorious than the Seraphim, who didst bear without corruption God the Word, thee, verily the God-bearing one, we magnify.

But if the Liturgy of S. Basil be celebrated, they sing instead of the foregoing,

IN thee, O full of grace, all creation rejoiceth, the hierarchy of Angels and the race of men, in thee, the sanctified temple, the spiritual paradise, the glory of virgins, of whom our God took flesh and became a child, even he that was God before the world. For he made thy womb his throne, and rendered it more extended than the heavens. In thee, O full of grace, all creation rejoiceth, glory to thee.

And on the Great Festivals of the Year, they substitute in this place the Irmos of the Ninth Ode of their proper Canon at Matins, to wit,

On Palm Sunday.

THE Lord is God, and hath appeared unto us. Come, let us keep the feast, and with gladness magnify Christ with palms and branches, crying in song, Blessed be he that cometh in the name of the Lord our Saviour.

On Easter Day, and in the Paschal Season.

AN Angel cried to the one full of grace, Hail! Virgin pure. And again I say, Hail! For thy Son, after three days, hath risen from the grave and raised the dead. Rejoice, ye people. Shine, shine, O new Jerusalem; for the glory of the Lord hath shone on thee. Rejoice now and exult, O Sion. And thou, pure Mother of God, be glad in the Resurrection of him whom thou didst bear.

On Pentecost Sunday.

HAIL! thou, O Queen, most glorious Virgin Mother. For no well-speaking eloquent lips can worthily extol thee; and every mind is at a loss to understand thy bringing forth. Wherefore, with one accord we glorify thee.

On Christmas Day.

MAGNIFY, my soul, her who is more honourable and glorious than the Hosts above. A mystery strange and wondrous I behold. The cave is heaven, the Virgin is the throne of Cherubim, the manger is the place where the Incomprehensible is laid, Christ our God, whom singing, we magnify.

On the Epiphany.

MAGNIFY, my soul, her who is more honourable and glorious than the Hosts above. O most pure Virgin, blessed Mother, the mystery of thy child-birth passeth thought, and by it we have gained a full salvation. Worthily we praise thee as our benefactress, and bring thee as a gift thanksgiving songs.

The Hymn to the Mother of God being ended, the Priest exclaimeth,

And chiefly, O Lord, remember the most holy Governing Synod (*or*, our Metropolitan, *or*, Archbishop, *or*, Bishop *N.*), the members of which (*or*, whom) preserve to thy holy Churches in peace, safety, honour, health, and length of days, and rightly dividing the word of thy truth.

Choir. And all men, and all women.

Priest. And grant us with one mouth and one heart to glorify and celebrate thine all-honourable and majestic name, of the Father, and of the Son, and of the Holy Ghost, now and ever, and to ages of ages.

Choir. Amen.

Priest. And the mercies of the great God and our Saviour, Jesus Christ, be with you all.

Choir. And with thy spirit.

Deacon. Commemorating all the Saints, again and again in peace let us pray to the Lord.

For the honourable Gifts now presented and hallowed, let us pray to the Lord.

That our man-loving God, who hath received them on his holy, heavenly, and spiritual altar, as the odour of a sweet smelling spiritual perfume, may send down on us his divine grace, and the gift of the Holy Ghost, let us pray to the Lord.

For our deliverance from all affliction . . . .

Help us, save us . . . .

That the whole day may be perfect . . . .

And the rest of the Ectenia of Supplication, concluding,

Having prayed for the unity of the faith, and the communion of the Holy Ghost, let us commend ourselves, and one another, and all our life to Christ, our God.

Choir. To thee, O Lord.

Priest. And make us worthy, O Master, with boldness, and without condemnation, to dare to call upon thee, our heavenly God and Father, and to say,

And we sing the Lord's Prayer.

Priest. For thine is the kingdom, and
the power, and the glory, of the Father, and
of the Son, and of the Holy Ghost, now
and ever, and to ages of ages.

Choir. Amen.

Priest. Peace to all. *Choir.* And to thy spirit.

Deacon. Bow your heads to the Lord.

Choir. To thee, O Lord. *Exclamation.*

Priest. Through the grace, compassion,
and love to men of thine only-begotten
Son, with whom, together with thy most holy,
and good, and life-creating Spirit, thou art
blessed, now and ever, and to ages of ages.

Choir. Amen.

Deacon. Let us attend.

Priest. Holy things for holy persons.

Choir. One holy, one Lord Jesus Christ,
to the glory of God the Father. Amen.

And they sing the Communion Hymn.

On Sundays. Praise the Lord from the
heavens, praise him in the highest. Alleluia,
alleluia, alleluia.

On Mondays. He maketh his Angels spirits,
and his Ministers a flame of fire. Alleluia,
alleluia, alleluia.

On Tuesdays. The righteous shall be had
in everlasting remembrance. Alleluia, alleluia, alleluia.

On Wednesdays. I will take the cup of salvation, and call upon the name of the Lord, Alleluia, alleluia, alleluia.

On Thursdays. Their sound is gone out into all lands, and their words unto the end of the world. Alleluia, alleluia, alleluia.

On Fridays. Thou hast wrought salvation in the midst of the earth, O God. Alleluia, alleluia, alleluia.

On Saturdays. Blessed are they whom thou choosest and takest unto thyself, O Lord, and their remembrance is from generation to generation. Alleluia, alleluia, alleluia.

On Palm Sunday. Blessed be he that cometh in the name of the Lord. Alleluia, alleluia, alleluia.

On Easter Day and in the Paschal Season. Receive ye the Body of Christ, and taste of the immortal Fount. Alleluia, alleluia, alleluia.

On Pentecost Sunday. Thy good Spirit shall lead me into the land of righteousness. Alleluia, alleluia, alleluia.

On Christmas Day. The Lord hath sent redemption unto his people. Alleluia, alleluia, alleluia.

On the Epiphany. The grace of God, which bringeth salvation, hath appeared unto us. Alleluia, alleluia, alleluia.

After the singing of the Communion Hymn the Priest saith,

Draw near with fear of God, and faith, and love.

Choir. Blessed be he that cometh in the name of the Lord. The Lord is God, and hath appeared unto us.

[*Now shall the Communicants, if there be any, receive the holy Sacrament.*

Prayer before Communion.

BELIEVE, Lord, and confess that thou art truly Christ, the Son of the living God, who camest into the world to save sinners, of whom I am the greatest.

I BELIEVE also that this is thy most holy and immaculate Body, and this thy precious Blood. Wherefore, I beseech thee, Have mercy upon me, and pardon my transgressions, voluntary and involuntary, in word and in deed, in knowledge and in ignorance, and make me worthy, without condemnation, to partake of thy most pure Mysteries, for the remission of sins, and for life eternal.

RECEIVE me to-day, O Son of God, as a partaker of thy mysterious Supper; for I will not betray this Mystery to thine enemies, nor give thee a kiss as Judas, but as the thief I will confess unto thee, Remember me, O Lord, in thy kingdom.

LET not the communion of thy holy Mysteries be to my judgment, nor to my condemnation, but to the healing of my soul and body.

And as the Priest giveth the holy Sacrament, he saith to each one,

THE servant (*or*, handmaid) of God, *N.,* partaketh of the precious and holy Body and Blood of our Lord, and God, and Saviour, Jesus Christ, for the forgiveness of *his* sins, and for life everlasting.

Also,

BEHOLD, this hath touched thy lips, and shall take away thy transgressions, and purge thy sins.

Meantime the Choir singeth,

RECEIVE ye the Body of Christ, and taste of the immortal Fount. Alleluia, alleluia, alleluia.]

Priest. O God, save thy people, and bless thine inheritance.

Choir. We have seen the true Light, we have received the heavenly Spirit, we have found the true Faith, and we worship the undivided Trinity, which hath saved us.

Priest. Always, now and ever, and to ages of ages.

Choir. Amen. *And singeth,*

LET our mouth be filled with thy praise, O Lord, that we may sing of thy glory, for that thou hast vouchsafed to make us partakers of thy holy, divine, immortal, and life-giving Mysteries. Preserve us by thy holiness all our days, that we may learn thy righteousness. Alleluia, alleluia, alleluia.

But on the Great Festivals they sing their proper Troparion instead of the foregoing.

Then saith the Deacon,

Having stood and partaken of the divine, holy, spotless, immortal, heavenly, life-giving, and terrible Mysteries of Christ, let us worthily give thanks to the Lord.

Choir. Lord, have mercy.

Deacon. Help us, save us, have mercy on us, and keep us, O God, by thy grace.

Choir. Lord, have mercy.

Deacon. Having prayed that the whole day may be perfect, holy, peaceful, and sinless, let us commend ourselves, and one another, and all our life to Christ our God.

Choir. To thee, O Lord. *Exclamation.*

Priest. For thou art our sanctification, and to thee we ascribe glory, to the Father, and to the Son, and to the Holy Ghost, now and ever, and to ages of ages.

Choir. Amen.

Priest. Let us depart in peace.

Choir. In the name of the Lord.

Deacon. Let us pray to the Lord.

Choir. Lord, have mercy.

And the Priest saith the following Prayer.

LORD, who blessest them that bless thee, and sanctifiest them that put their trust in thee, save thy people and bless thine inheritance. Preserve the fulness of thy Church, sanctify them that love the beauty of thine house, glorify them in return with thy divine power, and forsake not us who put our trust in thee. Give peace to the world, to thy churches, to our priests, and to our Sovereign, *N.*, to the army, and to all thy people. For every good gift and every perfect gift is from above, and cometh down from thee, the Father of light, and to thee we ascribe glory, thanks and worship, to the Father, and to the Son, and

11*

to the Holy Ghost, now and ever, and to ages of ages.

Choir. Amen. *And,*

BLESSED be the name of the Lord, from henceforth, and to all ages, *thrice.*

[*On Easter Day and in the Paschal Season they substitute for the foregoing,* Christ is risen from the dead . . . .]

Then is read Psalm 33 (34).

I will bless the Lord at all times . . . .
Vide page 15.

Deacon. Let us pray to the Lord.

Choir. Lord, have mercy.

Priest. The blessing of the Lord, his grace, and love to men be upon you, always, now and ever, and to ages of ages.

Choir. Amen.

Priest. Glory to thee, O Christ our God, our Hope, glory to thee.

Choir. Glory. Both now. Lord, have mercy, *thrice.* Give the blessing.

Priest. (He that arose from the dead, *or,* that vouchsafed to sit on the foal of an ass for our salvation, *or,* that sent down the most Holy Spirit in the likeness of fiery tongues upon his holy Disciples and Apostles, *or,* that vouchsafed to be born in a cave and laid in a manger for our salvation, *or,* that vouchsafed to be baptized by John in Jordan for our salvation, *according to the occasion of the Festival*), Christ our true God, through the prayers of his all-pure Mother, of the holy, glorious and all-praised Apostles, of our Father in the Saints, John Chrysostom, Archbishop of Constantinople, (*or, if his Liturgy be said*, Basil the Great, of Cæsarea in Cappadocia), and of all the Saints, have mercy upon us and save us, for he is good and the Lover of men.

Choir. Lord, have mercy, *thrice.*

And singeth the Many Years *for the Reigning House.*

XVI. AT THE LITURGY OF THE PRE-SANCTIFIED.

This Liturgy is said on the Wednesdays and Fridays of the first 6 Weeks of the Great Quadragesima, on the Thursday of the 5th. Week, and on the Monday, Tuesday, and Wednesday of Holy Passion Week. It may also be said, excepting on Saturdays and Sundays and on the Festival of the Annunciation, on other days during the Fast, to wit, on those of Festivals and their Vigils, and on the Commemoration of the Dedication of the Church.

The Office of the Typica being ended, as indicated at page 127, *the Priest giveth the blessing, and the Reader beginneth the Vespers, saying,*

O come, let us worship . . . . *thrice.*

Psalm 103 (104). *Glory. Both now.*

Alleluia, alleluia, alleluia, glory to thee, O God, *thrice.*

Then followeth the Ectenia of Peace. Vide page 2.

After the Exclamation, the Reader beginneth to read the 18 *th. Kathism of the Psalter, after each division of which is said the Little Ectenia, the first time with the Exclamation,* For thine is the might, and thine is the kingdom, the power, and the glory, of the Father . . . . *And the second time,* For thou art a good and man-loving God, and to thee we ascribe glory, to the Father . . . . *And the third time,* For thou art our God, the God of mercy and salvation, and to thee we ascribe glory, to the Father . . . .

Choir. Amen. *And beginneth the* Lord, I have cried, *with the properly appointed Stichera.*

Then is sung the Tranquil Light.

And the proper Prokimena and Lections follow, as are indicated in the Triodion.

[*In the lack of this book, the following Stichera, Prokimena and Lections may be said.*

Stichera in Tone 1.

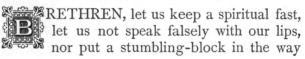RETHREN, let us keep a spiritual fast, let us not speak falsely with our lips, nor put a stumbling-block in the way

of our brother, but with repentance let us brighten the lamp of our souls, crying unto Christ, Forgive us our iniquities, O Lover of mankind.

RENOWNED Martyrs, earth retained you not, but heaven hath received you. The gates of Paradise were opened unto you, and, dwelling there, ye enjoy the tree of life. Pray unto Christ that he may grant peace and great mercy to our souls.

LET us desire a fasting of the soul to extinguish, by the Spirit's aid, our dangerous passions, to strengthen us to practise godly deeds, to lift our minds to heaven, and to gain us pardon for our sins from God most merciful.

LORD, I have spent my life with sinners shamefully, but like the prodigal, myself a prodigal, in penitence I cry, O heavenly Father, I have sinned, be gracious unto me, save and reject me not, though I am now far from thee and poor in godly works.

Others in Tone 4.

TO me, choked with life's passions and far from thee, O God the King of all things, and altogether hopeless, grant repentance and deliverance from evil, and amendment of life, and save me, a prodigal, in the greatness of thy goodness, O Jesus almighty, the Saviour of our souls.

THE divine Moses through fasting acquired purity of desire. Then imitate him, my poor soul, and hasten while it is day to cleanse thyself from evil through continence, that thou mayest find the Lord, who is good and man-loving, and granteth thee forgiveness, and graciousness, and redemption.

Glory. Both now.

And the proper Verse to the Virgin.

Prokimenon. Tone 4.

I HAVE trusted in the mercy of God for ever. *Verse.* Why boastest thou thyself, O tyrant, that thou canst do mischief?

The Lection from Genesis. Chap. VII. 6—9.

AND Noe was six hundred years old when the flood of water was upon the earth. And Noe went in, and his sons, and his wife, and his sons' wives with him, into the ark, because of the water of the flood. And of clean fowls, and of fowls that are not clean, and of clean cattle, and of cattle that are not clean, and of beasts, and of every kind of reptile that creepeth upon the earth, there went in two and two unto Noe into the ark, the male and the female, as the Lord God had commanded him.

Prokimenon. Tone 4.

WHEN the Lord turned back the captivity of his people, then did Jacob rejoice, and Israel was glad. *Verse.* The foolish body hath said in his heart, There is no God.

The Lection from Proverbs. Chap. IX. 12—19.

MY son, if thou be wise, thou shalt be wise for thine own self, but if thou turnest out evil, thou alone shalt bear the evil. He that receiveth instruction is wise, but to the froward becometh the place of a servant. He that resteth upon lies tendeth the wind, yea, he pursueth a winged bird. For he quitteth the paths of his own vineyard, and roameth in the confines of his own husbandry. He goeth in a way void of water, and through a land given up unto thirst, and he gathereth fruitlessness with his hands. A woman that is foolish and bold becometh scanty of bread, or otherwise she knoweth not shame. She sitteth at the door of her house, on a seat that is open to the streets, and calleth to them that pass by, to them that go right on their ways, Whoso is simple, let him turn in hither unto me. And to them that lack understanding she calleth and saith, Taste ye the secret bread of pleasure, and drink ye the sweet stolen water. But he knoweth not that the children of earth perish by her, and that he will encounter the snares of hades. But turn thou from her, loiter not near her place, neither cast thine eyes upon her. For by so doing thou wouldest come unto strange water; but from strange water refrain thyself, neither drink thou out of strange fountains, that thou mayest live long time, and that years of life may be added unto thee.]

And after the First Lection the Priest exclaimeth,

Wisdom! Stand up! The Light of Christ appeareth unto all.

At the conclusion of the Lections, the Reader, or other appointed person, standing in the middle of the Church, singeth,

ET my prayer be set forth before thee as incense, the lifting up of my hands as the evening sacrifice.

During the singing of this verse the Choir on both sides and all the People kneel. When the Reader hath sung it, he kneeleth, and the Choir and People on the right stand up and repeat the same. And, having done so, they kneel again, and the Reader standeth up, and singeth,

LORD, I have cried unto thee, hear me: attend to the voice of my prayer when I cry unto thee.

Then he kneeleth, and the Choir and People on the left stand up, and sing,

Let my prayer be set forth . . . .

And they kneel again, and the Reader standeth up, and singeth,

SET a watch, O Lord, before my mouth, and keep the door of my lips.

And again he kneeleth, and the Choir and People on the right stand up, and sing,

Let my prayer be set forth . . . .

And again they kneel, and again the Reader standeth, and singeth,

INCLINE not my heart to evil words to make excuses for sins.

And yet again he kneeleth, while the Choir and People on the left stand up, and sing,

Let my prayer be set forth . . . .

And they kneel once more, and the Reader standeth up, and singeth,

LET my prayer be set forth before thee as incense.

And he goeth to his place, while all stand, and both Choirs loudly sing,

THE lifting up of my hands as the evening sacrifice.

Then followeth the Prayer of S. Ephrem with the Genuflections.

In Holy Passion Week here is read the Gospel, or, if a Festival, they read the Epistle and Gospel thereof.

Then the Great Ectenia.

Let us all say with our whole soul . . . .

Vide page 10.

After the Exclamation concluding this, followeth the Ectenia for the Catechumens. *Vide page* 148.

[*Now from the Wednesday of Mid-Lent, the following Ectenia is added in this place, after the Exclamation,* That they also, together with us . . . .

As many as are Catechumens, depart. Ye Catechumens, depart. As many as are about to be illuminated, depart. Pray, ye that are about to be illuminated. Let us pray to the Lord. *Choir.* Lord, have mercy. *And so after the succeeding petitions.*

Ye Faithful, for our brethren that are preparing for holy illumination, and for their salvation, let us pray to the Lord.

That the Lord our God may confirm and strengthen them, let us pray to the Lord.

That he may enlighten them with the light of knowledge and piety, let us pray to the Lord.

That he may grant unto them in due time the laver of regeneration, the forgiveness of sins, and the garment of incorruption, let us pray to the Lord.

That he may make them born again of water and of the Spirit, let us pray to the Lord.

That he may bestow upon them the perfection of faith, let us pray to the Lord.

That he may number them among his holy and elect flock, let us pray to the Lord.

Save them, have mercy on them, help them, and keep them, O God, by thy grace.

Ye that are about to be illuminated, bow your heads to the Lord.

Choir. To thee, O Lord. *Exclamation.*

Priest. For thou art our illumination, and to thee we ascribe glory, to the Father, and to the Son, and to the Holy Ghost, now and ever, and to ages of ages.

Choir. Amen.

Deacon. As many as are about to be illuminated, depart. Ye that are about to be illuminated, depart. As many as are Catechumens, depart. Let there be no Catechumens.]

As many as are Faithful, again and again in peace, let us pray to the Lord.

And the Ectenia of the Faithful, as in the Liturgies of S. Chrysostom and S. Basil. The second Exclamation however is, Through the grace of thy Christ, with whom thou art blessed, together with thy most holy, and good, and life-creating Spirit, now and ever, and to ages of ages.

Choir. Amen. *And continueth,*

NOW the heavenly Powers invisibly minister with us; for, behold, the King of glory is borne in. Behold, the mystic Sacrifice, having been perfected, is borne aloft by Angels.

Let us draw near with faith and love, that we may become partakers of life eternal. Alleluia, alleluia, alleluia.

Deacon. Let us accomplish our evening prayer to the Lord.

For the precious and pre-sanctified Gifts that are offered, let us pray to the Lord.

That our man-loving God, who hath received them on his holy . . . . *And the rest of the Ectenia, as at page* 157, *concluding with the* Our Father. *Exclamation.* For thine is the kingdom, and the power, and the glory, of the Father, and of the Son, and of the Holy Ghost, now and ever, and to ages of ages. *Choir.* Amen.

Priest. Peace to all.

Choir. And to thy spirit.

Deacon. Let us bow our heads to the Lord.

Choir. To thee, O Lord. *Exclamation.*

Priest. Through the grace, compassion, and love to men of thine only-begotten Son, with whom, together with thy most holy, and good, and life-creating Spirit, thou art blessed, now and ever, and to ages of ages.

Choir. Amen. *Deacon.* Let us attend.

Priest. Holy things pre-sanctified for holy persons.

Choir. One holy, one Lord Jesus Christ, to the glory of God the Father. Amen.

And the Communion Hymn.

O TASTE and see that the Lord is good. Alleluia, alleluia, alleluia.

Priest. Draw near with fear of God, and faith, and love.

Choir. I will bless the Lord at all times, his praise shall continually be in my mouth.

Come, taste the Bread of heaven, and the Cup of salvation, and see that the Lord is good. Alleluia, alleluia, alleluia.

[*Here the Communicants, if there be any, shall receive the holy Sacrament.*]

Priest. O God, save thy people, and bless thine inheritance.

Always, now and ever, and to ages of ages.

Choir. Amen. Let our mouth be filled....

And the rest, as in the Liturgies of Saints Chrysostom and Basil, saving only that they shall say this whole evening *instead of* this whole day *in the Ectenia, that the Priest shall substitute for the prayer beginning,* Lord, who blessest them .... *the following,*

ALMIGHTY Lord, who in wisdom madest all things, who, after thine unspeakable foreknowledge and great goodness, dost sanctify unto us these sacred days for the cleansing of our souls and bodies, for the subduing of our passions, and for the hope of resurrection, and who after forty days didst give unto thy servant Moses the divinely written tables of the law; grant thou unto us, O Blessed One, that we may fight the good fight, may finish the course of the fast, may keep perfectly the faith,

12

may crush the heads of the invisible serpents, may become victorious over sin, and without condemnation may attain unto the time to worship thy holy Resurrection. For blessed and glorified is thine all-honourable and majestic name, of the Father, and of the Son, and of the Holy Ghost, now and ever, and to ages of ages. Amen.

And that the Dismissal shall be on this wise,

[*In Holy Passion Week*, He that for our salvation willingly endured passion,] Christ our true God, through the prayers of his all-pure Mother, through the might of his precious and life-giving Cross, through the prayers of our holy Father, Gregory the Divine, and of all the Saints, have mercy upon us and save us; for he is good and the Lover of men.

XVII. SUNDAY SERVICE IN THE SIXTH TONE.

—◦—

AT THE GREAT VESPERS.

With the Lord, I have cried, *Stichera on the Resurrection in Tone* 6.

THOU didst ascend the Cross, O Christ, to win victory over hades, that, together with thyself, thou mightest raise them that sat in the shades of death. O almighty Saviour, thou that art the Redeemer of the dead, from whose light springeth life, have mercy upon us.

Verse. If thou, O Lord, shouldest mark transgression, O Lord, who should stand? But with thee there is propitiation.

TO-DAY Christ treadeth down death, as he said. He is risen and giveth joy unto the world. Therefore in hymns we cry, O almighty Saviour, who art the Foun-

tain of life and of light inaccessible, have
mercy upon us.

Verse. For thy name's sake have I waited
for thee, O Lord : my soul hath waited for
thy word, my soul hath trusted in the Lord.

O LORD, who art everywhere present,
whither shall we sinners go to find thee?
To heaven? there thou dwellest. To hades?
there thou didst tread down death. Into
the depth of the sea? there is thine hand.
O Lord, we come to thee, and unto thee
falling down, we pray, O thou that didst
rise from the dead, have mercy upon us.

Verse. From the morning watch until
night, from the morning watch let Israel
trust in the Lord.

WE exult because of thy Cross, O Christ,
and sing and glorify thy Resurrection;
for thou art our God, and besides thee we
know none other.

Verse. For with the Lord is mercy, and
with him is plenteous redemption, and he
shall redeem Israel from all his transgressions.

EVER blessing the Lord, we sing his Resurrection; for, enduring crucifixion, death
by death he overthrew.

Verse. Praise the Lord, all ye nations,
praise him all ye peoples.

GLORY to thy might, O Lord, for thou hast abolished him that had the power of death, and hast renewed us by thy Cross, giving us life and immortality.

Verse. For his mercy is confirmed upon us, and the truth of the Lord remaineth for ever.

O LORD, thy Burial hath burst the bonds of hades, and thy Resurrection from the dead hath enlightened the world. Glory to thee, O Lord.

Glory. Both now. To the Virgin.

WHO would not bless thee, most pure Virgin? who would not sing thy holy child-birth? For he that shone for ever from the Father, even the only-begotten Son, came forth from thee unspeakably incarnate. He that is by nature God became by nature man for us. He was not divided into two persons, but appeared, without confusion, in two natures. Beseech him, O most pure and blessed one, to have mercy on our souls.

Then the Tranquil Light, *and the Prokimenon. Vide page* 8.

The Stichera with Verses. Tone 6.

THY Resurrection, O Saviour Christ, Angels sing in heaven. Vouchsafe to us also upon earth to extol thee with pure heart.

Verse. The Lord is King : he hath put on glorious apparel.

O GOD almighty, thou didst shatter the gates of brass and burst the bonds of hades, and thou didst raise the fallen race of men. Therefore with one accord we cry, O Lord, who didst rise from the dead, glory to thee.

Verse. He hath made the whole world so sure that it cannot be moved.

WILLING to restore our old estate, Christ was nailed to the Cross and placed in the grave, and the myrrh-bearing women, seeking him with tears, lamenting said, Alas! Saviour of all, how didst thou deign to dwell within a grave? And having dwelt there, who hath stolen thee? Whither art thou gone? And what place hideth thy quickening Body? Appear to us, O Lord, as thou didst say, and stay our wailing tears. As thus they wept, an Angel cried to them, Cease now your tears, and tell to the Apostles that the Lord is risen, granting propitiation and great mercy to the world.

Verse. Holiness becometh thine house, O Lord, for ever.

O CHRIST, thou hast been crucified, as thou didst will, and by the grave hast spoiled death, and on the third day, as God, hast risen with glory, bestowing life unending and great mercy on the world.

Glory. Both now. To the Virgin.

MY Maker and Redeemer, Christ the Lord, came forth from thee, most pure one, endued like me, and delivered Adam from the ancient curse. Therefore the Angel's greeting we exclaim to thee, the all-pure Mother of God, the Virgin true, Hail! Lady, mediatress, defender, and salvation of our souls.

Then, Lord, now lettest thou thy servant . . . . *Trisagion.* O most holy Trinity. *And, after* Our Father,

The Troparion in Tone 6.

ANGELIC powers are at thy tomb, and the guards are deadened, and Mary standeth at the grave seeking thy most pure Body. Thou madest hades captive, not being tempted by it. Thou didst meet the Virgin, and grantest life. O risen Lord, glory to thee.

To the Virgin.

THOU who didst call thy Mother blessed, of thine own will camest to suffer, and shining on the Cross that thou mightest bring back Adam, telledst the Angels, Rejoice with me, for the lost drachma is found.

O God, who in wisdom hast made all things, glory to thee.

AT THE GREAT MATINS.

After the Six Psalms, The Lord is God, and hath appeared . . . . *in Tone* 6.

And we say the Troparion.

Angelic powers are at thy tomb . . . .

Glory. Both now.

Thou who didst call thy Mother . . . .

And the usual Kathisms of the Psalter.

After the First Kathism, Kathismal Hymn in Tone 6.

THE grave being open and hades lamenting, Mary cried to the hidden Apostles, Come forth, ye workers of the vineyard, and proclaim the word of the Resurrection, The Lord is risen, granting great mercy to the world.

Glory. Both now. To the Virgin.

O MOTHER of God, Gideon did thy conception pre-narrate, and David told thy bringing forth. For as the dew came down upon the fleece, so did the Word into thy womb, and without seed thou bearedst fruit, O holy land, even the world's salvation, Christ our God, thou that art full of grace.

After the Second Kathism, Kathismal Hymn in Tone 6.

THE Life is placed in a grave, with a seal laid upon the stone. As a sleeping king the soldiers guarded Christ, and, invisibly beating down his enemies, the Lord arose.

Glory. Both now. To the Virgin.

O VIRGIN Mother of God, beseech thy Son, who of his own will was nailed to the Cross and from the dead arose, even Christ our God, to save our souls.

After the Blessed are they that are undefiled . . . . *i. e., Psalm* 118 (119),

The Troparia as at page 25.

Blessed art thou, O Lord . . . .

The assembly of Angels . . . .

After these, the Hypacoë in Tone 6.

O CHRIST, by thy voluntary and life-effecting death, thou didst, as God, overthrow the gates of hades and open unto us the ancient paradise, and, risen from the dead, hast saved our life from corruption.

Then the Graduals in Tone 6.

Antiphon I.

UNTO heaven have I lifted up mine eyes, even unto thee, O Word. Have compassion upon me, that I may live to thee.

Have mercy upon us who have been set at naught, making us again thy serviceable vessels, O Word.

Glory. Both now.

In the Holy Spirit is an all-saving fount. On whom he breatheth, according to their worth, he quickly raiseth from things of earth, he lifteth them, exalteth them, and placeth them on high.

Antiphon II.

IF the Lord were not with us, we none could have withstood the enemy's attacks. For they that overcome are thereby exalted.

Let not my soul as a bird be caught in their teeth, O Word. Alas! how shall I be delivered from the enemy, who am myself a lover of sin.

Glory. Both now.

Through the Holy Spirit cometh inspiration unto all, goodwill, understanding, peace and blessing; for he is co-worker with the Father and the Word.

Antiphon III.

THEY that trust in the Lord are terrible to enemies, and wonderful to all men; for they look on high.

Let not the inheritance of the righteous, who have thee, O Saviour, as their helper, stretch forth their hands unto iniquity.

Glory. Both now.

Of the Holy Spirit is the might in all things: him the Hosts above worship, and everything that hath breath below.

Prokimenon. Tone 6.

O LORD, stir up thy strength, and come and save us.

Verse. Hear, O thou Shepherd of Israel, thou that leadest Joseph like a flock.

The Lection from the holy Evangelist Matthew. Section 116.

AT that time, the eleven disciples went away into Galilee, into a mountain where Jesus had appointed them. And when they saw him, they worshipped him, but some doubted. And Jesus came and spake unto them, saying, All power is given unto me in heaven and in earth. Go ye therefore, and teach all nations, baptizing them in the name of the Father, and of the Son, and of the Holy Ghost, teaching them to observe all things whatsoever I have commanded you, and lo! I am with you alway, even unto the end of the world. Amen.

Then, Having seen the Resurrection of Christ . . . . *And the rest. Vide page* 28.

THE CANON ON THE RESURRECTION.

Tone 6.　Ode I.　İrmos.

ISRAEL, passing through the deep on foot, as on dry land, saw Pharao their pursuer overwhelmed, and cried, Let us sing a victorious song to God.

Refrain. Glory to thy holy Resurrection, O Lord.

O blessed Jesus, thou didst stretch forth thine hands upon the Cross, and so fulfil thy Father's will. Therefore we sing a victorious song to thee.

Death, as a bidden servant, approached thee in fear, O Lord of life, and thou thereby dost grant us endless life and resurrection.

Glory.

At Pilate's judgment-seat, unlawfully accused, willed to stand, as one condemned, the Judge; and God, before whom tremble heaven and earth, is smitten on the face by wicked hands.

Both now.　To the Virgin.

O pure one, thou hast in truth appeared creation's Queen, whose unsown womb conceived thine own Creator, when he did will incomprehensibly to be made man.

Ode III. Irmos.

O LORD, *my God, there is none holy like to thee, who dost exalt thy faithful people's horn, stablishing us, O Blessed One, upon the rock of thy confession.*

Creation saw thee crucified in flesh, O God, and feared; though, by thine upholding hand, who wast crucified for us, it is most firmly stablished.

Death, slain by death, lieth condemned and prone; for this strong one bore not the divine approach, and died, and resurrection is bestowed on all.

Glory.

Glory to thine Arising, O our almighty Saviour; for out of death, and hades, and corruption thou hast delivered us, and singing unto thee we cry, There is none holy like to thee, O Lord, thou Lover of mankind.

Both now. To the Virgin.

The wonder of thy divine child-birth, O pure one, surpasseth nature's way; for thou didst conceive God within thy womb, and bring him forth, and ever remainest Virgin.

Ode IV. Irmos.

*C*HRIST *is my Might, my God and Lord; and the sacred Church, divinely breaking forth in song, with pure intention keepeth a feast unto the Lord.*

O Christ, the tree doth blossom with true life; for the Cross is raised, and, soaked with blood and water from thine immortal side, it groweth life for us.

No longer doth the serpent deity by guile suggest to me; for Christ, the divine Maker of human nature, hath now, without forbidding, opened the path of life to me.

Glory.

The grave, O Saviour, received thee, who willingly for our sake didst die; but in no wise could it hold thee, Word of God, for thou didst rise and save our souls.

Both now. To the Virgin.

The mystery of thy divine child-bearing, O ever-virgin Mother of God, cannot be told nor understood by those on earth nor those in heaven.

Ode V. Irmos.

SHINE, I pray thee, thy divine light, O blessed and true Word of God, on them that lovingly rise early unto thee, and bid them flee the night of sin.

Now do the Cherubim retire from me, O Lord, and the flaming sword is turned back, because they saw thee, O true Word of God, shewing the thief the way to Paradise.

No longer do I fear returning unto earth, O Christ my Lord, for thou, in thy great mercy, hast, through thy Resurrection, called me on high from earth's forgetfulness to immortality. *Glory.*

O Blessed One, thou, by thy death, hast spoiled the power of death, and opened the fount of life, and given us immortality. Therefore, in faith thy Burial and thy Resurrection we adore, O God, whereby thou hast enlightened all the world.

Both now. To the Virgin.

O thou, the world's most blessed Queen, save them that from their soul confess thee Mother of God; for thou art an invincible mediatress, who truly didst bear God.

Ode VI. Irmos.

BEHOLDING the sea of life swelling with a storm of temptations, I take refuge in thy calm haven, and cry unto thee, Raise up my life from corruption, O most Merciful One.

O Lord, when thou wast crucified, thou, by the nails, our condemnation didst annul; and, when thy side was pierced with the lance, thou didst tear up the handwriting against Adam, and set the world at liberty.

Adam was smitten in the heel and borne down to hades' depths; but the merciful God went down to deliver him, and to carry him on his shoulder, and to raise him with himself.

Glory.

Thou wast contained in the tomb, O Saviour, but not detained there; for, though thou willingly didst taste of death, O Word, thou didst arise as God almighty, and with thyself didst raise them that were held in hades' bonds, and didst change the sadness of the women into joy.

Both now. To the Virgin.

O most holy Lady, who didst bring into the world the Lord, the Pilot of mankind; calm the inconstant and evil surgings of my passions, and grant quiet to my heart.

Condakion. Tone 6.

CHRIST God, the Giver of life, hath raised the dead from the dark abodes by his quickening hand, and granted resurrection to the human race; for he is the Saviour, Resurrection, Life, and God of all.

Icos. (Stanza.)

O GOD, almighty and immortal Giver of life, thy Cross and Burial we thy faithful sing and worship; for thou didst bind hades captive, and with thyself didst raise the dead. Thou didst, as God, overcome the gates of death, and bring the might of hades down. Therefore we earth-born glorify thee lovingly, who didst arise and overthrow the adversary's power, raising them that believe in thee, and delivering the world from the serpent's darts and the adversary's wiles; for thou art the God of all things.

Ode VII. Irmos.

*A*S *the Angel made the furnace to bedew the pious Youths, so the command of God burned the Chaldæans, and bade the tyrant say, Blessed art thou, O God of our fathers.*

At thy Passion, O Lord, the sun lamented and clothed himself with darkness, and at noon the light through all the world grew dim, crying, Blessed art thou, O God of our fathers.

The lowest depths were filled with light at thy descent, O Christ, and our Forefather there was seen replete with joy, and, keeping festival, with joy he cried, Blessed art thou, O God of our fathers. *Glory.*

O strange event! He that redeemed Israel from Pharao's bondage is crucified by them of his own will, and looseth the bonds of sinners. To him in faith we sing, O God, the Redeemer, blessed art thou.

Both now. To the Virgin.

O Mother Virgin, through thee light

13

shineth throughout all the world; for thou didst bear the Maker and God of all. Pray him, most pure one, to bestow great mercy on us faithful ones.

Ode VIII. Irmos.

IN the flame thou didst bedew the faithful ones, and burn with water the just one's sacrifice; for thou doest all things by thy will alone, O Christ. Thee we set up for ever.

The Jews, of old a prophet-killing race, through envy now are slayers of God, since they raised thee upon the Cross, O Word of God, whom we set up for ever.

Thou didst not leave the heavens, yet wentest down to hades, and with thyself, O Christ, didst raise corrupt mankind, and art set up for ever. *Glory.*

The ears with trembling hear how the Most High, of his own will, came down on earth, and, by his Cross and Burial, destroyed the might of hades, and called all men to arise. Bless him, ye youths; sing him, ye priests; ye people, set him up for ever.

Both now. To the Virgin.

O glorious Virgin, in whom God's Spirit dwelt, thou didst conceive from Light the light-originating Word, and bring him forth. Therefore we sing thee evermore.

Then we sing,

The more honourable than the Cherubim . . . .

Ode IX. Irmos.

*M*AN *cannot look on God, and angel Hosts dare not behold him; but through thee, most pure one, the incarnate Word was seen of men, whom, with the heavenly Hosts, we magnify, and call thee blessed.*

Unpassionate thou didst remain, O Word of God, when thou in flesh wast joined to passions, but thou didst free mankind from passions, dealing with passions by thy Passion; for thou, our Saviour, art alone the Immortal and Almighty One.

O Lord, when death's corruption touched thee, thou didst keep thy Body from decay, and thy Spirit, life-giving and divine, was not detained in hades; but as from sleep thou didst arise, and raise us with thyself.

Glory.

We glorify God the Father with pure lips, and his co-unbeginning Son, and honour the unspeakable and glorious might of the most Holy Spirit; for thou, O undivided Trinity, art alone almighty.

Both now. To the Virgin.

O most pure Mother of God, through thine ineffable and unspeakable child-bearing, resurrection is bestowed on the dead; for Life, clothed in flesh from thee, now shineth unto all, dispersing the shades of death.

Exapostilarion.

O SAVIOUR, when thou wast risen from the tomb, to shew that thou wast man, thou stoodest in the midst of thy Disciples, and didst partake of meat, and teach the baptism of repentance. Then straightway into heaven thou didst ascend unto the Father, promising to send the Paraclete. Glory to thine Arising, O most divine God-Man.

Glory. Both now. To the Virgin.

THE Maker of creation and the God of all things took human flesh from thy pure blood, most holy Virgin, and my corrupted nature made anew. And thou moreover after giving birth remainedst as before. Therefore in faith we praise thee and exclaim, Hail! Queen of all the world.

With the Psalms of Praise, Stichera on the Resurrection in Tone 6.

Verse. Let every thing that hath breath praise the Lord. O praise God in his Saints, praise him according to the greatness of his majesty.

THY Cross, O Lord, is life and resurrection to thy people, and we that trust therein sing unto thee, our risen God, Have mercy on us.

Verse. Praise him with the sound of the trumpet, praise him with psaltery and harp.

THY Burial, O Lord, hath opened Paradise unto the race of men, and we that are delivered from corruption sing unto thee, our risen God, Have mercy on us.

Verse. Praise him with timbrel and choir, praise him with stringed instruments and organ.

TO Christ, who from the dead arose we sing, as also to the Father and the Spirit, exclaiming unto him, O thou that art our Resurrection and our Life, have mercy on us.

Verse. Praise him with well-tuned cymbals, praise him with loud cymbals. Let every thing that hath breath praise the Lord.

O CHRIST, thou didst arise the third day from the tomb, as it is written, and raisedst our Forefather with thyself. Therefore the race of men extolleth thee and praiseth thy Resurrection.

Glory.   The Evangelical Verse.

O CHRIST, the Peace of God to man, when, after thine Arising, thou camest to give peace to thy Disciples they were afraid, thinking they saw a spirit. But thou didst shew thine hands and feet, and quiet their disturbed souls. And to them that still believed not, thou didst, when partaking of the meat and recalling unto them thy teachings, open their minds that they might understand the scriptures, and, repeating unto them .the fatherly promise and blessing them, thou didst return to heaven. Therefore with them we worship thee. Glory to thee, O Lord.

Both now.   To the Virgin.

Most blessed art thou, Virgin . . . .

And the Doxology, and the rest. Vide page 39, *et seq.*

AT THE LITURGY.

With the Beatitudes in Tone 6.

REMEMBER me, O God, my Saviour, when thou comest in thy kingdom, and save me; for thou alone art the Lover of mankind.

Verse. Blessed are the pure in heart . . . .

ADAM, who was beguiled by a tree, thou didst save again by the tree of the Cross when the thief exclaimed, Remember me, O Lord, in thy kingdom.

Verse. Blessed are the peace-makers ....

THOU didst destroy the gates and bars of hades, O Giver of life, and hast raised all things, O Saviour, and they cry, Glory to thine Arising.

Verse. Blessed are they that are persecuted ....

REMEMBER me, O thou who didst spoil death by thy Burial and fill all things with joy by thy Resurrection; for thou art most merciful.

Verse. Blessed are ye when men shall revile ....

THE myrrh-bearing women went to the tomb, and heard the Angel say, Christ is risen, and hath enlightened all things.

Verse. Rejoice, and be exceeding glad....

O CHRIST, who wast nailed on the tree of the Cross, and didst save the world from guile, with one accord we sing to thee.

Glory.

To the Trinity.

LET us glorify the Father, and the Son, and the Holy Ghost, saying, O holy Trinity, save our souls.

Both now. To the Virgin.

O VIRGIN, who didst unspeakably conceive and bring forth thine own Creator, save them that honour thee.

Prokimenon in Tone 6.

O LORD, save thy people, and bless thine inheritance.

Verse. Unto thee have I cried, O Lord my God: keep not silence concerning me.

The Lection from the Epistle to the Ephesians. Section 233.

BRETHREN! Be strong in the Lord, and in the power of his might. Put on the whole armour of God, that ye may be able to stand against the wiles of the devil. For we wrestle not against flesh and blood, but against principalities, against powers, against the rulers of the darkness of this world, against spiritual wickedness in high places. Wherefore take unto you the whole armour of God, that ye may be able to withstand in the evil day, and having done all, to stand. Stand therefore, having your loins girt about with truth, and having

on the breastplate of righteousness, and your
feet shod with the preparation of the gospel
of peace; and above all, taking the shield
of faith, wherewith ye shall be able to quench
all the fiery darts of the wicked. And take
the helmet of salvation, and the sword of
the Spirit, which is the word of God.

*The Lection from the holy Evangelist Luke.
Section* 71.

AT that time, Jesus was teaching in
one of the synagogues on the sabbath
day. And, behold, there was a woman
which had a spirit of infirmity eighteen
years, and was bowed together, and could
in nowise lift up herself. And when
Jesus saw her, he called her to him, and
said unto her, Woman, thou art loosed from
thine infirmity. And he laid his hands
on her, and immediately she was made
straight, and glorified God. And the ruler
of the synagogue answered with indigna-
tion, because that Jesus had healed on
the sabbath day, and said unto the people,
There are six days in which men ought to
work, in them therefore come and be healed,
and not on the sabbath day. The Lord
then answered him and said, Thou hypocrite,
doth not each one of you on the sabbath
loose his ox or his ass from the stall, and

lead him away to watering? And ought not this woman, being a daughter of Abraham, whom Satan hath bound, lo, these eighteen years, be loosed from this bond on the sabbath day? And when he had said these things, all his adversaries were ashamed; and all the people rejoiced for all the glorious things that were done by him.

XVIII. PENITENTIAL SERVICE TO OUR LORD JESUS CHRIST.

AT VESPERS.

With the Lord, I have cried, *Stichera in Tone* 6.

WHEN thou, O righteous Judge, shalt sit upon thy throne of glory to execute a righteous judgment, when the fiery river shall carry all men before thy terrible judgment-seat, when the heavenly Hosts shall stand around, and every man according to his works be tried, then spare us, we earnestly beseech thee, and bless us to be numbered with the saved, O Christ, thou Lover of mankind.

Who would not lament for me because I have transgressed the commandments of the Most High? For by mine intemperance my place is hades and not paradise. Through desiring sweet food I am given up to death and am become a stranger to divine glory and life. But, Lord, accept my repentance for thy great mercy's sake, O Merciful One, thou Lover of mankind.

LOOK upon mine affliction and my pain, and upon the measurelessness of mine iniquity, upon the passions of my soul and the temptations of my mind. Hearken unto my despairing and condemned voice, and give me, Lord, a broken spirit, a contrite heart, and a fountain of tears, and pardon my many offences, for thy great mercy's sake. *Glory.*

O GOD, that desirest that every man should be saved; attend unto my prayer, and reject not my tears as vain. Who hath come unto thee weeping and hath not been saved? And who hath earnestly cried unto thee and hath not been heard? Yea, Lord, thou art quickly found to save them that pray to thee; for thy mercy cannot be overcome.

Both now. To the Virgin.

UNTO me, accursed, O most pure Virgin, shew the greatness of thy loving-kindness, the depth of thy tenderness, and the grace of thine unspeakable pity. Quiet my

sinful desires, grant me continence, and preserve my soul and body undefiled.

Then the Tranquil Light.

The Stichera with Verses.   Tone 6.

AT thy fearful advent, O Christ, let us
not hear: I know you not. For in
thee, O Saviour, we have put our
trust, even though, because of our negligence,
we have not kept thy commandments. Still
spare our souls, we pray thee.

Verse 1. Unto thee have I lifted up mine
eyes . . . . *Vide page* 58.

I HAVE no repentance, neither have I
tears. Therefore, O Christ my God, I
pray thee to convert me before the end
cometh, and to grant me penitence that I
may escape the torment.

Verse 2. Have mercy upon us, O Lord,
have mercy . . . . *Vide page* 58.

THY Martyrs, O Lord, did not deny thee,
neither did they swerve from thy commandments. Through their prayers have
mercy upon us.

Glory. Both now. To the Virgin.

O MOST pure God-bearing Virgin, none
that hath recourse to thee is sent away
ashamed, but when he asketh blessing, he
gaineth grace to pray acceptably.

On Tuesday and Thursday Evenings the following is substituted for the foregoing.

To the Virgin at the Cross.

O MOST pure God-bearing one, when thou sawest our Life hanging on the tree, thou didst weep as mother, and exclaim, My Son and God, save them that sing to thee with love.

AT MATINS.

After the Six Psalms and the Troparion of the Day, or the proper Song to the Trinity, as indicated at page 94, et seq., the first proper Kathism of the Psalter is read. Then,

Kathismal Hymn.   Tone 5.

WHEN the Judge shall sit and the Angels shall stand around, when the trumpet shall sound and the flame shall burn, what wilt thou do, O my soul, when thou lookest upon the Judge? For then shall thy wickedness stand forth, and thy secret sins be revealed. Therefore, before the end, cry unto the Judge, O God, cleanse and save me.

Glory. Both now. To the Virgin.

O SENTIENT vine, growing for us the divine Cluster, whence we have drunk the wine of incorruption; pour cleansing water on my soul, even contrition, by the grace of thy prayers.

After the second proper Kathism of the Psalter,

Kathismal Hymn. Tone 6.

I THINK of the terrible day, and I lament over my evil deeds. How shall I answer the immortal King? How shall I, a prodigal, dare to look upon the Judge? O loving Father, O only-begotten Son, and O Holy Ghost, have mercy upon me.

Glory. Both now. To the Virgin.

O MOST pure God-bearing Virgin, grant unto thy servant thy quick protection, and help, and mercy, and calm the waves ot my vain thoughts, and raise up my fainting soul; for thou canst do all thou willest.

Then is read Psalm 50 (51).

CANON TO OUR LORD JESUS CHRIST.

Tone 6. Ode I. Irmos.

A HELP and protection hath he become to me unto salvation, he is my God and I will glorify him, my fathers' God and I will exalt him; for he hath triumphed gloriously.

Refrain. Glory to thee, our God, glory to thee.

O God, when thou shalt come with thousands and ten thousands of Angels, and with the heavenly Principalities, vouchsafe that I, accursed, may meet thee in the clouds, O Christ.

Enter not into judgment with me, neither reveal my actions, nor search out my words, nor correct me for my passions, but in thy pity despise my wickedness, and save me, O Almighty One. *Glory.*

The unquenchable fire of hell terrifieth and affrighteth me, the bitter worm, the gnashing of the teeth. But pardon and forgive me, O Christ, and appoint my place with thine elect. *Both now.*

To the Virgin.

I am bowed down by many temptations and evil deeds, and with soul and body I bow down to thee, O pure one, and ceaslessly exclaim, Do thou convert me.

Ode III. Irmos.

O LORD, stablish my fainting heart upon the rock of thy commandments; for thou alone art holy and the Lord.

The Lord shall come, and who shall endure the terror of him? Who shall stand before his face? Then be ready, O my soul, to meet him.

O Lord, how shall I, who have disobeyed thy commandments, endure thine unendurable anger; but spare me, spare me in the hour of judgment. *Glory.*

O Lord, I cry unto thee, Have mercy upon me, have mercy upon me when thou shalt come with thine Angels to render unto all according to their deeds.

Both now.   To the Virgin.

O Lady, who art the door of grace, who openest the gates of heaven to the faithful; open unto me the shining doors of repentance, and deliver me from the gates of death.

Kathisma.   Tone 6.

IN the vale of weeping, in the place which thou hast appointed, when thou shalt sit, O Merciful One, to execute a righteous judgment; declare not my secrets, neither shame me before the Angels, but spare me, O God, and have mercy upon me.

Glory.   Both now.   To the Virgin.

O BLESSED God-bearing Virgin, the hope of the world, I entreat thine alone awful mediation. Shew thy gentleness to us, a favoured people, and pray the merciful God to deliver our souls from all that threateneth us, O thou blessed one.

Ode IV. *Irmos.*

THE Prophet heard of thine advent, O Lord, and was afraid; for thou didst will to be born of a Virgin and to appear unto men, and he cried, I have heard the report of thee and I feared. Glory to thy might, O Lord.

The day draweth nigh, already at the doors the judgment is, keep watch, O soul! where kings and princes, the rich together with the poor shall meet, and as each one hath wrought, so each shall worthily receive.

Inviolate is thy judgment-seat, thy judging darkened not by crafty words, or sophistry of orators, or parrying righteous evidence of witnesses. For unto thee, O God, the hidden things of all stand forth. *Glory.*

O Word of God, my Christ, let me not come to the land of weeping, let me not see the place of darkness, neither be bound hand and foot, and cast out of thy chamber and condemned, because my garment is a defiled one that perisheth not.

Both now. To the Virgin.

O most pure one, my stronghold, my refuge, mine unassailable wall, and my mediatress with God; deliver me from the eternal flame and hell.

Ode V. Irmos.

*R*ISING *early from the night, I pray thee,
O Lover of mankind, to enlighten and
instruct me in thy commandments, and to
teach me, O Saviour, to do thy will.*

An inexpressible trembling and fear shall
be; for the Lord shall come, and every one's
deeds shall be before him. Who is there
therefore that shall not greatly bewail?

Spare, spare, O Lord, thy creature, and
forgive me who have sinned; for thou alone
art in essence sinless, and save thee there
is none without defilement. *Glory.*

I have no tears, no repentance, no contrition; but, O God, my Saviour, grant these
to me. *Both now. To the Virgin.*

O undefiled Mother of God, my intentions
are defiled and accursed because of my
faults, but I pray thee, Have compassion
upon me, and save me by thy mediation.

Ode VI. Irmos.

I CRIED *with my whole heart to the merciful God, and he heard me from the depths
of hades, and raised my life from corruption.*

O Christ, my Saviour, when thou shalt
reveal thyself from heaven at thy terrible
advent, when the thrones shall be set and

14*

the books be opened, then spare, O spare thy creature.

When God shall sit in judgment then nothing shall be able to help thee, neither care, nor artifice, nor glory, nor friendship, nothing save the virtue of thy deeds, O my soul. *Glory.*

Let me not hear thy sentence rejecting me from thee, O Lord, neither that bidding me go into the fire of the condemned; but let me hear the voice for which the righteous long. *Both now.*

To the Virgin.

O most pure and undefiled one, who cleansest us before the face of God; pray that in the day of judgment we may escape the fearful torment who confess thee to be the true Mother of God.

Condakion.

GOD, when thou shalt come on earth with glory, when all shall quake, when the fiery river shall carry away to the judgment - seat, when the books shall be opened and all secrets revealed, then do thou save me from unquenchable fire, and bless me, O righteous Judge, to stand at thy right hand.

Icos. (Stanza.)

FEARFUL shall be thy judgment-seat and
righteous thy judgment, but my deeds
are wicked; yet, O merciful Lord, prevent
and save me, and deliver me from torment.
Let not my part be among the goats, but
bless me, O righteous Judge, to stand at
thy right hand.

Ode VII. Irmos.

*WE have sinned, we have prevaricated, we
have been unrighteous before thee. We
have neither loved, neither kept those things
that thou hast commanded. Still, reject us not
at the last, O God of our fathers.*

The Lord shall come to judge, and who
shall endure his appearing? Tremble, O
condemned soul, tremble and prepare to
meet thy deeds. May the Merciful, Blessed
and Gentle One convert thee, even the God
of our fathers.

I fall down before thee, and offer thee my
words as tears. I have sinned as the sinful
woman sinned not, and have transgressed
like as none other upon earth. But, Lord,
have pity on me whom thou didst make,
and call me back to thee. *Glory.*

Then shut not thy door upon me, O Lord,
O Lord; but open it unto me, a penitent,

who in the grief of my heart fall down before thee. O God, have mercy upon me.

Both now. To the Virgin.

When the Bridegroom shall come in the
night to judge the earth, then, O pure one,
vouchsafe to conduct me with a shining lamp
to meet him, and to worship his appearing.

Ode VIII. Irmos.

*H*IM *that heavenly Hosts glorify and Cherubim and Seraphim fear, let every spirit
and every creature sing, bless and set up for ever.*

O Lord, when I think of meeting thy
terrible second advent, I tremble at thy
threatenings, I fear thine anger and exclaim,
From this hour save me for ever.

O Merciful One, I trust in thy goodness,
I fall down before thee, and I ask thee to
pardon mine iniquity. O Lord reject me not.

*Let us bless the Lord, the Father, the Son,
and the Holy Ghost.*

O my God and Lord, the Judge of all
men; let me hear thy welcome voice in that
day, let me see thy great light, let me behold thy dwelling-place, let me contemplate
thy glory and rejoice for ever.

*Let us praise, let us bless, let us worship
the Lord, singing unto him and setting him
up for ever.*

To the Virgin.

In the day of judgment reveal thyself, O Lady, and mediate for me, and deliver me from the torment and from the fire, that I may be saved by thee, and may sing thine invincible goodness.

Ode IX. Irmos.

THE unspeakable birth from a seedless conception of a husbandless mother is an incorruptible fruit; for the birth of God regenerateth nature. Then do all generations right-believingly magnify thee as the divine-bride Mother.

The Lord shall come to torment the sinners and to save the righteous. Let us weep, let us lament, and let us take thought for that day on which every unknown and secret thing shall be revealed, and every man be meted after his deserts.

Daniel feared the hour of trial. What then shall I, accursed one, endure when the Lord shall come on the terrible day? Still grant me before the end to serve thee acceptably, and to attain unto thy kingdom.

Glory.

The fire is ready, the worm is prepared. Gladness, glory, rest, light without evening, and joy are for the righteous. Who then shall be blessed to escape the torment of the one, and to gain the inheritance of the other?

Both now.   To the Virgin.

The surge of passion dismayeth me, and pleasure overwhelmeth me. O most undefiled Virgin, who didst bear the Pilot, Christ; stretch forth thine hand to help and save me, thou who alone art the salvaton of them that in faith call thee blessed.

The Lucern.

O LORD, when the thrones shall be set and the books be opened, and thou, O Judge, shalt come to try the deeds of men; condemn not us, whom thine hands did make, to the fire of gehenna, but vouchsafe to us thy kingdom, O Saviour.

Glory.   Both now.   To the Virgin.

HE that was born of thy blood, O pure one, is perfect man and true God and Lord. O pray him to deliver us from eternal fire.

The Stichera with Verses.   Tone 6.

THE enemy found me void of good works, and wounded me with the arrows of sin. But thou, O God, as the Physician of my soul and body, heal the wounds of my soul, and have mercy upon me.

Verse 1. Let us be filled early with thy mercy . . . . *Vide page* 105.

O SAVIOUR, Physician of my soul and body, heal the wounds of my heart caused by my sins, and forgive mine iniquities, and grant me tears of repentance, and loose me from my trespasses. O Lord, have mercy upon me.

Verse 2. And let the brightness of the Lord our God . . . . *Vide page* 105.

O LORD, if we had not thy Saints to pray for us and thy goodness so merciful unto us, how should we have dared, O Saviour, to sing to thee whom Angels without ceasing glorify? O Searcher of hearts, spare our souls.

Glory. Both now. To the Virgin.

O PURE Mary, golden vessel of fragrance, receptacle of one of the undivided Trinity, in whom the Father took delight, and in whose holy womb the Son, through the operation of the most Holy Spirit, dwelt; pray that in the day of judgment we may obtain forgiveness of our sins.

AT LITURGY.

Verses with the Beatitudes in Tone 6.

REMEMBER me, O God, my Saviour, when thou comest in thy kingdom, and save me, for thou alone art the Lover of mankind.

O CHRIST, thou didst accept the tears of Peter : accept also my repentance, and grant me forgiveness of my sins.

THOU that dost enlighten the heavenly choirs, O Christ; do thou enlighten the eyes of my heart.

O BAPTIST and Forerunner of the Lord, thou didst preach repentance unto men. I pray thee to vouchsafe that I may repent from my soul.

THOU wast of thine own will nailed to the tree, O Christ, and by thy power didst destroy the sting of the proud.

AS mysterious rays ye have penetrated the world, O glorious Apostles, and with faith ye have enlightened the race of men.

THOU that hast glorified the Prophets, and Teachers, and Venerables, and Just; save our souls by their prayers, O Lover of mankind. *Glory.*

WE glorify the Father, and the Son, and the Holy Ghost, saying, O holy Trinity, save our souls. *Both now.*

O MOST pure one, thou art called blessed throughout all generations, for of a truth thou didst bear the blessed God.

The Epistle to the Colossians. Section 258.

BRETHREN! Put on therefore (as the elect of God, holy and beloved) bowels of mercies, kindness, humbleness of mind, meekness, long-suffering, forbearing one another, and forgiving one another, if any man have a quarrel against any; even as Christ forgave you, so also do ye. And above all these things put on charity, which is the bond of perfectness, and let the peace of God rule in your hearts, to the which also ye are called in one body, and be ye thankful. Let the word of Christ dwell in you richly in all wisdom, teaching and admonishing one another in psalms and hymns and spiritual songs, singing with grace in your hearts to the Lord.

The Gospel from S. Mark. Section 37.

THE Lord said : Whosoever will come after me, let him deny himself, and take up his cross, and follow me. For whosoever will save his life shall lose

it; but whosoever shall lose his life for my
sake and the gospel's, the same shall save
it. For what shall it profit a man, if he
shall gain the whole world, and lose his
soul? Or what shall a man give in ex-
change for his soul? Whosoever therefore
shall be ashamed of me and of my words
in this adulterous and sinful generation, of
him also shall the Son of man be ashamed,
when he cometh in the glory of his Father
with the holy Angels. And he said unto
them, Verily I say unto you that there be
some of them that stand here, which shall
not taste of death, till they have seen the
kingdom of God come with power.

XIX. THE OFFICE FOR THE HOLY COMMUNION OF THE DIVINE MYS-TERY OF THE BODY AND BLOOD OF CHRIST.

———⋄———

A. PRAYERS BEFORE HOLY COMMUNION.

Let him that purposeth to approach the most pure Mysteries recite Compline, and after the I believe in one God, *say with contrite heart the following Canon in Tone 2.*

Ode I. Irmos.

*C*OME, *ye people, and let us sing a hymn to Christ our God, who divided the sea and guided the people whom he delivered from the bondage of Egypt; for he hath been glorified.*

Verse. Create in me a clean heart, O God, and renew a right spirit within me.

O bountiful Lord, may thy holy Body and thy precious Blood become the bread of everlasting life to me, and the healing of manifold diseases.

Verse. Cast me not away from thy presence, and take not thy Holy Spirit from me.

Defiled as I am, O Christ, by unbecoming deeds, I am not worthy of the communion of thy most pure Body and divine Blood. Still, do thou vouchsafe the same to me.

Glory. Both now.

O thou most blessed Bride of God, the good soil which grew the Corn untilled and saving to the world; grant that partaking thereof I may be saved.

Ode III. Irmos.

STABLISHING me on the rock of faith, thou hast enlarged my mouth against mine enemies. Then doth my heart rejoice to sing, There is none holy as the Lord our God, nor any just save thee, O Lord.

O Christ, give me those tearful drops which cleanse my heart's impurity, that, with a conscience pure, I may approach with faith and fear, O Lord, to the communion of thy divine Gifts.

O thou that lovest mankind, may thy most pure Body and divine Blood be to the remission of my sins, to the communion of the Holy Ghost, to life everlasting, and to freedom from passions and afflictions.

Glory. Both now.

O thou most holy table of the Bread of life, which, for mercy's sake, came from above and giveth new life unto the world; grant that I may now, unworthy as I am, taste thereof in fear and live.

Ode IV. Irmos.

THOU camest from the Virgin, neither as a mediator, nor as an angel, but as the Lord himself incarnate, and hast saved all men. Therefore I cry to thee, Glory to thy might, O Lord.

O most Merciful One, thou didst will to take flesh for our sake, and to be slain as a lamb for the sins of men. Therefore I beseech thee, Cleanse my sins also.

O Lord, heal the wounds of my soul and sanctify me wholly, and grant, O Master, that I, a prodigal, may partake of thy divine and mystical Supper.

Glory. Both now.

O Lady, propitiate him who was born of thee towards me, and preserve me, thy servant, pure and undefiled, so that, by receiving the goodly Pearl, I may be sanctified.

Ode V. Irmos.

O *Lord, Giver of light and Creator of eternity, lead us in the light of thy commandments; for save thee, we know none other God.*

As thou, O Christ, didst foretell, so let it be unto thine unprofitable servant, and in me abide, as thou didst promise; for, lo! I eat thy divine Body and drink thy Blood.

O Word of God and God, may the coal of thy Body be to the enlightenment of my darkness, and thy Blood to the cleansing of my defiled soul.

Glory. Both now.

O Mary, Mother of God, thou honourable tabernacle of sweet odour; make me, by thy prayers, a chosen vessel, that I may receive the sanctification of thy Son.

Ode VI. Irmos.

G *ROVELLING in the abyss of sin, I invoke the unfathomable depth of thy mercy. O God, raise me from corruption.*

O Saviour, sanctify my mind, my soul, my heart and my body, and bless me, O Lord, to approach uncondemned thy terrible Mysteries.

Grant that I may be rid of my passions, increase in thy grace, and be confirmed in my life by the communion of thy holy Mysteries, O Christ.

Glory. Both now.

O God, O God, O holy Word, wholly sanctify me now approaching thy divine Mysteries, through the supplications of thy holy Mother.

Condakion. Tone 2.

FORBID me not now, O Christ, to receive the Bread, which is thy Body, and thy divine Blood; and, reprobate though I am, let me partake, O Lord, of thy most pure and awful Mysteries. Let these not be to my judgment, but to everlasting and immortal life.

Ode VII. Irmos.

THE wise children did not serve the golden image, and themselves went into the furnace and reviled their gods, and cried in the midst of the flame, and the Angel bedewed them. For the prayer of your lips was heard.

O Christ, Fountain of blessings, may the communion of thine immortal Mysteries be to me now light and life, and freedom from pain, and to my growth and increase in

15

divine virtues, that I may glorify thee who alone art good.

Grant that now approaching thine immortal and divine Mysteries in fear and love and piety, I may be delivered, O Lover of mankind, from passions and enemies, and from every affliction ; and vouchsafe that I may sing to thee, Blessed art thou, O Lord God of our fathers.

Glory. Both now.

O thou God-favoured one, who didst above comprehension bear the Saviour Christ, I, thy servant, pray thee now, the impure the pure, Cleanse me, desiring now to approach the most pure Mysteries, from all defilement of flesh and spirit.

Ode VIII. Irmos.

O YE works of the Lord, sing unto God, who came down unto the Hebrew children in the fiery furnace and changed the flame to dew, and set him up for ever.

O Christ, grant that I now, uncondemned, may become a partaker of thy heavenly, terrible and holy Mysteries, and of thy divine and mystical Supper, O God, my Saviour.

Seeking refuge in thy loving-kindness, O Blessed One, I cry to thee with fear, Abide in me, O Saviour, and let me also, as thou didst say, abide in thee; for, lo! trusting in

thy mercy, I eat thy Body and I drink thy
Blood.

Glory. Both now.

I tremble in taking this fire lest I should
be consumed as wax or as grass. O fearful
mystery! O the loving-kindness of God!
How is it that I, being but dust, partake of
the divine Body and Blood, and am made
incorruptible?

Ode IX. Irmos.

*T*HE *Son of the unbeginning Father, the
God and Lord incarnate of the Virgin,
hath appeared to us, to enlighten the darkened
and to gather the scattered. Therefore do
we all magnify thee, the all-praised Mother
of God.*

O taste and see that it is Christ the Lord,
who, for our sake, made like to us of old,
once offered up himself as an offering to his
Father, and now is ever slain, sanctifying
the communicants.

O Lord, let me be sanctified in body and
soul, let me be enlightened and saved, and
become thy dwelling through the communion
of thy holy Mysteries, having thee, O most
merciful Benefactor, living in me, with the
Father and the Spirit. *Glory.*

May thy Body and thy precious Blood,
O my Saviour, be as fire and light to me,

15*

consuming the substance of sin and burning the tares of my passions, and wholly enlightening me, that I may worship thy Divinity. *Both now.*

God took flesh from thy pure blood. Therefore do all generations sing thee, O Lady, and the hosts of spirits glorify thee; for, through thee, they clearly behold him that ruleth all things endued with human nature.

And straightway. It is very meet to bless thee . . . . *Vide page* 61.

Then, Trisagion. O most holy Trinity . . . . *After the* Our Father,

The Troparion of the occurring Festival.

If it is not one, the following in Tone 6. Have mercy upon us . . . .

Glory. O Lord, have mercy upon us . . . .

Both now. O blessed Mother of God . . . .

Vide page 72.

Lord, have mercy, *forty times.*

And the Prayer to the most holy Mother of God.

O thou Virgin spotless . . . . *Vide page* 77.

On the morrow, the usual Office
of Hours.

And after the Beatitudes,

*The Lection from the Epistle of Paul the
Apostle to the Corinthians. Section* 149.

BRETHREN! I have received of the
Lord that which also I delivered unto
you, That the Lord Jesus the same
night in which he was betrayed took bread,
and when he had given thanks, he brake it,
and said, Take, eat, this is my body, which
is brokcn for you: this do in remembrance
of me. After the same manner also he took
the cup, when he had supped, saying, This
cup is the new testament in my blood: this
do ye, as oft as ye drink it, in remembrance
of me. For as often as ye eat this bread,
and drink this cup, ye do shew the Lord's
death till he come. Wherefore whosoever
shall eat this bread, and drink this cup of
the Lord unworthily, shall be guilty of the
body and blood of the Lord. But let a man
examine himself, and so let him eat of the
bread and drink of the cup. For he that
eateth and drinketh unworthily, eateth and
drinketh condemnation to himself, not discerning the Lord's body. For this cause
many are weak and sickly among you, and

many sleep. For if we would judge ourselves, we should not be judged. But when
we are judged, we are chastened of the
Lord, that we should not be condemned
with the world.

*The Lection from the holy Evangelist John.
Section 23.*

THE Lord said unto them that came
unto him of the Jews, I am the bread
of life. Your fathers did eat manna
in the wilderness, and are dead. This is the
bread which cometh down from heaven, that
a man may eat thereof, and not die. I am
the living bread which came down from
heaven : if any man eat of this bread, he
shall live for ever, and the bread that I will
give is my flesh, which I will give for the
life of the world. The Jews therefore strove
among themselves, saying, How can this man
give us his flesh to eat? Then Jesus said
unto them, Amen, Amen, I say unto you,
Except ye eat the flesh of the Son of man,
and drink his blood, ye have no life in you.
Whoso eateth my flesh, and drinketh my
blood, hath eternal life, and I will raise him
up at the last day.

After the reading of the Gospel,

Remember us, O Lord • . . , *And the rest,
as written in the Typica.* Vide page 129.

After this, continue with all attention,

Through the prayers of our holy Fathers . . . .
O heavenly King . . . . *Trisagion. After
the* Our Father, Lord, have mercy, *twelve
times. Glory. Both now.* O come, let us
worship . . . . *thrice. And the following
Psalms.*

Psalm 22 (23).

THE Lord is my Shepherd, therefore can
I lack nothing. He shall feed me in
a green pasture, and lead me forth
beside the waters of comfort. He shall convert my soul, and bring me forth in the
paths of righteousness for his name's sake.
Yea, though I walk through the valley of
the shadow of death, I will fear no evil; for
thou art with me, thy rod and thy staff comfort me. Thou shalt prepare a table before
me against them that trouble me. Thou hast
anointed my head with oil, and thy cup
inebriateth me as with strong wine. And thy
mercy shall follow me all the days of my
life, that I may dwell in the house of the
Lord for ever.

Psalm 23 (24).

THE earth is the Lord's, and all that
therein is, the compass of the world
and they that dwell therein. For he
hath founded it upon the seas, and prepared

it upon the floods. Who shall ascend into the hill of the Lord? or who shall rise up in his holy place? Even he that hath clean hands and a pure heart, that hath not lift up his mind unto vanity, nor sworn to deceive his neighbour. He shall receive blessing from the Lord, and righteousness from the God of his salvation. This is the generation of them that seek him, even of them that seek thy face, O God of Jacob. Lift up your gates, O ye princes, and be ye lift up, ye everlasting gates, and the King of glory shall come in. Who is this King of glory? It is the Lord strong and mighty, even the Lord mighty in battle. Lift up your gates, O ye princes, and be ye lift up, ye everlasting gates, and the King of glory shall come in. Who is this King of glory? Even the Lord of hosts, he is the King of glory.

Psalm 115 (116).

I BELIEVED, and therefore have I spoken, but I was sore troubled. I said in my haste, All men are liars. What reward shall I render unto the Lord for all the benefits he hath done unto me? I will take the cup of salvation, and call upon the name of the Lord. I will pay my vows now in the presence of all his people. Right dear in the sight of the Lord is the death of his saints. Behold, Lord, how that I am thy servant, and the son of thine handmaid: thou hast broken my bonds in sunder. I will offer to thee the sacrifice of thanksgiving, and will call upon the name of the Lord. I will pay my vows unto the Lord in the sight of all his people, in the courts of the Lord's house, even in the midst of thee, O Jerusalem.

Glory. Both now.

Alleluia, alleluia, alleluia, glory to thee, O God, *thrice.*

Then the following Troparia. Tone 8.

O LORD, who wast born of the Virgin, despise my transgressions, and cleanse my heart, making it a temple for thy most pure Body and Blood, and cast me not away from thy presence, O thou who hast mercy without measure. *Glory.*

How shall I, unworthy, dare to partake of thy holy Sacrament? If, with the worthy, I venture to approach thee, my garment will denounce me, for it is not a supper one, and I shall call forth the condemnation of my most sinful soul. O Lord, cleanse the defilement of my soul, and save me, for thou lovest mankind. *Both now.*

Because of the multitude of my trans-

gressions I come to thee, O pure Mother
of God, asking for salvation. Visit thou my
ailing soul, and beseech thy Son and our
God to grant me remission of the evils I
have wrought, O thou most blessed one.

But in Holy and Great Quadragesima say,

WHEN, on the evening of the washing
of feet, the glorious Disciples were being
enlightened, then was it that the malicious
Judas, ailing with the love of silver, was
darkened, and betrayed thee, the righteous
Judge to the unrighteous judges. Beware
then, thou that settest thine heart on riches,
beware him whom the same hath brought
to strangling. Flee from that insatiate soul
which dared such things against the Master.
O Lord, good unto all, glory to thee.

Then, Lord, have mercy, forty times.

And as many genuflections as thou wilt.

Then say these lines,

IF thou wishest, O man, to eat the Body
of the Lord,

Approach in fear, lest thou be scorched,
for it is fire,

And, drinking the divine Blood unto communion,

First reconcile thyself to them that have
sorrowed thee,

Then venture and eat the mystical food.

Other lines,

BEFORE partaking of the fearful Sacrifice
Of the life-creating Body of the Lord,
After this manner pray in fear,

Prayer of Saint Basil the Great.

O Lord Jesus Christ our God, Source of life and immortality, Creator of all things visible and invisible, co-eternal Son with the everlasting Father, who, out of thy great loving-kindness, didst in the latter days become incarnate, and wast crucified for us ungrateful and thankless ones, and hast renewed with thine own Blood our nature corrupted by sin; do thou thyself, immortal King, accept the repentance of thy sinful servant, incline thine ear towards me, and hearken unto my supplications. For I have sinned, O Lord, I have sinned against heaven and against thee, and I am not worthy to raise mine eyes to the height of thy glory; I have also angered thy goodness by transgressing thy commandments and by not obeying thine ordinances. But thou, O Lord, who art long-suffering and of great mercy, hast not given me over to perish in my sins, always awaiting my conversion. For thou hast said by thy Prophets, O thou Lover of mankind, that thou hast not pleasure in the death of a sinner, but rather

that he should return and live. Thou willest
not, O Lord, that the works of thy hands
should be lost, neither hast thou pleasure
in the perdition of men, but desirest that
all should be saved and come to the knowledge of the truth. Therefore even I, although
unworthy of heaven, or yet of earth and of
this temporal life, having submitted my whole
self to sin and made myself a slave of pleasure, defiling thine image, being still thy
creature and thy handiwork, despair not of
salvation, reprobate as I am ; and, emboldened
by thine immeasurable compassion, I come
unto thee. Receive me then, even me, O
man-loving Lord, like the adulteress, like the
thief, like the publican, like the prodigal,
and take away the heavy load of my sins,
O thou who takest away the sins of the
world, who healest the infirmities of men,
who callest unto thyself the weary and the
burdened and givest them rest, who camest
not to call the righteous but sinners to repentance. And do thou cleanse me from
every defilement of the flesh and of the
spirit, and teach me to perfect holiness in
the fear of thee, that, in the pure testimony
of my conscience, receiving my portion of
thy holy things, I may be united with thy
holy Body and Blood, and have thee to dwell
and to remain within me, with the Father

and thy Holy Spirit. Yea, O Lord Jesus Christ my God, grant that the communion of thy holy and life-giving Mysteries may not be to my condemnation, neither let me communicate of them unworthily on account of the ailings of my soul and body; but grant me unto the last breath of my life to partake uncondemned of my share of thy holy things, to the fellowship of the Holy Spirit, as a provision for life eternal, and for a favourable answer at thy terrible judgment-seat; that I, even I, may also become with thine elect a partaker of thine incorruptible blessings, which thou hast prepared for them that love thee, O Lord, in whom thou art glorified to ages. Amen.

Prayer of our Father in the Saints, John Chrysostom.

I KNOW, O Lord my God, that I am not worthy nor sufficient that thou shouldest come under the roof of my soul's habitation, for it is all deserted and in ruins, and thou hast not in me where worthily to lay thy head. But as from the height of thy glory thou didst humble thyself for us, bear now also with my humility; and as thou didst deign to lay thyself down in a manger in a cave, so deign now also to enter into the manger of my mute soul and defiled body; and as thou didst not refuse to enter into the house of Simon the leper and to sup there with sinners, so also deign to enter into the habitation of my humble soul, leprous and sinful; and as thou didst not reject the sinful woman who approached and touched thee, so also have pity on me, a sinner, coming to thee and touching thee. And grant that I may partake of thy precious Body and thine honourable Blood to the sanctification, enlightenment and strengthening of my humble soul and body, to the alleviation of the burden of my many sins, to my preservation from all the snares of the devil, to victory over my sinful and evil habits, to the mortification of my passions, to the fulfilment of thy commandments, to the increase of thy divine grace, and to the inheritance of thy kingdom. For it is not in lightness of heart, O Christ my God, that I venture to approach thee, but trusting in thine infinite goodness, and in the fear that being drawn afar from thee I may become the prey of our spiritual enemy. Therefore do I pray unto thee, O Lord, who alone art holy, that thou wouldest sanctify my soul and body, my heart and mind, and, renewing me entirely, wouldest implant in my members the fear of thee. And be thou my Help and Guide, governing my life in the ways of peace, and making me worthy to obtain with thy Saints a place at thy right hand, through the prayers and supplications of thy most pure Mother, of thy bodiless Ministers and honourable Powers, and of all thy Saints who from ages have found favour before thee. Amen.

Prayer of Saint Simeon the Meditative.

ONLY pure and all-holy Lord, who, through immeasurable compassion for man, didst take upon thyself the whole burden of our mortality in thy miraculous conception by the operation of the Holy Spirit and by the good will of the eternal Father; thyself, O Jesus Christ, the Wisdom, the Peace, and the Power of God, who didst deign to take upon thyself thy life-giving and saving passion, the cross, the nails, the spear and death itself; deaden, I beseech thee, my bodily passions which destroy my soul. O thou who by thy burial didst vanquish the kingdom of hell, bury my evil imaginations in good thoughts, and disperse within me the spirits of evil. O thou who in thy life-giving resurrection on the third day didst raise again our fallen forefather Adam, raise me who am dead in sin, and give me the means of repentance. O thou who didst in thy glorious ascension deify the flesh that thou hadst taken upon thee, and didst honour it by a seat at the right hand of God, enable me by partaking of thy holy Sacrament to obtain a place on thy right hand with thy redeemed. O thou who by the descent of the Holy Ghost, the Paraclete, didst render thy holy disciples worthy vessels, do thou render me also a receptacle for his habitation. O thou who shalt come again to judge the world, bless me also to meet thee, my Creator and Judge, in the clouds with all thy Saints, that I may for ever praise and glorify thee, with thine eternal Father, and thy most holy, and good, and life-giving Spirit, now and ever, and to ages of ages. Amen.

Another Prayer of the same Saint.

CHRIST my God, as though I were standing before thy terrible and impartial judgment-seat, awaiting my sentence and rendering an account of mine evil deeds, so, even at this present hour before the day of my judgment has yet come, I stand before thy holy Altar, before thy terrible and holy Angels, and, bowed down by my conscience, I bring before thee my evil and wicked doings, and confess them, and reveal them. O Lord, look down on my humility, and forgive all my sins. See, my transgressions number more than the hairs of my head. What evil have I not done? What sin have I not committed? What wickedness have I not imagined in my soul? Have I not sinned indeed by pride, boasting, slander, idle speech, improper laughter, intemperance, hatred, envy, avarice, self-love, ambition, falsehood? Have I not defiled all my senses, all my members, and have I not been a ready agent of Satan? I know well, O Lord, that mine iniquities have gone over my head; but I also know that the multitude of thy bounties is without measure, and the mercy of thy great goodness is unspeakable, and there is no sin that can overcome thy loving-kindness. Therefore, O most wonderful King, O most good Lord, do thou shew thy mercies in me, a sinner, manifest in me the power of thy goodness and the might of thy loving-kindness, and receive me who turn to thee. Accept me as thou didst accept the prodigal, the thief, and the sinful woman. Accept me, though in word and in deed, by my evil passions and unreasonable imaginations, I have sinned without measure against thee. And as at the eleventh hour thou didst receive them that came unto thee, though nothing worthy had they done, so also receive me, a sinner; for greatly have I sinned,

16

and am defiled, and I have grieved thy Holy Spirit, and offended thy loving-kindness in word, in deed, and in thought, by night and by day, openly and secretly, knowingly and unknowingly; and full well I know that thou wilt shew unto me my sins such as I have committed them, and that thou wilt demand an account from me of that wherein I have offended without excuse. But, O Lord, O Lord, rebuke me not in thy righteous wrath, neither chasten me in thy hot displeasure. Have mercy upon me, O Lord, for though I am weak, I am also thy creature. Thou, O Lord, hast stablished thy fear in me, and yet I have done evil in thy sight. Against thee, thee only, have I sinned, but, I beseech thee, enter not into jugdment with thy servant. For if, O Lord, thou wilt be extreme to mark what is done amiss, O Lord, who shall abide before thee? I shall not, for I am but an abyss of evil, and am neither worthy nor sufficient to look up and behold the height of heaven on account of the multitude of my sins. For what sins have I not committed? What evil hath not possessed me? Every sin have I committed, every uncleanness have I taken into my soul, and I have been unprofitable before thee and before men. Oh! who will raise me fallen into such great and dire sins?

O Lord my God, I have put my trust in thee. If there is any hope of salvation for me, if thy loving mercy can overcome the multitude of my transgressions, be thou my Saviour, and, according to thy goodness and mercy, loosen, remit and forgive all wherein I have sinned; for my soul is full of trouble, and there is no hope of salvation in me. Have mercy upon me, O God, according to thy loving-kindness; deal not with me according to my sins; but turn, preserve, and deliver my soul from the evils besetting it, and from all its wicked undertakings. Save me for thy mercy's sake, that where sin abounded thy grace may much more abound; and I will glorify thee always, all the days of my life. For thou art the God of the penitent, and the Saviour of sinners, and to thee we ascribe glory, with thine eternal Father, and thy most holy, and good, and life-giving Spirit, now and ever, and to ages of ages. Amen.

Prayer of the Divine Damascene.

LORD Jesus Christ our God, who alone hast power to remit the sins of men; do thou, O most Good and most Merciful One, remit the sins that I have committed wilfully, or in ignorance, and enable me, uncondemned, to receive thy

16*

divine, glorious, most pure and life-giving Mysteries, not to judgment, not to punishment, not to increase of sin, but to purification and sanctification, to a closer communion with the kingdom and the life to come, as a bulwark and a help to my soul, to the turning away from evil, and to the blotting out of my many sins. For thou art the God of mercy and bounties, and thou lovest mankind; and to thee we ascribe glory, with the Father and the Holy Spirit, now and ever, and to ages of ages. Amen.

Prayer of Saint Basil the Great.

KNOW, O Lord, that I receive unworthily thy most pure Body and thy precious Blood, that I am guilty, O Lord, and that I eat and drink to my own condemnation, not discerning the Body and Blood of Christ my God; but, trusting in thy mercy, I come unto thee who hast said, He that eateth my Flesh and drinketh my Blood shall abide in me and I in him. Have compassion upon me therefore, O Lord, and make not an example of me, thy sinful servant; but do with me according to thy great mercy, and grant that these holy things may rather operate in me to the healing, purifying, enlightening, guarding, saving and sanctifying of my soul and body,

to the overthrow of every imagination, evil
action, or work of the devil, to loving and
acknowledging thee, to the amendment and
steadfastness of my life, to the increase of
virtue, to the keeping of thy commandments,
to the fellowship of the Holy Spirit, to the
hope of eternal life, and to be an acceptable
apology before thine awful judgment seat.
Amen.

Prayer of Saint Simeon the New Divine.

FROM soiled lips,
From fouled heart,
From tongue impure,
From soul defiled,
Accept a prayer, my Christ,
And of me despise,
Neither the words, neither the manner,
Nor the shamelessness.
Grant me daringly to say
That which I wish, my Christ,
Or rather, teach thou me
What me behoveth to do and say.
I have sinned more than that sinful woman,
Who, learning where thou wast,
Did purchase myrrh,
And came daringly to anoint
The feet of thee, my Christ,
My Master, and my God.
Since thou didst not reject her,

Coming with her heart to thee,
So loathe not me, O Word of God;
But give me thy feet
To touch and kiss,
And with a flood of tears,
As with most precious myrrh,
To daringly anoint.
Wash me in my tears,
And with them cleanse me, Word of God;
And forgive mine iniquities,
And grant me pardon.
Thou knowest the multitude of evils in me,
Thou knowest my wounds,
And seest my sores;
But thou knowest also my faith,
Thou seest my good intentions,
And hearest my sighs.
There is nothing hidden from thee, O
my God,
My Creator, my Redeemer,
Not even a tear-drop,
Nor a part of that drop.
My substance yet imperfect
Thine eyes did behold,
And in thy book
Even things not yet done
Are found written by thee.
Look upon my lowliness,
Look upon my grief how great it is,
And all my sins

Forgive me, God of all things,
That, with pure heart,
And fearing mind,
And contrite soul,
I may partake of thy spotless
And most pure Mysteries,
Which quicken and deify
All them that eat and drink
In purity of heart.
For thou, my Lord, hast said,
He that eateth my Flesh
And drinketh my Blood
In me shall he abide,
And I abide in him.
True is every word
Of my Master and my God.
For, partaking of thy divine
And deifying blessings,
I am no more alone,
But with thee, O my Christ,
The tri-solar light
Which enlighteneth the world.
Let me not then remain alone
Without thee, O Life-giver,
My breath, my life,
My gladness,
And the salvation of the world.
For this cause have I come to thee,
As thou seest, with tears
And contrite soul,

Deliverance from mine iniquities
Praying to be granted me,
And of thy life-giving
And perfect Mysteries
To partake uncondemned;
So that thou mayest abide, as thou hast said,
With me, a thrice-accursed one,
Lest, finding me separated
From thy grace, the tempter
Should beguile me,
And, being tempted, draw me
From thy divine-effecting words.
For this cause I fall down to thee,
And earnestly I cry to thee,
As thou didst receive the prodigal,
And the sinful woman who came to thee,
So receive me, a sinner,
And a prodigal, O Compassionate One,
Who, with smitten soul,
Now come to thee.
I know, O Saviour, that no one
Hath sinned so as I have,
Nor done such deeds
As I have wrought;
But this I also know
That not the greatness of iniquity,
Nor the multitude of sins,
Surpasseth of my God
The abundant long-suffering
And exceeding love to men;

But that, in merciful compassion,
Them that earnestly repent
Thou cleansest and enlightenest,
And makest partakers of light,
And communicants of thy Divinity,
Making no distinctions,
And, strange thing to Angels
And to the thoughts of men!
Conversest with them ofttimes,
As with thy true friends.
This it is that emboldeneth me,
This it is that inspireth me, O my Christ;
And, trusting in the riches
Of thy benefactions unto us,
Joyful and yet trembling,
I partake of fire,
Myself but grass, and, strange the wonder!
Am unconsumedly bedewed,
As of old the bush
Did burn unconsumedly.
And now, with thankful mind,
With thankful heart,
And with thankful songs
Of my soul and body,
I worship, and magnify,
And glorify thee, O my God;
For thou art blessed
Now and for ever.

Prayer of Saint John Chrysostom.

O GOD, loosen, remit and forgive my sins against thee, whether in word, in deed, or in thought, willingly or unwillingly, knowingly or unknowingly committed, forgive them all; for thou art good and lovest mankind. And, through the prayers of thy most holy Mother, of thy heavenly Servants and holy Powers, and of all the Saints who have found favour in thy sight, bless me to receive uncondemned thy holy and immaculate Body and thy precious Blood, to the healing of my soul and body, and to the driving away of my evil imaginations; for thine is the kingdom, the power, and the glory, Father, Son, and Holy Ghost, now and ever, and to ages of ages. Amen.

Another of Saint Chrysostom.

O LORD and God, I am not worthy that thou shouldest enter the habitation of my soul; but as thou willest, according to thy loving-kindness, to dwell in me, I venture to approach thee. Thou biddest me open the gates of my soul, which thou alone hast made, that thou mayest enter therein with thy wonted loving-kindness, that thou mayest enter and enlighten my darkened mind. I believe thou wilt do

this, for thou didst not cast away the sinful
woman coming to thee in tears, nor didst
thou reject the penitent publican, nor the
thief on the cross who acknowledged thy
kingdom, nor didst thou leave the repentant
persecutor to himself, but didst number all
them that came to thee in repentance among
thy friends, O thou that alone art blessed,
always, now, and to everlasting ages. Amen.

Another Prayer of Saint Chrysostom.

LORD Jesus Christ my God, loosen,
remit, cleanse and forgive me, thine
unworthy and miserable servant, all
my sins, iniquities, and errors, as often as
I have sinned against thee from my youth
up to the present day and hour, whether
wittingly or in ignorance, whether in word or
deed, in thought or imagination, or in all
my feelings. And, through the prayers of
thy pure Mother, the blessed ever-virgin
Mary, my alone sure hope and protection,
enable me without condemnation to partake
of thy holy, immortal, life-giving, and terrible
Mysteries, unto the remission of sins and
life everlasting, unto the sanctification, enlightenment, strength and health of my soul
and body, to the complete overthrow and
destruction of my evil thoughts, prejudices
and imaginations; for thine is the kingdom,

the power, and the glory, the honour and
the worship, with the Father and thy Holy
Ghost, now and ever, and to ages of ages.
Amen.

Prayer of Saint John Damascene.

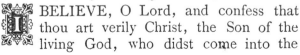I STAND before the gates of thy temple,
and yet do my grievous thoughts not
leave me. But thou, O Christ my
God, who didst justify the publican, didst
have mercy upon the Canaanite, and didst
open the gates of paradise to the thief on
the cross; open unto me thy bowels of compassionate mercy, and receive me coming
unto thee and touching thee like the sinful
woman and like the sick woman; for she
touched but the hem of thy garment, and
was healed, and the other embracing thy
feet received forgiveness of her sins. But
I, a miserable sinner, that dare to partake
of thy precious Body, let me not be consumed; but receive me like unto them, and
enlighten my spiritual senses, destroying my
sinful errors, through the prayers of thy holy
Mother and of the heavenly Hosts; for blessed
art thou to ages of ages. Amen.

Prayer of Saint John Chrysostom.

I BELIEVE, O Lord, and confess that
thou art verily Christ, the Son of the
living God, who didst come into the

world to save sinners, of whom I am the greatest. And I believe that this is thy most pure Body, and this thy most precious Blood. I therefore pray thee, Have mercy upon me, and forgive me my sins, voluntary and involuntary, in word and in deed, in knowledge or in ignorance committed; and vouchsafe me, uncondemned, to partake of thy most pure Mysteries, to the remission of sins, and to life eternal. Amen.

On approaching to communicate, say the following lines of Saint Simeon.

BEHOLD 1 approach the divine Communion!

My Creator, consume me not in the partaking of it;

For thou art a consuming fire to the unworthy :

Purify me now from every stain.

Then say,

OF thy mysterious Supper to-day, O Son of God, accept me as a partaker; for I will not reveal thy Mystery to thine enemies, nor give thee a kiss as Judas, but as the thief I will confess thee, Remember me, O Lord, in thy kingdom.

And again these lines :

O MAN, behold the divine Blood, and tremble ;

For it is a fire consuming the unworthy.

The divine Body both deifieth and nourisheth;

It deifieth the spirit, and strangely nourisheth the mind.

Also the Troparia.

THOU hast sweetened me, O Christ, by thy love, and hast changed me by thy divine favour. Consume my sins with thy spiritual fire, and enable me to be so filled with the love of thee, that, leaping for joy, I may magnify thy presence, O Blessed One.

Into the brilliant company of thy Saints how shall I, unworthy and sinful, enter? If I dare to enter into the bridechamber, my garment will put me to shame, for it is not a wedding one, and I shall be bound hand and foot and cast out by thine Angels. Purify, Lord, my polluted soul, and save me in thy loving-kindness.

Prayer.

GRANT, O Lord Jesus Christ my God, that I may not partake of this thy holy Sacrament to my condemnation, because of mine unworthiness, but to the purification and sanctification of my soul and body, and as an earnest of thine everlasting kingdom and life. For it is good for me to cleave unto my God, putting in the Lord the hope of my salvation. Amen.

B. PRAYERS OF THANKSGIVING AFTER HOLY COMMUNION.

When thou hast received the blessed communion of the life-giving, mystical Gifts, first give praise, be exceedingly thankful, and fervently from thy soul say,

GLORY to thee, our God. Glory to thee, our God. Glory to thee, our God.

Then the following Prayer of Thanksgiving.

I THANK thee, O Lord my God, that thou hast not rejected me, a sinner, but hast permitted me to become a partaker of thy holy Mysteries. I thank thee that thou hast enabled me, an unworthy one, to receive thy pure and heavenly Gifts. But thou, O Lord most merciful, who didst die for us, and didst rise again, and hast bestowed upon us these awful and life-giving Mysteries to the benefit and sanctification of our souls and bodies; grant that they may operate in me to the healing of my soul and body, to the overthrow of every evil thing, to the enlightenment of my heart, to the peace of my spiritual faculties, to invincible faith, to sincere love, to increase of wisdom, to the keeping of thy commandments, to growth in grace and to the inheritance of thy kingdom, that, preserved by them in thy sanctification, I may ever call to mind thy grace, and live, not unto myself, but unto thee, our Lord and Benefactor. And thus, when this life on earth shall have passed away in the hope of life eternal, may I attain unto everlasting rest, where the hymn of them that glorify thee is unceasing, and infinite the sweetness of them that behold the unspeakable goodness of thy face. For thou art the true desire and inexpressible oy of them that love thee, O Christ our God, and all creation glorifieth thee to all eternity. Amen.

Prayer of Saint Basil the Great.

LORD Christ our God, King of ages, and Creator of the universe, I thank thee for all the good things thou hast bestowed on me, but above all, for the participation in thy pure and life-giving Mysteries. I therefore pray thee, good and merciful Lord, keep me under thy roof and in the shadow of thy wings, and grant me, in a pure conscience, to my latest breath, worthily to partake of thy holy Sacrament to the remission of sins and to life eternal. For thou art the Bread of life, the Source of sanctification, the Giver of all good ; and to thee we ascribe all glory, with the Father and the Holy Ghost, now and ever, and to ages of ages. Amen.

Prayer of Saint Simeon the Meditative, in Verses.

THOU who, of thine own good will, dost give thy Body as food unto me, Thou who art a fire consuming the unworthy;

Consume me not, O my Creator,

But rather enter into my limbs, my joints, my inmost heart,

And burn the tares of my transgressions.

Cleanse thou my soul, and sanctify my thoughts.

Strengthen my limbs, together with my bones.

Enlighten my five senses. Stablish me wholly in thy fear.

Ever cover me; preserve and protect me from all soul-corrupting words and deeds.

Make me chaste, purify and wash me; garnish me, instruct and enlighten me.

Shew me to be the habitation of thy one Spirit, and in nowise the dwelling-place of sin;

That from me, thy dwelling through the reception of thy Sacrament, all evil, every lust may flee as from fire.

I invoke as supplicants for me all the

Saints, the Bodiless Powers, thy Baptist, thy wise Apostles, and with them, thy pure, most holy Mother.

Receive their prayers graciously, O my Christ, and render thy servant a son of light.

For thou art our Sanctification, O Blessed One, and the Light of our souls, and to thee, as God and Lord, we ascribe glory every day.

Another Prayer.

MAY thy holy Body, O Lord Jesus Christ our God, be for eternal life unto me, and thy precious Blood to the remission of sins; and may this Eucharist be to my joy, health and gladness. And at thy terrible second Advent grant that I, a sinner, may stand at the right hand of thy glory, through the prayers of thy most pure Mother and of all the Saints. Amen.

Another Prayer. To the holy Mother of God.

O MOST holy Mother of God, light of my darkened soul, my hope, protection, refuge, comfort and joy; I thank thee that thou hast enabled me, an unworthy one, to be a partaker of the most pure Body and the most precious Blood of thy Son. Enlighten the eyes of my heart, thou who hast borne the true Light. Thou who didst bear the Fountain of immortality, quicken thou me, deadened by sin. As the very loving Mother of the merciful God, do thou have mercy upon me, and grant me a repentant and contrite heart and humility of mind, and vouchsafe that to my latest breath I may uncondemned receive the sanctification of the most pure Mysteries, to the healing of my soul and body. And give me tears of repentance and thanksgiving, that I may hymn and praise thee all the days of my life, for thou art blessed and glorified to ages. Amen.

XX. EXTRACTS FROM THE LENTEN TRIODION.

———⋄———

ON THE SUNDAY OF THE PUBLICAN AND PHARISEE.

The Troparion on the Resurrection in the proper Tone, with its Verse to the Virgin.

Condakion of the Triodion.   Tone 4.

LET us avoid the high-flown speech of the Pharisee, and learn the majesty of the Publican's humble words, penitentially cried, O Saviour of the world, cleanse us, thy servants.

ON THE SUNDAY OF THE PRODIGAL SON.
(SEPTUAGESIMA.)

The Troparion on the Resurrection in the proper Tone, with its Verse to the Virgin.

Condakion of the Triodion.   Tone 3.

I HAVE wickedly strayed away from thy fatherly glory, and wasted the riches thou gavest me among sinners. Then do I raise the prodigal's cry unto thee, O bountiful Father, I have sinned against thee : take me back as a penitent, and make me as one of thy hired servants.

ON THE SATURDAY OF MEAT FARE.

Troparion for the Departed. Tone 2.

 THOU Creator, who in the depth of wisdom orderest all things in loving-kindness unto men, and grantest unto all expedient things; give rest, O Lord, unto the souls of thy servants; for in thee, our Maker, Author and God, they have put their trust.

To the Virgin. Same Tone.

WE have thee as a fortress and a haven, and as an accepted mediatress with God whom thou didst bear, O unwedded Mother of God, the salvation of the faithful.

Condakion. Tone 8.

O CHRIST, rest the souls of thy servants with the Saints, where there is no sickness, nor sorrow, nor lamentation, but life everlasting.

ON THE SUNDAY OF MEAT FARE.
(SEXAGESIMA.)

The Troparion on the Resurrection in the proper Tone, with its Verse to the Virgin.

Condakion of the Triodion. Tone 1.

O GOD, when thou shalt come on earth with glory, when all shall quake, when the fiery river shall carry away to the judgment-seat, when the books shall be opened and all secrets revealed, then do thou save me from unquenchable fire, and bless me, O righteous Judge, to stand at thy right hand.

NOTE :— *In this Week of Cheese Fare cheese and eggs are permitted on Wednesday and Friday, as well as on the other days.*

ON THE SATURDAY OF CHEESE FARE,

We commemorate all our venerable and God-bearing Fathers who have been illustrious in asceticism.

Troparion. Tone 4.

GOD of our Fathers, who ever dealest with us according to thy clemency ; remove not thy mercy from us, but, by their intercessions, direct our life in peace.

To the Virgin.

O HOLY Mother of the unapproachable Light, with angelic hymns we honour thee, and with reverence magnify thee.

Condakion. Tone 8.

AS preachers of piety and silencers of impiety, thou hast made the company of the God-bearers lights upon the earth. By their intercessions, O Lord, preserve in perfect peace them that glorify and magnify thee, that they may praise and sing to thee, Alleluia.

ON THE SUNDAY OF CHEESE FARE.
(QUINQUAGESIMA.)

The Troparion on the Resurrection in the proper Tone, with its Verse to the Virgin.

Condakion of the Triodion. Tone 6.

O LORD, Teacher of wisdom, Giver of understanding, Instructor of the unwise and Defence of the poor; stablish and enlighten mine heart. Thou Word of the Father, give unto me words, for I will not restrain my lips from calling upon thee. O Merciful One, have pity on me, a fallen one.

NOTE:—*After the Sunday of Cheese Fare beginneth the Fast of the Holy and Great Quadragesima, which continueth until the Day of Holy Pascha.*

ON THE FIRST SATURDAY OF THE FAST,

We commemorate the miracle wrought by the Great Martyr Theodore the Guard.

Troparion. Tone 2.

GREAT are the triumphs of faith! In a well of fire as in refreshing water the holy martyr Theodore rejoiced;

for, sacrificed as sweet bread, he worshipped the Trinity. Through his intercessions, O Christ God, save our souls.

Glory. Both now. To the Virgin.

MOST glorious and above understanding are thy mysteries, O Mother of God; for spotless and virgin thou art acknowledged a true Mother who didst bear the true God. Pray unto him to save our souls.

Condakion. Tone 8.

ACCEPTING in thine heart the faith of Christ as a breastplate, thou didst, O Athlete, overcome the hostile powers, and now, as Victor, art eternally crowned with a heavenly diadem.

ON THE FIRST SUNDAY OF THE FAST,

Called, of Orthodoxy, we commemorate the Prophets Moses and Aaron and the rest, and the restoration of the holy and honourable Icons.

The Troparion on the Resurrection in the proper Tone. Glory.

And the following in Tone 2.

TO thy most pure Icon we bow down, O Blessed One, praying for forgiveness of our sins, Christ our God; for, of thine own will, thou didst condescend to ascend the Cross in flesh, and thereby to deliver thy creatures from the yoke of the enemy. Therefore, we thankfully cry unto thee, Thou hast filled all things with joy, O our Saviour, thou who camest to save the world. *Both now.*

To the Virgin.

Most glorious and above understanding.... *Vide preceding page.*

Condakion. Tone 8.

O MOTHER of God, the incomprehensible Word of the Father hath been comprehended by us through his incarnation from thee, and the defiled image, being imbued with divine goodness, is made as of old. Confessing our salvation, we, in word and in deed, represent this.

ON THE SECOND SUNDAY OF THE FAST,

Is sung the Office of our Father in the Saints, Gregory, Archbishop and Wonderworker of Thessalonica.

The Troparion on the Resurrection in the proper Tone, and that to the Saint in Tone 8.

WONDERWORKING Gregory, thou light of Orthodoxy, pillar and teacher of the Church, ornament of monks, invincible champion of divines, the boast of Thessalonica and preacher of grace; ever pray that our souls may be saved.

Condakion. Same tone.

THEE, the divinely speaking Gregory, do we with one accord extol as the divine and sacred organ of wisdom and the harmonious trumpet of theology. Do thou, O guiding Father, as the mind present with the First Mind, guide our minds to that Same, that we may cry, Hail! thou preacher of grace.

ON THE THIRD SUNDAY OF THE FAST,

We celebrate the veneration of the honourable and life-effecting Cross.

The Troparion on the Resurrection in the proper Tone, and that to the Cross in Tone 1.

O Lord, save thy people and bless . . . . *Vide page* 52.

Condakion. Tone 6.

NO longer doth the fiery weapon bar the gates of Eden; for the wood of the Cross, that glorious help, hath come upon them. The sting of death and the victory of hades are done away; for thou, my Saviour, didst come and tell them that are in hades, Come ye again into Paradise.

ON THE FOURTH SUNDAY OF THE FAST,

We sing the Office of our venerable Father, John Climacus.

The Troparion on the Resurrection in the

proper Tone, and that to the Venerable in Tone 1.

THOU, our God-bearing Father John, didst appear as a dweller in the desert, an angel in flesh, and a wonderworker. By fasting, vigil, and prayer thou didst obtain heavenly gifts, and healest the sick and the souls of them that come to thee in faith. Glory to him who gave thee this power! Glory to him who crowned thee! Glory to him who through thee worketh all manner of healings!

Condakion. *Tone* 3.

THE Lord hath placed thee on the height of true abstinence, like a bright star shining unto the ends of the earth, thee, our Teacher and Father John.

ON THURSDAY OF THE FIFTH WEEK,

We sing the Office of the Great Canon.

Irmi of the Great Canon. Tone 6.

I. A help and protection hath he become to me unto salvation, he is my God, and I will glorify him, my fathers' God, and I will exalt him; for he hath triumphed gloriously.

II. Give ear, O ye heavens, and I will speak, and I will sing Christ incarnate of the Virgin.

See now, see now, that I am he, God, who of old did rain manna in the desert, and draw water from the rock for my people, by mine own right hand and power.

III. O Lord, stablish my mind on the rock of thy commandments.

O Lord, stablish my fainting heart on the rock of thy commandments; for thou alone art holy and the Lord.

IV. The Prophet heard of thine advent, O Lord, and was afraid; for thou didst will to be born of a Virgin, and to appear unto men, and he cried, I have heard the report of thee, and I feared. Glory to thy might, O Lord.

V. Rising early from the night, I pray thee, O Lover of mankind, to enlighten and instruct me in thy commandments, and to teach me, O Saviour, to do thy will.

VI. I cried with my whole heart to the merciful God, and he heard me from the depths of hades, and raised my life from corruption.

Condakion.

MY soul, my soul, arise! Why sleepest thou? The end draweth near, and thou wilt be troubled. Awake then, that Christ God, who is everywhere and who filleth all things, may spare thee.

VII. We have sinned, we have prevaricated, we have been unrighteous before thee. We have neither loved, neither kept those things that thou hast commanded. Still, reject us not at the last, O God of our fathers.

VIII. Him that heavenly Hosts glorify, and Cherubim and Seraphim fear, let every spirit and every creature sing, bless and set up for ever.

IX. The unspeakable birth from a seedless conception of a husbandless mother is an incorruptible fruit; for the birth of God regenerateth nature. Then do all generations right-believingly magnify thee as the divine-bride Mother.

NOTE:—*These Irmi, sung at Matins to-day, are also sung at the Great Compline on Monday, Tuesday, Wednesday and Thursday of the First Week of the Fast.*

ON SATURDAY OF THE FIFTH WEEK,

We sing the Acathist Hymn to the most holy Mother of God.

Troparion. Tone 8.

TAKING the command secretly to heart, the Angel cometh under Joseph's roof, and saith to the one that knew no husband, He that by his descent hath bent the heavens down, is contained whole and unchangeably in thee, and beholding him taking in thee the form of man, I fearingly cry unto thee, Hail! O unmarried Bride.

Condakion. Tone 8.

TO thee, O Virgin, the chosen guide, thy servants sing a triumphal song, ascribing thanks to thee for the deliverance from evils, and, since thou hast an invincible might, deliver us, we beseech thee, from every ill, that we may cry unto thee, Hail! O unmarried Bride.

ON THE FIFTH SUNDAY OF THE FAST,

We sing the Office of our venerable Mother, Mary of Egypt.

The Troparion on the Resurrection in the proper Tone, and that to the Venerable in Tone 8.

IN thee, O Mother, is a pattern of certain salvation; for, taking up the Cross, thou didst follow Christ, and didst teach in very deed to despise the flesh, for it passeth away, and to care for the soul, which is immortal. Therefore doth thy spirit, O venerable Mary, rejoice with the Angels.

Icos. (Stanza.) Tone 4.

LET us now extol in hymns the lamb and daughter of Christ, Mary the ever-

memorable, who appeared as the lamb of
Egypt, and yet escaped all its wiles, and
became a perfect growth in the Church by
exercising herself in fasting and prayer
above the measure of human nature. Therefore hath the Almighty raised on high the
life and deeds of the glorious Mary.

ON THE SATURDAY OF THE HOLY AND RIGHTEOUS LAZARUS.

Troparion. Tone 1.

CHRIST God, thou didst, before thy
very Passion, confirm the truth of the
general Resurrection by raising Lazarus from the dead. Then do we also, as
youths bearing the standard of victory, cry
unto thee, the Conqueror of death, Hosanna
in the highest! Blessed be he that cometh
in the name of the Lord.

Condakion. Tone 2.

CHRIST, the Joy of all, the Truth, the
Light and Life, and the Resurrection of
the world, hath appeared to them that are
on earth, and is become an image of the
Resurrection, granting unto all divine forgiveness.

ON THE SUNDAY OF PALMS.

Stichera at the Great Vespers, with the Lord, I have cried, *in Tone* 6.

TO-DAY the grace of the Holy Spirit gathereth us together, and, all bearing thy Cross, we say, Blessed be he that cometh in the name of the Lord. Hosanna in the highest. *Glory. Both now.* To-day the grace of the Holy Spirit . . . .

Troparion. Tone 1.

O Christ God, thou didst before thy very Passion . . . .

Another, in Tone 4.

BURIED with thee in baptism, O Christ our God, we have been blessed with life immortal through thy Resurrection, and, hymning thee, we cry, Hosanna in the highest! Blessed be he that cometh in the name of the Lord.

Hypacoë after Ode III. Tone 6.

THE lawless Jews first praised him with the branches, then nailed him to the tree, even Christ our God. But we, with faith unchanging, ever honouring him as Benefactor, cry ceaselessly to him, Blessed art thou that comest to recall from exile Adam.

Condakion. Tone 6.

ON the throne in heaven, and on earth borne by a colt, O Christ our God, thou didst receive the praises of Angels and the hymns of children, crying unto thee, Blessed art thou that comest to recall from exile Adam.

Magnifying.

WE magnify thee, O Christ, Giver of life, Hosanna in the highest we also cry to thee. Blessed be he that cometh in the name of the Lord.

ON HOLY AND GREAT MONDAY.

At Matins after the Alleluia, *we sing the Troparion in Tone* 8.

Behold the Bridegroom cometh . . . . *Vide page* 85.

Condakion. Tone 8.

JACOB bewaileth the loss of Joseph, and the virtuous one sitteth in a chariot honoured as a king; for, as he would not become a slave to the pleasures of Egypt, he was exalted by him that looketh upon the hearts of men and bestoweth incorruptible crowns.

ON HOLY AND GREAT TUESDAY.

At Matins. Behold the Bridegroom cometh . . . .

18

Condakion. Tone 2.

O MY soul, considering the hour of thine end, and fearing the cutting down of the fig tree, do thou carefully cultivate the talent given unto thee, being watchful and crying, Let us not remain outside the house of Christ.

ON HOLY AND GREAT WEDNESDAY.

At Matins. Behold the Bridegroom cometh . . . .

Condakion. Tone 4.

O BLESSED One, I have transgressed more than the sinful woman, but in no-wise do I bring unto thee floods of tears. Still, in silence I fall down, longing with love to embrace thy most pure feet, so that thou, O Lord, mayest grant me forgiveness of my trespasses, when I cry unto thee, Deliver me, O Saviour, from the defilement of my deeds.

ON HOLY AND GREAT THURSDAY.

At Matins after the Alleluia, *we sing the Troparion in Tone* 8.

WHEN, on the evening of the wash-ing of feet, the glorious Disciples were being enlightened, then was it that the malicious Judas, ailing with the

love of silver, was darkened, and betrayed
thee, the righteous Judge, to the unrighteous
judges. Beware then, thou that settest thine
heart on riches, beware him whom the same
hath brought to strangling. Flee from that
insatiate soul which dared such things
against the Master. O Lord, good unto all,
glory to thee.

Condakion. Tone 2.

THE hands with which he took the Bread,
the betrayer secretly holdeth forth, and
taketh the price of him who with his own
hands made man, and remaineth perverse,
even Judas, the slave and flatterer.

Icos. (Stanza.)

HAVING all approached in fear to the
mystical table, let us, with pure souls,
take the Bread, remaining with the Lord,
that we may witness how he washeth the
feet of his Disciples, and that we may do
as we behold, submitting ourselves one to
another, and washing the feet of one another. For Christ thus commanded unto his
Disciples, and foretold that it should be
done. Yet Judas, the slave and flatterer,
heeded it not.

ON THE SAME DAY IN THE EVENING.

THE PASSION OF THE LORD.

The Priest beginneth, Blessed be our God . . . .

Reader. Amen. Glory to thee, our God . . . . O heavenly King . . . . *Trisagion. After* Our Father, *&c.,* O come, let us worship . . . . *thrice. And the rest as at the beginning of Matins. Vide page* 52.

And after the Six Psalms and the Ectenia of Peace, we begin to sing the Alleluia *antiphonally, loudly, and in sweet melody, according to Tone* 8. *Likewise the Troparion in the same Tone.*

When, on the evening of the washing of feet . . . . *Vide page* 274.

This is sung thrice, and the Little Ectenia followeth.

Then the Warden distributeth the tapers which are lighted during the Lections. And the Deacon exclaimeth,

A ND that he would make us worthy to hear the holy Gospel, let us beseech the Lord God.

Choir. Lord, have mercy, *thrice.*

Deacon. Wisdom! Stand up! Let us hear the holy Gospel.

Priest. Peace to all.

Choir. And to thy spirit.

And the Priest loudly announceth,

THE Lection from the holy Evangelist John, (*or*, Matthew, *or*, Mark, *or*, Luke).

Choir. Glory to thee, Lord, glory to thee.

Deacon. Let us attend.

NOTE:—*On this wise are all the Lections preceded.*

And the Priest readeth

GOSPEL I. FROM S. JOHN.

THE Lord said unto his disciples, Now is the Son of man glorified, and God is glorified in him. If God be glorified in him, God shall also glorify him in himself, and shall straightway glorify him. Little children, yet a little while I am with you. Ye shall seek me; and as I said unto the Jews, Whither I go, ye cannot come; so now I say to you. A new commandment I give unto you, that ye love one another; as I have loved you, that ye also love one another. By this shall all men know that ye are my disciples, if ye have love one to another. Simon Peter said unto him, Lord, whither goest thou? Jesus answered him, Whither I go, thou canst not follow me now; but thou shalt follow me afterwards. Peter said unto him, Lord, why cannot I follow thee now? I will lay down my life for thy sake. Jesus answered him, Wilt thou lay down thy life for my sake? Verily, verily, I say unto thee, The cock shall not crow, till thou hast denied me thrice. Let not your heart be troubled; ye believe in God, believe also in me. In my Father's house are many mansions: if it were not so, I would have told you. I go to prepare a place for you. And if I go and prepare a place for you, I will come again, and receive you unto myself; that where I am, there ye may be also. And whither I go ye know, and the way ye know. Thomas saith unto him, Lord, we know not whither thou goest; and how can we know the way? Jesus saith unto him, I am the way, the truth, and the life: no man cometh unto the Father, but by me. If ye had known me, ye should have known my Father also; and from henceforth ye know him, and have seen him. Philip saith unto him, Lord, shew us the Father, and it sufficeth us. Jesus saith unto him, Have I been so long time with you, and yet hast thou not known me, Philip? He that hath seen me hath seen the Father; and how sayest thou then, Shew us the Father? Believest thou not that I am in the Father, and the Father in me? The words that I speak unto you I speak not of myself; but the Father that dwelleth in me, he doeth the works. Believe me that I am in the Father, and the Father in me; or else believe me for the very works' sake. Verily, verily, I say unto you, He that believeth on me, the works that I do shall he do also; and greater works than these shall he do; because I go unto my Father. And whatsoever ye shall ask in my name, that will I do, that the Father may be glorified in the Son. If ye shall ask anything in my name, I will do it. If ye love me, keep my commandments. And I will pray the Father, and he shall give you another Comforter, that he may abide with you for ever; even the Spirit of truth, whom the world cannot receive, because it seeth him not, neither knoweth him: but ye know him; for he dwelleth with you, and shall be in you. I will not leave you comfortless: I will come to you. Yet a little while, and the world seeth me no more; but ye see me: because I live, ye shall live also. At that day ye shall know that I am in my Father, and ye in me, and I in you. He that hath my commandments, and keepeth them, he it is that loveth me; and he that loveth me shall be loved of my Father, and I will love him, and will manifest myself to him. Judas saith unto

him, not Iscariot, Lord, how is it that thou
wilt manifest thyself unto us, and not unto
the world? Jesus answered and said unto
him, If a man love me, he will keep my
words; and my Father will love him, and
we will come unto him, and make our abode
with him. He that loveth me not keepeth
not my sayings; and the word which ye hear
is not mine, but the Father's which sent me.
These things have I spoken unto you, being
yet present with you. But the Comforter,
which is the Holy Ghost, whom the Father
will send in my name, he shall teach you
all things, and bring all things to your remembrance, whatsoever I have said unto you.
Peace I leave with you, my peace I give
unto you: not as the world giveth, give
I unto you. Let not your heart be troubled,
neither let it be afraid. Ye have heard how
I said unto you, I go away, and come
again unto you. If ye loved me, ye would
rejoice, because I said, I go unto the Father;
for my Father is greater than I. And now
I have told you before it come to pass, that,
when it is come to pass, ye might believe.
Hereafter I will not talk much with you;
for the prince of this world cometh, and
hath nothing in me. But that the world may
know that I love the Father; and as the
Father gave me commandment, even so I

do. Arise, let us go hence. I am the true vine, and my Father is the husbandman. Every branch in me that beareth not fruit he taketh away; and every branch that beareth fruit, he purgeth it, that it may bring forth more fruit. Now ye are clean through the word which I have spoken unto you. Abide in me, and I in you. As the branch cannot bear fruit of itself, except it abide in the vine; no more can ye, except ye abide in me. I am the vine, ye are the branches: he that abideth in me, and I in him, the same bringeth forth much fruit; for without me ye can do nothing. If a man abide not in me, he is cast forth as a branch, and is withered; and men gather them, and cast them into the fire, and they are burned. If ye abide in me, and my words abide in you, ye shall ask what ye will, and it shall be done unto you. Herein is my Father glorified, that you bear much fruit; so shall ye be my disciples. As the Father hath loved me, so have I loved you: continue ye in my love. If ye keep my commandments, ye shall abide in my love; even as I have kept my Father's commandments, and abide in his love. These things have I spoken unto you, that my joy might remain in you, and that your joy might be full. This is my commandment, That ye love one another, as I have loved you. Greater love hath no man than this, that a man lay down his life for his friends. Ye are my friends, if ye do whatsoever I command you. Henceforth I call you not servants, for the servant knoweth not what his lord doeth; but I have called you friends, for all things that I have heard of my Father I have made known unto you. Ye have not chosen me, but I have chosen you, and ordained you, that ye should go and bring forth fruit, and that your fruit should remain; that whatsoever ye shall ask of the Father in my name, he may give it you. These things I command you, that ye love one another. If the world hate you, ye know that it hated me before it hated you. If you were of the world, the world would love his own; but because ye are not of the world, but I have chosen you out of the world, therefore the world hateth you. Remember the word that I said unto you, The servant is not greater than his lord. If they have persecuted me, they will also persecute you; if they have kept my saying, they will keep yours also. But all these things will they do unto you for my name's sake, because they know not him that sent me. If I had not come and spoken unto them, they had not had sin; but now they have no cloke for their sin. He that hateth

me hateth my Father also. If I had not
done among them the works which none
other man did, they had not had sin; but
now have they both seen and hated both me
and my Father. But this cometh to pass,
that the word might be fulfilled that is
written in their law, They hated me without
a cause. But when the Comforter is come,
whom I will send unto you from the Father,
even the Spirit of truth, which proceedeth
from the Father, he shall testify of me;
and ye also shall bear witness, because ye
have been with me from the beginning. These
things have I spoken unto you, that ye
should not be offended. They shall put you
out of the synagogues; yea, the time cometh,
that whosoever killeth you will think that he
doeth God service. And these things will
they do unto you, because they have not
known the Father, nor me. But these things
have I told you, that when the time shall
come, ye may remember that I told you of
them. And these things I said not unto you
at the beginning, because I was with you.
But now I go my way to him that sent
me; and none of you asketh me, Whither
goest thou? But because I have said these
things unto you, sorrow hath filled your heart.
Nevertheless I tell you the truth, It is
expedient for you that I go away; for if I

go not away, the Comforter will not come
unto you; but if I depart, I will send him
unto you. And when he is come, he will
reprove the world of sin, and of righteousness,
and of judgment: of sin, because they believe not on me; of righteousness, because
I go to my Father, and ye see me no more;
of judgment, because the prince of this
world is judged. I have yet many things to
say unto you, but ye cannot bear them now.
Howbeit when he, the Spirit of truth,
is come, he will guide you into all truth;
for he shall not speak of himself, but whatsoever he shall hear, that shall he speak;
and he will shew you things to come. He
shall glorify me; for he shall receive of mine,
and shall shew it unto you. All things that
the Father hath are mine; therefore said I,
that he shall take of mine, and shall shew it
unto you. A little while and ye shall not
see me; and again, a little while, and ye
shall see me, because I go to the Father.
Then said some of his disciples among
themselves, What is this that he saith unto
us, A little while, and ye shall not see me;
and again, a little while, and ye shall see
me, and, Because I go to the Father? They
said therefore, What is this that he saith,
A little while? We cannot tell what he saith.
Now Jesus knew that they were desirous

to ask him, and said unto them, Do ye in-
quire among yourself of that I said, A little
while, and ye shall not see me; and again,
a little while, and ye shall see me? Verily,
verily, I say unto you, That ye shall weep
and lament, but the world shall rejoice; and
ye shall be sorrowful, but your sorrow shall
be turned into joy. A woman when she is
in travail hath sorrow, because her hour is
come; but as soon as she is delivered of
the child, she remembereth no more the
anguish, for joy that a man is born into the
world. And ye now therefore have sorrow;
but I will see you again, and your heart shall
rejoice, and your joy no man taketh from you.
And in that day ye shall ask me nothing.
Verily, verily, I say unto you, Whatsoever
ye shall ask the Father in my name, he will
give it you. Hitherto have ye asked nothing
in my name: ask, and ye shall receive, that
your joy may be full. These things have I
spoken unto you in proverbs, but the time
cometh, when I shall no more speak unto you
in proverbs, but I shall shew you plainly of
the Father. At that day ye shall ask in my
name; and I say not unto you, that I will
pray the Father for you; for the Father himself loveth you, because ye have loved me,
and have believed that I came out from God.
I came forth from the Father, and am

come into the world: again, I leave the world, and go to the Father. His disciples said unto him, Lo, now speakest thou plainly, and speakest no proverb. Now are we sure that thou knowest all things, and needest not that any man should ask thee: by this we believe that thou camest forth from God. Jesus answered them, Do ye now believe? Behold, the hour cometh, yea, is now come, that ye shall be scattered, every man to his own, and shall leave me alone; and yet I am not alone, because the Father is with me. These things I have spoken unto you, that in me ye might have peace. In the world ye shall have tribulation; but be of good cheer, I have overcome the world. These words spake Jesus, and lifted up his eyes to heaven and said, Father, the hour is come: glorify thy Son, that thy Son also may glorify thee; as thou hast given him power over all flesh, that he should give eternal life to as many as thou hast given him. And this is life eternal, that they might know thee the only true God, and Jesus Christ, whom thou hast sent. I have glorified thee on the earth: I have finished the work which thou gavest me to do. And now, O Father, glorify thou me with thine own self with the glory which I had with thee before the world was. I have manifested thy name unto the men

which thou gavest me out of the world:
thine they were, and thou gavest them me;
and they have kept thy word. Now they
have known that all things whatsoever thou
hast given me are of thee. For I have given
unto them the words which thou gavest me;
and they have received them, and have
known surely that I came out from thee, and
they have believed that thou didst send me.
I pray for them: I pray not for the world
but for them which thou hast given me;
for they are thine. And all mine are thine,
and thine are mine; and I am glorified in
them. And now I am no more in the world,
but these are in the world, and I come to
thee. Holy Father, keep through thine own
name those whom thou hast given me; that
they may be one, as we are. While I was
with them in the world, I kept them in thy
name: those that thou gavest me I have
kept, and none of them is lost, but the son
of perdition; that the scripture might be fulfilled. And now come I to thee; and these
things I speak in the world, that they might
have my joy fulfilled in themselves. I have
given them thy word; and the world hath
hated them, because they are not of the
world, even as I am not of the world. I
pray not that thou shouldest take them out
of the world, but that thou shouldest keep

them from the evil. They are not of the world, even as I am not of the world. Sanctify them through thy truth: thy word is truth. As thou hast sent me into the world, even so have I also sent them into the world. And for their sakes I sanctify myself, that they also might be sanctified through the truth. Neither pray I for these alone, but for them also which shall believe on me through their word; that they all may be one; as thou, Father, art in me, and I in thee, that they also may be one in us; that the world may believe that thou hast sent me. And the glory which thou gavest me I have given them; that they may be one, even as we are one; I in them, and thou in me, that they may be made perfect in one; and that the world may know, that thou hast sent me, and hast loved them, as thou hast loved me. Father, I will that they also, whom thou hast given me, be with me where I am; that they may behold my glory, which thou hast given me: for thou lovedst me before the foundation of the world. O righteous Father, the world hath not known thee; but I have known thee, and these have known that thou hast sent me. And I have declared unto them thy name, and will declare it; that the love wherewith thou hast loved me may be in them, and I in them. When Jesus had spoken these words, he went forth with his disciples over the brook Kidron, where was a garden, into the which he entered, and his disciples.

And after this and every Lection we sing,

GLORY to thy long-patience, O Lord, glory to thee.

Then we sing the Antiphons.

Antiphon I. Tone 8.

THE princes of the people were gathered together against the Lord, and against his Christ.

They laid a lawless accusation against me, O Lord. O Lord, do thou not forsake me.

Let us present our senses pure unto Christ, and, as his friends, let us sacrifice our souls for him; let us not be overwhelmed with cares of life like Judas, but in our occupations let us cry, Our Father, which art in heaven, deliver us from evil.

Glory. Both now. To the Virgin.

O unmarried Virgin, thou didst bring forth, and virgin didst remain. Mother unwedded, God-bearing Mary, pray Christ our God to save our souls.

Antiphon II. Tone 6.

JUDAS ran to the wicked scribes, and said, What will you give me, and I will betray

19

him to you? And thou meantime wast invisibly present among the very men that counselled against thee. O Searcher of hearts, spare our souls.

Let us minister unto God, as Mary at the supper, and avoid Judas' love of silver, that we may ever be with Christ our God.

Glory. Both now. To the Virgin.

Him that is loving-kind unto all men, whom thou, O Virgin, didst inexpressibly bring forth, cease not to pray to deliver from dangers them that betake themselves to thee.

Antiphon III. Tone 2.

BECAUSE of the raising of Lazarus, O man-loving Lord, the Hebrew children sang, Hosanna! unto thee. But the malicious Judas willed not to understand.

At thy Supper, O Christ God, thou didst foretell to thy Disciples that one of them should betray thee. But the malicious Judas willed not to understand.

To John's question, O Lord, who is it that shall betray thee? thou didst reveal him by the sop. But the malicious Judas willed not to understand.

The Jews sought to slay thee by means of thirty pieces of silver and a false kiss.

But the malicious Judas willed not to understand.

At thy washing of feet, O Christ God, thou didst persuade thy Disciples, Do as ye behold. But the malicious Judas willed not to understand.

Watch and pray, lest ye fall into temptation, thou didst say, O our God, unto thy Disciples. But the malicious Judas willed not to understand. *Glory. Both now.*

To the Virgin.

O God-bearing one, save thy servants from dangers; for, after God, we all betake ourselves to thee, as the strong bulwark and mediatress.

Then the little Ectenia (which precedeth all the Kathismata), and we sing,

Kathisma. Tone 7.

FEEDING the Disciples at the Supper, and foreseeing the intended betrayal, thou didst mete this part to Judas, knowing him to be perverse, and wishing to prove unto all men that thou gavest thyself up of thine own free-will that thou mightest deliver the world from the power of the adversary. O thou that art long-patient, glory to thee.

And the Priest readeth

GOSPEL II. FROM S. JOHN.

A T that time, Jesus went forth with his disciples over the brook Kidron, where was a garden, into the which he entered, and his disciples. And Judas also, which betrayed him, knew the place; for Jesus ofttimes resorted thither with his disciples. Judas then, having received a band of men and officers from the chief priests and Pharisees, cometh thither with lanterns and torches and weapons. Jesus therefore, knowing all things that should come upon him, went forth and said unto them, Whom seek ye? They answered him, Jesus of Nazareth. Jesus saith unto them, I am he. And Judas also, which betrayed him, stood with them. As soon then as he had said unto them, I am he, they went backward, and fell to the ground. Then asked he them again, Whom seek ye? And they said, Jesus of Nazareth. Jesus answered, I have told you that I am he: if therefore ye seek me, let these go their way; that the saying might be fulfilled, which he spake, Of them which thou gavest me have I lost none. Then Simon Peter having a sword drew it, and smote the high priest's servant, and cut off his right ear. The servant's name was Malchus. Then said Jesus unto Peter, Put up thy sword into the sheath: the cup which my Father hath given me, shall I not drink it? Then the band and the captain and officers of the Jews took Jesus, and bound him. And led him away to Annas first; for he was father in law to Caiaphas, which was the high priest that same year. Now Caiaphas was he, which gave counsel to the Jews, that it was expedient that one man should die for the people. And Simon Peter followed Jesus, and so did another disciple: that disciple was known unto the high priest, and went in with Jesus into the palace of the high priest. But Peter stood at the door without. Then went out that other disciple, which was known unto the high priest, and spake unto her that kept the door, and brought in Peter. Then saith the damsel that kept the door unto Peter, Art not thou also one of this man's disciples? He saith, I am not. And the servants and officers stood there, who had made a fire of coals; for it was cold. And they warmed themselves, and Peter stood with them, and warmed himself. The high priest then asked Jesus of his disciples, and of his doctrine. Jesus answered him, I spake openly to the world; I ever taught in the synagogue, and in the temple, whither the Jews always

resort; and in secret have I said nothing.
Why askest thou me? Ask them which heard
me what I have said unto them: behold,
they know what I said. And when he had
thus spoken, one of the officers which stood
by struck Jesus with the palm of his hand,
saying, Answerest thou the high priest so?
Jesus answered him, If I have spoken evil,
bear witness of the evil; but if well, why
smitest thou me? Now Annas had sent
him bound unto Caiaphas the high priest.
And Simon Peter stood and warmed himself. They said therefore unto him, Art not
thou also one of his disciples? He denied
it, and said, I am not. One of the servants
of the high priest, being his kinsman whose
ear Peter cut off, saith, Did not I see thee in
the garden with him? Peter then denied
again; and immediately the cock crew. Then
led they Jesus from Caiaphas unto the hall
of judgment. And it was early; and they
themselves went not into the judgment hall,
lest they should be defiled; but that they
might eat the passover.

Antiphon IV. Tone 5.

TO-DAY Judas forsaketh his Teacher and
receiveth the devil. He is blinded by
the love of silver, and, being darkened, falleth
away from the light. For how could he

look up, he that sold the Luminary for thirty pieces of silver? Yet he that suffered for the world dawneth upon us, and unto him we cry, Thou that didst suffer for and with mankind, glory to thee.

To-day Judas counterfeiteth the fear of God and becometh an alien from grace, being a disciple he becometh a betrayer, under the wonted kiss he hideth his guile, and senselessly preferreth thirty pieces of silver before the love of his Master, becoming the guide of the wicked assembly. But we who have salvation, even Christ, the same let us glorify.

Let us acquire brotherly love as brethren in Christ, and let us not be without sympathy unto our neighbours, lest we be condemned for the sake of riches, like the unmerciful servant, and, like the repentant Judas, find them of no avail. *Glory. Both now.*

To the Virgin.

Glorious things have been spoken of thee in all places, O God-bearing Mary; for thou, the all-praised and unmarried one, didst bring forth in flesh the Creator of all things.

Antiphon V. Tone 6.

THE Teacher's disciple maketh agreement concerning the price, and selleth the

Lord for thirty pieces of silver, with a false kiss betraying him to death unto the transgressors.

To-day the Creator of heaven and earth spake unto his Disciples, The hour is nigh, and Judas the betrayer draweth near unto me. Let no one deny me when they see me on the Cross between two thieves. For I suffer as man, but, as Lover of man, I will save them that believe in me.

Glory. Both now. To the Virgin.

Thou that in a manner altogether unspeakable didst conceive and bring forth thine own Creator, save, O Virgin, them that magnify thee.

Antiphon VI. Tone 7.

TO-DAY Judas is on the watch to betray the Lord, the eternal Saviour of the world, who satisfied the multitude with five loaves. To-day the transgressor denieth his Teacher, and, having been his disciple, betrayeth his Master. He selleth him for silver who fed man with manna.

To-day the Jews have nailed the Lord to the Cross, even him that divided the sea with a rod 'and guided them in the wilderness. To-day they have pierced with a spear the side of him that laid stripes upon

Egypt for their sake, and have given vinegar to drink unto him that showered manna
as food for them.

O Lord, drawing nigh unto thy voluntary
Passion, thou didst say unto thy Disciples,
If but an hour ye cannot watch with me,
how do ye promise to die for my sake?
Behold how Judas slumbereth not, but hasteneth
to betray me to the wicked. Arise and pray,
lest any of you deny me when you see me
on the Cross. O thou that art long-patient,
glory to thee.

Glory. Both now. To the Virgin.

Hail! O God-bearing one, who didst
contain within thee him whom the heavens
contain not. Hail! O Virgin, thou proclama-
tion of the Prophets, through whom Em-
manuel hath shone upon us. Hail! O Mother
of Christ our God.

Kathisma. Tone 7.

WHAT motive made thee, Judas, the betrayer of the Saviour? Hath he severed
thee from the company of the Apostles, de-
prived thee of the gift of healing, rejected
thee from the companionship of the others
at the supper table? Hath he refused to
wash thy feet when washing those of the
rest? How forgetful art thou of numerous

blessings, and thine ungrateful temper is plainly seen, while his incomparable long-patience and great mercy are proclaimed.

GOSPEL III. FROM S. MATTHEW.

AT that time, the soldiers that had laid hold on Jesus led him away to Caiaphas the high priest, where the scribes and the elders were assembled. But Peter followed him afar off unto the high priest's palace, and went in and sat with the servants to see the end. Now the chief priests, and elders, and all the council, sought false witness against Jesus, to put him to death; but found none: yea, though many false witnesses came, yet found they none. At the last came two false witnesses, and said, This fellow said, I am able to destroy the temple of God, and to build it in three days. And the high priest arose, and said unto him, Answerest thou nothing? What is it which these witness against thee? But Jesus held his peace. And the high priest answered and said unto him, I adjure thee by the living God, that thou tell us whether thou be the Christ, the Son of God. Jesus saith unto him, Thou hast said: nevertheless I say unto you, Hereafter shall ye see the Son of man sitting on the right hand of power, and coming in the clouds of heaven. Then the high priest rent his clothes, saying, He hath spoken blasphemy; what further need have we of witnesses? Behold, now ye have heard his blasphemy. What think ye? They answered and said, He is guilty of death. Then did they spit in his face, and buffeted him, and others smote him with the palms of their hands, saying, Prophesy unto us, thou Christ. Who is he that smote thee? Now Peter sat without in the palace; and a damsel came unto him, saying, Thou also wast with Jesus of Galilee. But he denied before them all, saying, I know not what thou sayest. And when he was gone out into the porch, another maid saw him, and said unto them that were there, This fellow was also with Jesus of Nazareth. And again he denied with an oath, I do not know the man. And after a while came unto him they that stood by, and said to Peter, Surely thou also art one of them; for thy speech bewrayeth thee. Then began he to curse and to swear, saying, I know not the man. And immediately the cock crew. And Peter remembered the word of Jesus, which said unto him, Before the cock crow, thou shalt deny me thrice. And he went out, and wept bitterly.

Antiphon VII. Tone 8.

WHEN thou didst endure, O Lord, to be taken by the wicked, thou spakest thus, Though ye have struck the Shepherd and dispersed the twelve lambs, my Disciples, yet could I have brought against you more than twelve legions of Angels. But I am long-patient, that the unknown and secret things I have revealed to you through the Prophets may be fulfilled. Glory to thee, O Lord.

Thrice Peter denied thee, and straightway understood what had been told him, and brought tears of repentance to thee. O God, cleanse and save me. *Glory. Both now.*

To the Virgin.

Let us all sing the holy Virgin as the saving porch and pleasant paradise, and shading cloud of everlasting light, saying unto her, Hail!

Antiphon VIII. Tone 2.

SAY, ye wicked men, What have you heard from our Saviour? Hath he not laid down the teachings of the law and of the Prophets? How can you then purpose to betray to Pilate him that is the Word of God from God, and the Redeemer of our souls?

Let him be crucified, they cried, even they that ever enjoyed thy gifts, and the evil-doer instead of the Well-doer they preferred to have, they, the slayers of the righteous. But thou didst keep silence, enduring their harshness, for thou didst will to save us, O thou Lover of mankind.

Glory. Both now. To the Virgin.

Since we have not daring on account of our many sins, do thou, O God-bearing Virgin, pray him that was born of thee, for the Mothers's prayer availeth much to procure the Lord's clemency. Despise not, O most pure one, the supplications of sinners, for he that vouchsafed to suffer for us is merciful and powerful to save.

Antiphon IX. Tone 3.

THEY put down thirty pieces of silver as the price of the Priceless, whom the children of Israel thus valued. Watch and pray, lest ye enter into temptation. The spirit indeed is willing, but the flesh weak. Therefore, watch!

They gave me bitter things to eat, and in my thirst they brought me vinegar. But thou, O Lord, raise me, and I will reward them.

Glory. Both now. To the Virgin.

We Gentiles sing thee, O pure God-bearing one, for thou didst bring forth

Christ our God, who, through thee, hath delivered mankind from the curse.

Kathisma. Tone 8.

O HOW could Judas, once thy disciple, seek to betray thee? He, supping with thee hypocritically, a traitor himself and unjust, goeth and saith to the priests, What will ye give me, and I will betray unto you him that destroyeth the law and profaneth the sabbath? O long-patient Lord, glory to thee.

GOSPEL IV. FROM S. JOHN.

AT that time, led they Jesus from Caiaphas unto the hall of judgment; and it was early; and they themselves went not into the judgment hall, lest they should be defiled; but that they might eat the passover. Pilate then went out unto them, and said, What accusation bring ye against this man? They answered and said unto him, If he were not a malefactor, we would not have delivered him up unto thee. Then said Pilate unto them, Take ye him, and judge him according to your law. The Jews therefore said unto him, It is not lawful for us to put any man to death; that the saying of Jesus might be fulfilled, which he spake, signifying what death he should die. Then Pilate entered into the judgment hall

again, and called Jesus, and said unto him,
Art thou the King of the Jews? Jesus answered him, Sayest thou this thing of thyself,
or did others tell it thee of me? Pilate answered, Am I a Jew? Thine own nation and
the chief priests have delivered thee unto
me: what hast thou done? Jesus answered,
My kingdom is not of this world: if my kingdom were of this world, then would my servants fight, that I should not be delivered
to the Jews; but now is my kingdom not
from hence. Pilate therefore said unto him,
Art thou a king then? Jesus answered, Thou
sayest that I am a king. To this end was
I born, and for this cause came I into the
world, that I should bear witness unto the
truth. Every one that is of the truth heareth
my voice. Pilate saith unto him, What is
truth? And when he had said this, he went
out again unto the Jews, and saith unto
them, I find in him no fault at all. But ye
have a custom, that I should release unto you
one at the passover: will ye therefore that
I release unto you the King of the Jews?
Then cried they all again, saying, Not this
man, but Barabbas. Now Barabbas was a
robber. Then Pilate therefore took Jesus,
and scourged him. And the soldiers platted
a crown of thorns, and put it on his head,
and they put on him a purple robe, and

said, Hail, King of the Jews! And they smote
him with their hands. Pilate therefore went
forth again, and saith unto them, Behold, I
bring him forth to you, that ye may know
that I find no fault in him. Then came
Jesus forth, wearing the crown of thorns,
and the purple robe. And Pilate saith unto
them, Behold the man! When the chief
priests therefore and officers saw him, they
cried out, saying, Crucify him, crucify him.
Pilate saith unto them, Take ye him, and
crucify him; for I find no fault in him.
The Jews answered him, We have a law,
and by our law he ought to die, because
he made himself the Son of God. When
Pilate therefore heard that saying, he was
the more afraid; and went again into the
judgment hall, and saith unto Jesus, Whence
art thou? But Jesus gave him no answer.
Then saith Pilate unto him, Speakest thou
not unto me? Knowest thou not that I have
power to crucify thee, and have power to
release thee? Jesus answered, Thou couldest
have no power at all against me, except it
were given thee from above; therefore he
that delivered me unto thee hath the greater
sin. And from thenceforth Pilate sought to
release him; but the Jews cried out, saying,
If thou let this man go, thou art not Cæsar's
friend: whosoever maketh himself a king

speaketh against Cæsar. When Pilate therefore heard that saying, he brought Jesus forth, and sat down in the judgment-seat in a place that is called the Pavement, but in the Hebrew, Gabbatha. And it was the preparation of the passover, and about the sixth hour; and he saith unto the Jews, Behold your King! But they cried out, Away with him, away with him, crucify him. Pilate saith unto them, Shall I crucify your King? The chief priests answered, We have no king but Cæsar. Then delivered he him therefore unto them to be crucified.

Antiphon X. Tone 6.

THOU that clothest thyself with light as with a garment didst stand naked at the judgment-seat, and on the cheek receivedst blows from hands which thou didst make. Yea, the wicked people nailed the Lord of glory to the Cross. Then was the veil of the temple rent in twain, the sun was darkened, unable to behold the outraged God, whom all things fear. Him let us worship.

The disciple denied thee, but the thief exclaimed, Remember me, O Lord, in thy kingdom. *Glory. Both now.*

To the Virgin.

Give peace unto the world, O Lord, thou that from the Virgin didst vouchsafe to take flesh for the sake of thy servants, that with one accord we may glorify thee, O Lover of mankind.

Antiphon XI. Tone 6.

FOR the good things thou hast wrought, O Christ, unto the Hebrew race, they have condemned thee to crucifixion and given thee vinegar and gall to drink. But render unto them O Lord, according to their works; for they understood not thy condescension.

The Hebrew men, content not with thy betrayal, wagging their heads, came mocking and reviling thee. But render unto them, O Lord, according to their works; for in vain they strove against thee.

Neither the quaking earth nor the rent rocks convinced the Jews, neither the torn temple veil, nor the rising of the dead. But render unto them, O Lord, according to their works; for in vain they strove against thee.

Glory. Both now. To the Virgin.

From thee, O God-bearing Virgin, we have been made to know the God incarnate, thou only pure and only blessed one. Therefore unceasingly we sing and magnify thee.

Antiphon XII. Tone 8.

THUS saith the Lord to the Jews, My people, what have I done unto thee, or in what have I hindered thee? I gave sight to thy blind, I cleansed thy lepers, I restored the paralytic. My people, what have I done unto thee, and what hast thou done in return for me? For manna, thou hast returned hyssop; for water, vinegar; for my love thou hast nailed me to the Cross. But no longer will I withhold myself from others: I will call the Gentiles mine, and these shall glorify me, with the Father and the Spirit, and I will give to them eternal life.

To-day the veil of the temple is rent in twain to the exposure of the wicked, and the sun hideth his rays, beholding the Lord crucified.

Ye lawgivers of Israel, ye Jews and Pharisees, the company of the Apostles crieth unto you, Behold the Temple that ye have destroyed, behold the Lamb that ye have crucified and committed to the tomb; but he shall arise of his own will. Be not misled, ye Jews; for this is he that saved you in the sea and fed you in the wilderness: he is the Life and the Light, and the Peace of all the world.

Glory. Both now. To the Virgin.

Hail! O thou gate of the King of glory, through which the Most High alone hath passed, and afterwards left sealed to the salvation of our souls.

20*

Kathisma. Tone 8.

O GOD, when thou didst stand before Caiaphas, and thou, the Judge, didst submit thyself to Pilate, then did the heavenly Powers quake with fear, yea, when moreover thou didst ascend the tree between two thieves, and thou, the Sinless One, wast counted among transgressors in order to save man. O most meek Lord, glory to thee.

GOSPEL V. FROM S. MATTHEW.

AT that time, Judas, seeing that Jesus was condemned, repented himself, and brought again the thirty pieces of silver to the chief priests and elders, saying, I have sinned in that I have betrayed the innocent blood. And they said, What is that to us? See thou to that. And he cast down the pieces of silver in the temple, and departed, and went and hanged himself. And the chief priests took the silver pieces, and said, It is not lawful for to put them into the treasury, because it is the price of blood. And they took counsel, and bought with them the potter's field, to bury strangers in. Wherefore that field was called, The field of blood, unto this day. Then was fulfilled that which was spoken by Jeremy the Prophet, saying, And they took the thirty pieces of silver, the price of him that was valued, whom they of the children of Israel did value; and gave them for the potter's field, as the Lord appointed me. And Jesus stood before the governor; and the governor asked him, saying, Art thou the King of the Jews? And Jesus said unto him, Thou sayest. And when he was accused of the chief priests and elders, he answered nothing. Then said Pilate unto him, Hearest thou not how many things they witness against thee? And he answered him to never a word; insomuch that the governor marvelled greatly. Now at that feast the governor was wont to release unto the people a prisoner, whom they would. And they had then a notable prisoner, called Barabbas. Therefore when they were gathered together, Pilate said unto them, Whom will ye that I release unto you? Barabbas, or Jesus which is called Christ? For he knew that for envy they had delivered him. When he was set down on the judgment-seat, his wife sent unto him, saying, Have thou nothing to do with that just man; for I have suffered many things this day in a dream because of him. But the chief priests and elders persuaded the multitude that they should ask Barabbas, and destroy Jesus. The governor answered and said unto them, Whether of the twain will ye that I release unto you? They said, Barabbas. Pilate saith unto them, What shall I do then with Jesus which is called Christ? They all say unto him, Let him be crucified. And the governor said, Why, what evil hath he done? But they cried out the more, saying, Let him be crucified. When Pilate saw that he could prevail nothing, but that rather a tumult was made, he took water, and washed his hands before the multitude, saying, I am innocent of the blood of this just person: see ye to it. Then answered all the people, and said, His blood be on us, and on our children. Then released he Barabbas unto them; and when he had scourged Jesus, he delivered him to be crucified. Then the soldiers of the governor took Jesus into the common hall, and gathered unto him the whole band of soldiers. And they stripped him, and put on him a scarlet robe. And when they had platted a crown of thorns, they put it upon his head, and a reed in his right hand; and they bowed the knee before him, and mocked him, saying, Hail, King of the Jews! And they spit upon him, and took the reed, and smote him on the head. And after that they had mocked him, they took the robe off from him, and put his own raiment on him, and led him away to crucify him. And as they came out, they found a man of Cyrene, Simon by name: him they compelled to bear his Cross.

Antiphon XIII. Tone 6.

THE Jewish assembly desired Pilate to crucify thee, O Lord, and though they found no accusation against thee, they freed the criminal Barabbas and condemned thee, the Just One, thereby inheriting the charge of bloodguiltiness. But give them, O Lord, their reward; for in vain they strove against thee.

Him before whom all things fear and tremble, and whom all tongues sing, even Christ, the Power of God and the Wisdom of God, him do the priests smite upon the cheek and offer vinegar to drink. Yet all these things thou didst vouchsafe to suffer, desiring to save us from our transgressions by thine own Blood, O Lover of mankind.

Glory. Both now. To the Virgin.

O God-bearing one, who by word didst above word bring forth thine own Creator, beseech the same to save our souls.

Antiphon XIV. Tone 8.

O LORD, who didst accept as thy companion the thief that had defiled his hands in blood, do thou likewise number us with him, for thou art good and lovest mankind.

Few were the words spoken by the thief upon the cross, yet great was found his faith, and in an instant was he saved, entering first the opened gates of Paradise. Thou that didst accept his repentance, O Lord, glory to thee.

Glory. Both now. To the Virgin.

Hail! thou that through the Angel didst receive the world's joy. Hail! thou that didst bring forth thy Creator and Lord. Hail! thou that wast counted worthy to become the Mother of Christ our God.

Antiphon XV. Tone 6.

TO-DAY is suspended on the tree he that suspendeth the earth upon the waters, *thrice.* He that is the King of Angels is crowned with thorns. He that covereth the heavens with clouds is covered with derisive purple. He that freed Adam in the Jordan is buffeted. The Bridegroom of the Church is pierced with nails. The Son of the Virgin is wounded with a spear. We bow down, O Christ, to thy Passion, *thrice.* Let us also see thy glorious Resurrection.

Not like the Jews do we keep festival, for our Pascha is Christ God sacrificed for us. Still, let us cleanse ourselves from every defilement, and in sincerity pray to him, Arise, O Lord, save us as the Lover of mankind.

Thy Cross, O Lord, is life and resurrection to thy people, and, trusting in the same, we sing thee, O our crucified God. Have mercy upon us. *Glory. Both now.*

To the Virgin.

Beholding thee hanging on the Cross, O Christ, she that brought thee forth exclaimed, What is the strange mystery I behold, my Son? How dost thou die upon the tree, with thy flesh fixed thereupon, O thou Bestower of life?

Kathisma. Tone 4.

THOU hast redeemed us from the curse of the law by thy precious Blood: being nailed to the Cross and wounded with the lance, thou hast shed immortality upon men. O our Saviour, glory to thee.

GOSPEL VI. FROM S. MARK.

AT that time, the soldiers led Jesus away into the hall, called Prætorium; and they call together the whole band. And they clothed him with purple, and platted a crown of thorns, and put it about his head, and began to salute him, Hail, King of the Jews! And they smote him on

the head with a reed, and did spit upon
him, and bowing their knees worshipped
him. And when they had mocked him, they
took off the purple from him, and put his
own clothes on him, and led him out to
crucify him. And they compel one Simon,
a Cyrenian, who passed by, coming out of
the country, the father of Alexander and
Rufus, to bear his Cross. And they bring
him unto the place Golgotha, which is, being
interpreted, The place of a skull. And they
gave him to drink wine mingled with myrrh;
but he received it not. And when they had
crucified him, they parted his garments, casting lots upon them, what every man should
take. And it was the third hour, and they
crucified him. And the superscription of his
accusation was written over, The King of the
Jews. And with him they crucify two thieves;
the one on his right hand, and the other on
his left. And the scripture was fulfilled, which
saith, And he was numbered with the transgressors. And they that passed by railed on
him, wagging their heads, and saying, Ah,
thou that destroyest the temple, and buildest
it in three days, save thyself, and come
down from the Cross. Likewise also the
chief priests mocking said among themselves
with the scribes, He saved others; himself
he cannot save. Let Christ the King of Israel

descend now from the Cross, that we may see and believe in him.

Then we sing the Beatitudes in Tone 4.

IN thy kingdom remember us, O Lord, when thou comest in thy kingdom.

Blessed are the poor in spirit, for theirs is the kingdom of heaven.

Blessed are they that mourn, for they shall be comforted.

Blessed are the meek, for they shall inherit the earth.

Through the tree Adam became an exile from Paradise. Through the tree of the Cross the thief became an inhabitant thereof. For the one, having tasted, transgressed the commandment of his Maker; but the other, being crucified, confessed his hidden God. Remember us also, O Saviour, in thy kingdom.

Blessed are they which do hunger and thirst after righteousness, for they shall be filled.

The wicked have bought the Maker of the law of his disciple, and placed him as a malefactor at the judgment-seat of Pilate, crying, Crucify him, even him that gave them manna in the wilderness. But we, imitating the righteous thief, cry out in faith, Remember us also, O Saviour, in thy kingdom.

Blessed are the merciful, for they shall obtain mercy.

The assembly of God-slayers, even the wicked nation of the Jews, cried madly unto Pilate, saying, Crucify him, even the innocent Christ, and give us rather Barabbas. But we lift up unto him the voice of the right-judging thief. Remember us also, O Saviour, in thy kingdom.

Blessed are the pure in heart, for they shall see God.

Thy life-giving side, as a fountain springing out of Eden, watereth that reasonable Paradise, which is thy Church, O Christ, and branching off in her into four rivers, the four Gospels, nourisheth the world, maketh all creation joyful, and teacheth the nations faithfully to worship thy kingdom.

Blessed are the peace-makers, for they shall be called the children of God.

Thou wast crucified for me that thou mightest send forth forgiveness unto me. Thou wast pierced in the side that thou mightest spring forth unto me streams of life. Thou wast affixed with nails that I, by the depth of thy Passion being convinced of the height of thy power, might cry unto thee, O life-giving Christ, Glory to thy Cross, O Saviour, and to thy Passion.

Blessed are they which are persecuted for

righteousness' sake, for theirs is the kingdom of heaven.

When thou wast crucified, O Christ, all creation beholding trembled, the foundations of the earth shook with fear of thy power, the luminaries became darkened, and the veil of the temple was rent, the mountains groaned, and the rocks were rent, while the believing thief crieth unto thee with us, O Saviour, Remember me.

Blessed are ye when men shall revile you and persecute you, and shall say all manner of evil against you falsely for my sake.

Upon the Cross, O Lord, thou didst tear up the bond of our sins, and, numbered among the dead, thou didst bind the tyrant of them there, delivering all by thy Resurrection from the bonds of death, through which we are enlightened, O man-loving Lord, and cry unto thee, Remember us also, O Saviour, in thy kingdom.

Rejoice, and be exceeding glad, for great is your reward in heaven.

Thou that wast lifted on the Cross, and didst annul the might of death, and didst, O Lord, as God, blot out the handwriting against us; vouchsafe, O Christ our God, thou only Lover of mankind, the repentance of the thief to us who worship thee in faith, and cry to thee, Remember us also in thy kingdom. *Glory.*

Ye faithful, let us with one accord pray worthily to glorify the Father, Son, and Holy Ghost, the divine Unity existing in three Persons, abiding unconfounded, Oneness undivided and unapproachable, by whom we are delivered from the fiery punishment.

Both now. To the Virgin.

Thy Mother, O Christ, who without seed brought thee forth in flesh, and after bringing forth truly remained an undefiled Virgin, the same we bring unto thee as mediatress, O most merciful Master, that we at all times may gain forgiveness of our iniquities, even us who cry, Remember us also, O Saviour, in thy kingdom.

Prokimenon. Tone 4.

THEY parted my garments among them, and upon my vesture did they cast lots.

Verse. O God, my God, attend unto me: why hast thou forsaken me?

GOSPEL VII. FROM S. MATTHEW.

AT that time, when the soldiers were come unto a place called Golgotha, that is to say, A place of a skull, they gave him vinegar to drink mingled with gall; and when he had tasted thereof, he would not drink. And they crucified him, and parted his garments, casting lots; that it might be fulfilled, which was spoken by the Prophet, They parted my garments among them, and upon my vesture did they cast lots. And sitting down they watched him there; and set up over his head his accusation written, This is Jesus the King of the Jews. Then were there two thieves crucified with him, one on the right hand, and another on the left. And they that passed by reviled him, wagging their heads, and saying, Thou that destroyest the temple, and buildest it in three days, save thyself. If thou be the Son of God, come down from the Cross. Likewise also the chief priests mocking him, with the scribes and elders, said, He saved others; himself he cannot save. If he be the King of Israel, let him now come down from the Cross, and we will believe him. He trusted in God: let him deliver him now, if he will have him; for he said, I am the Son of God. The thieves also, which were crucified with him, cast the same in his teeth. Now from the sixth hour there was darkness over all the land unto the ninth hour. And about the ninth hour Jesus cried with a loud voice, saying, Eli, Eli, lama sabachthani? that is to say, My God, my God, why hast thou forsaken me? Some of them that stood there, when they heard that, said, This man calleth for Elias. And straightway one of them ran, and took a spunge, and filled it with vinegar, and put it on a reed, and gave him to drink. The rest said, Let be, let us see whether Elias will come to save him. Jesus, when he had cried again with a loud voice, yielded up the ghost. And, behold, the veil of the temple was rent in twain from the top to the bottom; and the earth did quake, and the rocks rent; and the graves were opened; and many bodies of the saints which slept arose, and came out of the graves after his Resurrection, and went into the holy city, and appeared unto many. Now when the centurion, and they that were with him, watching Jesus, saw the earthquake, and those things that were done, they feared greatly, saying, Truly this was the Son of God.

Then the Reader intoneth Psalm 50 (51). And after this the Priest readeth

GOSPEL VIII. FROM S. LUKE.

AT that time were also two other, malefactors, led with him to be put to death. And when they were come to the place, which is called Calvary, there they crucified him, and the malefactors, one on the right hand, and the other on the left.

Then said Jesus, Father, forgive them; for they know not what they do. And they parted his raiment and cast lots. And the people stood beholding. And the rulers also with them derided him, saying, He saved others; let him save himself, if he be Christ, the chosen of God. And the soldiers also mocked him, coming to him, and offering him vinegar, and saying, If thou be the king of the Jews, save thyself. And a superscription also was written over him in letters of Greek, and Latin, and Hebrew, This is the King of the Jews. And one of the malefactors which were hanged railed on him, saying, If thou be Christ, save thyself and us. But the other answering rebuked him, saying, Dost not thou fear God, seeing thou art in the same condemnation? And we indeed justly; for we receive the due reward of our deeds, but this man hath done nothing amiss. And he said unto Jesus, Lord, remember me when thou comest into thy kingdom. And Jesus said unto him, Verily I say unto thee, To-day shalt thou be with me in paradise. And it was about the sixth hour, and there was a darkness over all the earth until the ninth hour. And the sun was darkened, and the veil of the temple was rent in the midst. And when Jesus had cried with a loud voice, he said,

Father, into thy hands I commend my spirit. And having said thus, he gave up the ghost. Now when the centurion saw what was done, he glorified God, saying, Certainly this was a righteous man. And all the people that came together to that sight, beholding the things which were done, smote their breasts, and returned. And all his aquaintance, and the women that followed him from Galilee, stood afar off, beholding these things.

And straightway we sing the following TRIODE, *of which the Acrostich is,*
Προσάββατόν τε, *or, in English,*
Ere the Sabbath,
A Work of the Master Cosmas.

Ode V. Tone 6. Irmos.

EARLY at morn I come to thee, O Word of God, to thee that for thy pity's sake didst without change empty thyself, and, without passion, submit thyself to passion. O Lover of mankind, grant peace to me, a fallen one.

Refrain. Glory to thee, our God, glory to thee.

Rewashed our feet, and cleansed ourselves again by the communion of thy divine Sacrament, O Christ, we thy servants accompany thee from Sion to the great mount of Olivet, hymning thee, O Lover of mankind.

Glory. Both now.

Exclaimedst thou, Look ye, my friends, but have no fear. For now the hour is nigh, in which I must be taken and slain by wicked hands. Disperse ye all and leave me, until I reassemble you to preach me, the Lover of mankind.

Then again the Irmos, Early at morn I come . . . .

Condakion. Tone 8.

COME ye all, and let us sing him that was crucified for us; for Mary beheld him on the tree, and said, Though thou dost endure the Cross, thou art my Son and God.

Icos. (Stanza.)

THE gentle Mary, beholding her own Lamb dragged to the slaughter, with other women following, lamenting cried, Whither goest thou, my Child? In whose favour makest thou such haste? There is not again a marriage in Cana, thither now to speed that thou mayest make them water into wine. Shall I go with thee, Child, or shall I wait for thee? O Word, give me one word and pass me not in silence by, thou that hast kept me pure; for thou art my Son and God.

Ode VIII. Irmos.

THE divine Children despised the monument of an evil divinity, but the haughty lawless Sanhedrim counselleth vain things against Christ, and seeketh to slay him that holdeth their life in his hands. Him doth all Creation bless, glorifying him to ages.

Have now sleep shaken from your eyelids, saidst thou, O Christ, to the Disciples. Keep watch in prayer, lest ye perish in temptation; and thou, O Simon, above all; for to the stronger cometh the greater trial. Mark thou me, O Peter, whom doth all creation bless, glorifying me to ages.

Exclaimed Peter, Not one profane word will I let fall from my lips, O Master. With thee will I gladly die, even though all forsake thee; for neither flesh nor blood, but thine own Father hath revealed thee to me, whom doth all creation bless, glorifying thee to ages.

Spake the Lord, O man, in nowise hast thou penetrated the depth of the divine wisdom and knowledge, neither dost thou apprehend the unfathomableness of my judgment. Being flesh, boast not; for thrice thou wilt deny me, whom doth all creation bless, glorifying me to ages.

As soon as it is asked, thou wilt deny,

O Simon Peter, him in whom thou dost believe, and a certain maid coming to thee will frighten thee, said the Lord; and bitterly wilt thou weep, although thou hast me very gracious, whom doth all creation bless, glorifying me to ages.

Let us praise, let us bless, let us worship the Lord, singing unto him and setting him up for ever.

And again the Irmos, The divine children despised . . . .

Ode IX. Irmos.

BEING more honourable than the Cherubim, and incomparably more glorious than the Seraphim, who didst bear without corruption God the Word, thee, verily the God-bearing one, we magnify.

Bestood thee, O Christ, the pernicious band of wicked God-slayers, and thee, the Creator of all things, they wounded as unjust, even thee whom we magnify.

As a sheep they wounded thee, O Lord of all things, they, the impious, knowing not the law, and vainly studying the Prophets' words, and they unjustly sacrificed thee, thee whom we magnify.

The priests and scribes bade the heathen take away the life that was betrayed, smiting, of their wicked envy, him that is by nature Giver of life, him whom we magnify.

How many dogs came about thee, Lord, smiting thee on the cheek, and cursing thee, and falsely witnessing against thee. But thou enduredst all things, and savest all men.

And again the Irmos, Being more honourable . . . .

Exapostilarion. Tone 3.

TO-DAY, O Lord, thou didst make the thief worthy of Paradise; and by the tree of the Cross, enlighten thou me also and save me, *thrice.*

GOSPEL IX. FROM S. JOHN.

AT that time, there stood by the Cross of Jesus his Mother, and his Mother's sister, Mary the wife of Cleophas, and Mary Magdalene. When Jesus therefore saw his Mother, and the Disciple standing by, whom he loved, he saith unto his Mother, Woman, behold thy son! Then saith he to the Disciple, Behold thy Mother! And from that hour that Disciple took her unto his own home. After this, Jesus knowing that all things were now accomplished, that the scripture might be fulfilled, saith, I thirst. Now there was set a vessel full of vinegar; and they filled a spunge with vinegar, and put it upon hyssop, and put it to his mouth. When Jesus therefore had received the vinegar, he said, It is finished. And he bowed his head, and gave up the ghost. The Jews therefore, because it was the preparation, that the bodies should not remain upon the cross on the sabbath day, (for that sabbath day was an high day,) besought Pilate that their legs might be broken, and that they might be taken away. Then came the soldiers, and brake the legs of the first, and of the other which was crucified with him. But when they came to Jesus, and saw that he was dead already, they brake not his legs; but one of the soldiers with a spear pierced his side, and forthwith came thereout blood and water. And he that saw it bare record, and his record is true; and he knoweth that he saith true, that ye might believe. For these things were done, that the scripture should be fulfilled, A bone of him shall not be broken. And again another scripture saith, They shall look on him whom they pierced.

Then the Psalms of Praise with Stichera in Tone 3.

WO wicked deeds hast thou wrought, my first-born son, Israel. Thou hast forsaken me, the Fountain of living water, and dug unto thyself a well of destruction. Thou hast crucified me upon a tree, and hast asked for Barabbas and set him free. The heaven was awed thereat, and the sun hid his beams; yet thou, O Israel, wast not ashamed, but gave me over to death. Forgive them, holy Father, for they know not what they do.

EVERY member of thy holy flesh suffered dishonour for us: thy head, the thorns; thy face, the spittings; thy cheeks, the buffets; thy lips, the vinegar mixed with gall; thine ears, the scoffing blasphemies; thy shoulders, blows; thy hand, the reed; thy whole body, distension on the Cross; thy limbs, the nails; thy side, the spear. O thou almighty Saviour, who didst both suffer for us and deliver us from passions, descend to us in loving-kindness, and, raising us up, have mercy upon us.

WHEN thou wast crucified, O Christ, all creation, beholding, feared, and the ends of the earth were moved with awe at thy might; for by thy lifting up to-day the Hebrew race was cast down. The veil of the temple was rent in twain; the tombs were opened; the centurion, seeing the marvel, trembled; while thy Mother, standing by maternally lamenting, cried, How should

I not grieve and my heart not melt when I behold thee naked, and hanging condemned upon a tree. O thou that wast crucified and wast buried, and didst rise from the dead, Lord, glory to thee.

Glory. Tone 6.

THEY stripped me of my garments, and put upon me a purple robe; they put upon my head a crown of thorns, and in my right hand they placed a reed, that I might dash them in pieces like a potter's vessel. *Both now.*

THEY gave my back to the scourges, and my face lacked not the spittings. I stood at Pilate's judgment-seat and endured the Cross, for the salvation of the world.

GOSPEL X. FROM S. MARK.

AT that time, there came Joseph of Arimathæa, an honourable counsellor, which also waited for the kingdom of God, and went in boldly unto Pilate, and craved the Body of Jesus. And Pilate marvelled if he were already dead; and calling unto him the centurion, he asked him whether he had been any while dead. And when he knew it of the centurion, he gave the Body to Joseph. And he bought fine linen and took him down, and wrapped him in the linen, and laid him in a sepulchre which was hewn out of a rock, and rolled a stone unto the door of the sepulchre. And Mary Magdalene and Mary the mother of Joses beheld where he was laid.

Then,

To thee is due glory, O Lord our God, and to thee we ascribe glory . . . .

And the Doxology.

Glory to God in the highest . . . . *Vide page* 105.

Then the Ectenia,

Let us accomplish our morning prayer . . . . *And the rest. Vide page* 12.

GOSPEL XI. FROM S. JOHN.

AT that time, Joseph of Arimathæa, being a disciple of Jesus, but secretly for fear of the Jews, besought Pilate that he might take away the Body of Jesus; and Pilate gave him leave. He came therefore, and took the Body of Jesus. And there came also Nicodemus, which at the first came to Jesus by night, and brought a mixture of myrrh and aloes, about an hundred pound weight. Then took they the Body of Jesus, and wound it in linen clothes with the spices, as the manner of the Jews is to

bury. Now in the place where he was crucified there was a garden; and in the garden
a new sepulchre, wherein was never man yet
laid. There laid they Jesus.

And we sing the Stichera with Verses,

Tone 1.

ALL creation was changed with fear,
seeing thee, O Christ, hanging on
the Cross. The sun was darkened,
and the foundations of the earth were shaken.
All things suffered with their Creator. O
thou that willingly endured for us, Lord,
glory to thee.

Verse. They parted my garments among
them, and upon my vesture did they cast lots.

Tone 2.

O IMPIOUS and lawless people, why have
ye imagined vain things? Why have
ye condemned the Life of all things unto
death? O great wonder! The world's
Creator is delivered into the hands of sinners,
and the Lover of mankind is lifted up upon
a tree, that he may deliver them that are
bound in hades, and these exclaim, O long-
patient Lord, glory to thee.

Verse. They gave me bitter things to eat,
and in my thirst they brought me vinegar.

TO-DAY the blameless Virgin, beholding
thee, O steadfast Word, upon the Cross,

with motherly lamenting pity moaned bitterly in heart, and, groaning grievously in depth of soul, stood with dishevelled hair, and beat her breast, and wailing cried, Alas! my Son divine. Alas! Light of the world. Why fadeth from mine eyes the Lamb of God? Wherefore the bodiless Hosts, constrained with fear, exclaimed, O Lord incomprehensible, glory to thee.

Verse. God is our King of old, who hath wrought salvation in the midst of the earth.

SEEING thee hanging on the tree, O Christ, thee, the Creator and God of all things, she that without seed bore thee cried bitterly, My Son, where is the beauty of thy form? I cannot bear to look on thee unjustly crucified. Then hasten to arise, that I may see thy third day Resurrection from the dead. *Glory.*

Tone 8.

O LORD, when thou wast raised on the Cross, trembling and fear fell on creation. Yet thou forbadest earth to swallow them that crucified thee, but gavest thyself to hades to send up its prisoners, and to give new birth to mortals. O Judge of quick and dead, thou camest to bestow not death but life. Glory to thee, O Lover of mankind. *Both now.*

ALREADY the pen of the sentence is being wetted by the unjust judges, and Jesus is sentenced and condemned to death on the Cross. And creation suffereth, beholding the Lord on the tree. O thou good Lord, who sufferest for me in thy flesh, glory to thee.

GOSPEL XII. FROM S. MATTHEW.

ON the morrow that followeth the day of the preparation, the chief priests and Pharisees came together unto Pilate, saying, Sir, we remember that that deceiver said, while he was yet alive, After three days I will rise again. Command therefore that the sepulchre be made sure until the third day, lest his disciples come by night, and steal him away, and say unto the people, He is risen from the dead: so the last error shall be worse than the first. Pilate said unto them, Ye have a watch: go your way, make it as sure as ye can. So they went, and made the sepulchre sure, sealing the stone, and setting a watch.

Then,

IT is a good thing to give thanks unto the Lord, and to sing praises unto thy name, O Most High.

Trisagion. O most holy Trinity . . . .

Our Father... *And the Troparion. Tone* 4.

THOU hast redeemed us from the curse of the law by thy precious Blood. Having been nailed to the Cross and pierced by the spear, thou hast shed immortality on men. O our Saviour, glory to thee.

Then, the Great Ectenia.

Have mercy upon us, O God . . . . *And the rest. Vide page* 10.

And the Dismissal.

HE that spittings, and blows, and revilings, the Cross and death endured for the salvation of the world, Christ our true God . . . .

And the Choir singeth the Many years.

THE HOURS ON HOLY AND GREAT FRIDAY.

About the Second Hour of the Day, the Priest having vested and given the blessing, we say the usual Prayers, O heavenly King.... *Trisagion.* O most holy Trinity . . . . Our Father . . . . For thine is . . . . Lord, have mercy, *twelve times. Glory. Both now.*

THE FIRST HOUR.

O come, let us worship . . . . *thrice.*
Psalms 5, 2, *and* 21 (22).

Glory. Both now. Alleluia, *thrice.* Lord, have mercy, *thrice.*

Glory. Troparion. Tone I.

WHEN thou wast crucified, O Christ, then didst thou overcome the tyrant and destroy the power of the enemy. For it was not an Angel nor a man, but the Lord himself that saved us. Glory to thee, O Lord.

Both now. To the Virgin.

What shall we call thee .... *Vide page* 108.

Then we sing the following Stichera in Tone 8.

First Choir. To - day the veil of the temple .... *Vide page* 307.

The Second Choir repeateth the same.

First Choir. Verse. Why did the heathen rage, and the people imagine vain things.

O Christ the King, thou didst come as a sheep to the slaughter, and as a blameless lamb thou wast nailed on the Cross by wicked men for our sins, O Lover of mankind.

Second Choir. Verse. The kings of the earth set themselves, and the princes were gathered together against him.

O Christ the King, thou didst come ....

First Choir. Glory. When thou didst endure .... *Vide page* 300.

Second Choir. Both now. When thou didst endure ....

Prokimenon. Tone 4.

HE was brought out, and they spake against him. *Verse.* Blessed is he that considereth the poor and needy.

The Lection from the Prophecy of Zacharias.

Thus saith the Lord, I took . . . . *ending,* into the treasury, as the Lord commanded me. *Chap.* XI. 10—13.

The Lection from the Epistle of Paul to the Galatians.

Brethren! God forbid that I should glory . . . . *ending,* be with your spirit. Amen. *Chap.* VI. 14—18.

The Lection from the holy Evangelist Matthew.

At that time, when morning was come . . . . *ending,* the mother of the sons of Zebedee. *Chap.* XXVII. 1—56.

And straightway,

Order my steps . . . . *Vide page* 109.

After the Our Father, *Condakion.*

O come ye all, and let us sing . . . . *Vide page* 323.

Lord, have mercy, *forty times.*

The Prayer.

Thou that in all times . . . . *Vide page* 76.

Lord, have mercy, *thrice.*

The more honourable than the Cherubim . . . .

In the name of the Lord, father, give the blessing.

Priest. God be merciful unto us . . . .

And the concluding Prayer of the First Hour.

Christ the true Light . . . . *Vide page* III.

THE THIRD HOUR.

O come, let us worship . . . . *thrice.*

Psalms 34 (35), 108 (109), *and* 50 (51).

Glory. Both now. Alleluia, *thrice.* Lord, have mercy, *thrice.*

Glory. Troparion. Tone 6.

O LORD, the Jews have condemned thee, the Life of all things, unto death. They that by a rod passed through the Red Sea have nailed thee to the Cross. They that drew honey out of the rock have offered gall unto thee. But thou didst willingly endure all things to deliver us from the thrall of the enemy. O Christ our God, glory to thee.

Both now. To the Virgin.

O Mother of God, thou art the true vine . . . . *Vide page* 113.

Then we sing the Stichera in Tone 8.

First Choir. Through fear of the Jews thy friend and comrade Peter denied thee, O Lord; but, repenting, he lamenting said,

22

Despise not my tears, O Pitiful One, though I said I would keep the faith and have not kept it. Accept our penitence also, and have mercy upon us.

The Second Choir repeateth the same.

First Choir. Verse. Consider my words, O Lord, give ear unto my crying.

O Lord, when the soldiers mocked before thine honourable Cross, then were the hosts of Spirits awed; for a crown of outrage was on thine head who dost vivify the earth, and a vesture of scorn covered thee who coverest the heavens with clouds. But such was thy dispensation to reveal thy love. O Christ most merciful, glory to thee.

Second Choir. Verse. Hearken unto the voice of my prayer, my King and my God.

O Lord, when the soldiers . . . .

First Choir. Glory. O Lord, when thou wast extended on the Cross, thou spakest thus, What have I done that ye desire to crucify me, ye Jews? I made your paralytic whole, I raised your dead to life, I stayed the issue of blood, I had mercy on the Canaanite. What have I done that ye desire to slay me, O ye Jews? But ye shall look upon him whom now ye pierce, O ye transgressors.

Second Choir. Both now. O Lord, when thou wast extended . . . .

Prokimenon. Tone 4.

FOR I am ready for scourges, and my grief is continually before me. *Verse.* O Lord, rebuke me not in thy wrath, neither chasten me in thy hot displeasure.

The Lection from the Prophecy of Esaias.

The Lord hath given me . . . . *ending,* lie down in sorrow. *Chap.* L. 4—11.

The Lection from the Epistle of Paul to the Romans.

Brethren! When we were yet without strength . . . . *ending,* we shall be saved by his life. *Chap.* v. 6—10.

The Lection from the holy Evangelist Mark.

At that time the soldiers . . . . *ending,* which came up with him unto Jerusalem. *Chap.* xv. 16—41.

And straightway,

Blessed be the Lord God . . . . *Vide page* 113.

After the Our Father, *Condakion.*

O come ye all . . . . *Vide page* 323.

And the rest, concluding with the Prayer,

Master, God, Father almighty . . . . *Vide page* 115.

THE SIXTH HOUR.

O come, let us worship . . . . *thrice.*

Psalms 53 (54), 139 (140), *and* 90 (91).

22*

Glory. Both now. Alleluia, *thrice.* Lord, have mercy, *thrice.*

Glory. Troparion. Tone 2.

THOU hast perfected salvation in the midst of the earth, O Christ our God, thou hast stretched out thy most pure hands upon the Cross, gathering together all nations, who cry unto thee, Glory to thee, O Lord.

Both now. To the Virgin.

As we have not daring. *Vide page* 67.

Then we sing the Stichera in Tone 8.

First Choir Thus saith the Lord to the Jews . . . . *Vide page* 306.

The Second Choir repeateth the same.

First Choir. Verse. They gave me bitter things to eat, and in my thirst they brought me vinegar.

Ye lawgivers of Israel . . . . *Vide page* 307.

Second Choir. Verse. Save me, O God, for the waters are come in, even unto my soul.

Ye lawgivers of Israel . . . .

First Choir. Glory. Come, ye Christ-bearing people, and let us note what Judas the betrayer and the wicked priests have plotted together against our Saviour. To-day they have wrought that death should hold the immortal Word, whom they betrayed to Pilate, and have crucified. But suffering thus, our Saviour spake and said, Forgive them this sin, O Father, so may the gentiles know my Resurrection from the dead.

Second Choir. Both now. Come, ye Christ-bearing people . . . .

Prokimenon. Tone 4.

O LORD, our Lord, how wonderful is thy name in all the earth. *Verse.* For thy greatness is exalted above the heavens.

The Lection from the Prophecy of Esaias.

Thus saith the Lord, Behold my servant. . . . *ending,* hath an husband. *Chap.* LII. 13—LIII. 1.

The Lection from the Epistle of Paul to the Hebrews.

Brethren! He that sanctifieth . . . . *ending,* succour them that are tempted. *Chap.* II. 11—18.

The Lection from the holy Evangelist Luke.

At that time, there were also two other. . . . *ending,* seeing these things. *Chap.* XXIII. 32—49.

And straightway,

Let thy compassions soon overtake us . . . . *Vide page* 116.

After the Our Father, *Condakion.*

O come ye all . . . . *Vide page* 323.

And the rest, concluding with the Prayer, O God and Lord of hosts . . . . *Vide page* 118.

THE NINTH HOUR.

O come, let us worship . . . . *thrice.*
Psalms 68 (69), 69 (70), *and* 85 (86).
Glory. Both now. Alleluia, *thrice.* Lord,
have mercy, *thrice.*[1]

Glory. Troparion. Tone 8.

The thief, seeing the Prince . . . . *Vide
page* 122.

To the Virgin.

Thou that for our sakes . . . . *Vide page* 120.

Then we sing the Stichera in Tone 7.

First Choir. There was wonder to behold
the Maker of heaven hanging on the Cross.
The sun was darkened and the day turned
back to night, and earth sent up the dead
bodies from the graves. With these we
worship thee. Save us, O Lord.

The Second Choir repeateth the same.

First Choir. Verse. They parted my garments among them, and upon my vesture
did they cast lots. *Tone* 2.

When the transgressors nailed thee, the
Lord of glory, to the Cross, then saidest
thou to them, Wherein have I grieved you?
and how have I angered you? Before me,
who delivered you from affliction? And now,
how have ye rewarded me? For good, ye
have rendered evil; for the pillar of fire, ye

have nailed me to a cross; for the cloud,
ye have digged a grave for me; for manna,
ye have offered me gall; for water, given
me vinegar to drink. Henceforth I call the
gentiles, and these shall glorify me, with the
Father and the Holy Ghost.

Second Choir. Verse. They gave me bitter
things to eat, and in my thirst they brought
me vinegar. When the transgressors . . . .

Glory. Both now.

*The following is read in a loud voice and
with all reverence by the Reader in the middle
of the Church, and then sung in verses by
both Choirs.*

To-day is suspended . . . . *Vide page* 312.

Prokimenon. Tone 6.

THE fool hath said in his heart, There is
no God. *Verse.* There is none that doeth
good, no, not one.

The Lection from the Prophecy of Jeremias.

O Lord, thou hast given . . . . *ending,* every
man to his land. *Chap.* XI. 18—XII. 15.

*The Lection from the Epistle of Paul to
the Hebrews.*

Brethren! Having boldness . . . . *ending,*
into the hands of the living God. *Chap.* X.
19—31.

The Lection from the holy Evangelist John.

At that time they lead Jesus . . . . *ending*, him whom they pierced. *Chap.* XVIII. 28— XIX. 37.

And straightway,

O cast us not away at the last . . . . *Vide page* 121.

After the Our Father, *Condakion.*

O come ye all . . . . *Vide page* 323.

And the rest, concluding with the Prayer,

Master, Lord Jesus Christ . . . . *Vide page* 122.

Then we begin to sing the Beatitudes, loudly and in sweet melody.

In thy kingdom remember us, O Lord . . . .

And the rest, as written in the Typica, singing the Condakion,

O come, ye all . . . . *in the proper place thereof.*

And, in conclusion, the Dismissal of the Hours.

AT VESPERS ON HOLY AND GREAT FRIDAY.

About the Tenth Hour of the Day the bells are rung for Vespers, which, after the Priest's blessing, we begin to sing as customarily. And with the Lord, I have cried *we sing the following Stichera in Tone* I.

All creation was changed . . . .
O impious and lawless people . . . .
To-day the blameless Virgin . . . .
Seeing thee hanging on the . . . . *Vide*
page 331, *et seq.*

Tone 6.

TO-DAY the Lord of creation standeth before Pilate, and the Creater of all things is betrayed to the Cross, as a lamb going thereunto of his own will. He that showered manna is affixed with nails, his side is pierced, and with a sponge his lips are touched. The Redeemer of the world is smitten on the cheek, and the Maker of all things by his own servants is chastised. O the loving-kindness of the Lord! For for them that crucified him he invoked his Father, saying, Forgive them this sin, for the transgressors know not what they do. *Glory.*

HOW hath the lawless Synagogue adjudged creation's King to death, respecting not the benefits he before bestowed on them, of which reminding them, he said, My people, what have I done to you? Have I not filled with wonders Juda's land? Have I not raised the dead by word alone? Have I not healed weakness and disease? What then have ye given in return to me? And why are ye unmindful of me? Instead of healings ye have given me stripes; instead of life, to die; upon a tree have hanged me, Well-doer, as evil-doer; as lawless, me, Lawgiver; as condemned, me, King of all. O long-patient Lord, glory to thee. *Both now.*

A FEARFUL and strange mystery hath appeared wrought to-day. The Invisible is held. Adam's Deliverer from the curse is bound. He that trieth the hearts and reins is tried. He that shutteth the depths is shut in prison. He standeth before Pilate before whom stand with fear the Hosts of heaven. The Creator is smitten by hands he made. The Judge of quick and dead is sentenced to a tree. He that destroyeth hades is closed in a grave. Thou that endurest all things lovingly, and savest all men from the curse, glory to thee, forbearing Lord.

Then the Tranquil Light .... *Vide page* 8. *And straightway the Lections.*

Prokimenon. Tone 4.

THEY parted my garments among them, and upon my vesture did they cast lots. *Verse.* O God, my God, make haste unto me, why hast thou forsaken me?

The Lection from Exodus.

And the Lord spake unto Moses .... *ending,* but my face I will not shew unto thee. *Chap.* XXXIII. 11—23.

Prokimenon. Tone 4.

PLEAD thou my cause, O Lord, against them that strive against me. *Verse.* They rendered unto me evil for good.

The Lection from Job.

The Lord blessed . . . . *Chap.* XLII. 12, *ad fin.*

The Lection from the Prophecy of Esaias, with its Prokimenon. As in the Sixth Hour. Vide page 341.

Prokimenon. Tone 6.

THEY laid me in the lowest pit, in dark places, and in the shadow of death. *Verse.* O Lord God of my salvation, I have cried day and night before thee.

The Lection from the First Epistle of Paul to the Corinthians.

Brethren! The preaching of the Cross . . . . *ending,* and him crucified. *Chap.* I. 18—II. 2.

Alleluia. *Tone* 5.

SAVE me, O God, for the waters are come in, even unto my soul. *Verse.* They gave me bitter things to eat, and in my thirst they brought me vinegar. *Verse.* Let their eyes be darkened, that they may not see.

The Lection from the holy Evangelists, Matthew, Luke, and John.

At that time all the chief priests . . . . *to*, and another on the left. *Matt.* XXVII. 1—38. And one of the malefactors . . . . *to*, To-day shall thou be with me in paradise. *Luke* XXIII. 39—43. And they that passed by . . . . *to*, Truly this was the Son of God. *Matt.* XXVII. 39—54. The Jews therefore . . . . *to*, They shall look on him whom they pierced. *John* XIX. 31—37. And many women were there . . . . *to*, sitting over against the sepulchre. *Matt.* XXVII. 55—61.

Then the Great Ectenia. Vide page 10.

The Prayer, Vouchsafe, O Lord . . . . *Vide page* II.

ₛ *And the Ectenia of Supplication. Vide page* 12. *And, after this,*

The Stichera with Verses. Tone 2.

O CHRIST, the Life of all things, when the Arimathæan took thee dead from off the tree, he laid thee out in myrrh, and with loving heart and hands made haste to wrap thy precious Body in fine linen, and, though cast down with fear, rejoicing cried, Glory to thy condescension, O Lover of mankind.

Verse. The Lord reigneth, he is clothed with majesty.

WHEN thou, Redeemer of all, wast, for the sake of all, laid in a new sepulchre, hades, that scorneth all things, saw and feared. Its bars were shattered and its gates were crushed. The tombs were opened and the dead arose. Then Adam, giving thanks, rejoicing cried, Glory to thy condescension, O Lover of mankind.

Verse. For he hath made the whole world so sure that it cannot be moved.

WHEN thou, O Christ, who art in essence God, didst in thy Body will to be closed in a grave, being thyself uncircumscribed and limitless, then didst thou close the abodes of hades and of death, and empty all their kingdom, and then didst also grant this thy bright, glorious, and divinely blessed Sabbath Day.

Verse. Holiness becometh thine house, O Lord, unto length of days.

WHEN the heavenly Hosts saw thee, O Christ, falsely accused hy roaming sinners, and the stone sealed hy hands that pierced thy precious side, they trembled at thine unspeakable long-patience; yet, for our salvation, they rejoiced and cried, Glory to thy condescension, O Lover of mankind.

Glory. Both now. Tone 5.

THEE that coverest thyself with light as with a garment, thee, Joseph and Nicodemus take down from the tree, and, seeing thee dead, naked and unburied, receive thee with loving tears, and, deeply sighing, say, Alas, alas, sweet Jesus! Yet but a little while ago the sun, seeing thee hanging on the Cross was cast about with darkness, the earth with fear was moved, and the temple's veil was rent. And, lo! now I see thee of thine own will subject to death for me. How shall I bury thee, my God? In what linen fold thee? With what hands touch thy precious Body? What hymn sing at thy burial, O divine Love? I magnify thy Passion, I hymn thy Grave and Resurrection, and I cry, Glory to thee, O Lord.

After the Lord, now lettest thou thy servant depart . . . . *Trisagion, and the rest, the following Troparia in Tone 2.*

THE honourable Joseph, taking down thy most pure Body from the tree, wrapped it in pure fine linen with sweet spices, and placed it and closed it in a new sepulchre.

THE Angel, appearing before the myrrh-bearing women at the sepulchre, cried, Myrrh is fitting for the dead, but Christ hath appeared free from corruption.

And the Dismissal.

AT MATINS ON HOLY AND GREAT SATURDAY.

About the Seventh Hour the bells are rung for Matins. And after the Six Psalms we sing the The Lord is God *to Tone 2.*

Then the following Troparia to the same Tone.

The honourable Joseph .... *Vide page* 350.

Glory.

WHEN thou, the Living, the Immortal, didst condescend unto death, then didst thou slay hades by the light of thy Godhead. And when thou didst raise the dead from the lowermost parts of the earth, all the heavenly Hosts cried, O Christ, Giver of life, our God, glory to thee. *Both now.*

The Angel, appearing .... *Vide page* 350.

Then they sing the Seventeenth Kathism of the Psalter, on this wise:

Stasis 1.

BLESSED art thou, O Lord, O teach me thy statutes.

Blessed are they that are undefiled in the way, that walk in the law of the Lord.

Thou, O Christ, that art the life, art placed in a grave, and angel Hosts, awe-stricken, glorify thy condescension.

Blessed are they that keep his testimonies, and that seek him with the whole heart.

O Life, how dost thou die and dwell in a grave, whilst thou destroyest the kingdom of death and raisest the dead from hades?

They that do no wickedness walk in his ways.

We magnify thee, O Jesus the King, and reverence thy Burial and thy Passion, by which thou hast saved us from corruption.

Thou hast charged that we shall diligently keep thy commandments.

Within a narrow sepulchre art thou to-day laid, O Jesus, the King of all, who hast the limits of the earth itself appointed, and dost raise up the dead. *Glory.*

We hymn thee, O Word and God of all things, with the Father and thy Holy Spirit, and glorify thy divine sepulture. *Both now.*

We bless thee, pure Mother of God, and faithfully reverence the three days' burial of thy Son and our God.

Then the Little Ectenia, with the Exclamation, For blessed is thy name, and glorified is thy kingdom, of the Father . . . .

Stasis 2.

IT is meet to magnify thee, O Giver of life, who, with hands extended on the Cross, deliverest us from the power of the adversary.

Thy hands have made me and fashioned me. O give me understanding, that I may learn thy commandments.

It is meet to magnify thee, O Creator of all things; for, by thy Passion, we are delivered from passions, and are saved from corruption.

They that fear thee will be glad when they see me, because I have put my trust in thy word.

The earth trembled, and the sun, O Saviour, hid himself, whilst thou, O Christ, ever-shining Light, disappeared, according to the body, in the grave.

I know, O Lord, that thy judgments are right, and that thou of very faithfulness hast caused me to be troubled.

Thou hast slept, O Christ, within the grave the sleep natural for a living being, and hast raised the race of man from the heavy sleep of sin.

Glory.

O unbeginning God, co-eternal Word, and Holy Spirit, strengthen the sceptres of right-believing Princes against enemies; for thou art good. *Both now.*

Thou that didst bear the very Life, most spotless and pure Virgin; stay in the churches all causes of offence, and grant us peace; for thou art good.

23

Then again the Little Ectenia, with the Exclamation, For holy art thou, our God, and thou restest on a throne of glory of the Cherubim, and to thee we ascribe glory, with thine unbeginning Father, and thy most holy, and good, and life-creating Spirit, now . . . .

Stasis 3.

TO thy burial, O my Christ, all nations bring their songs.

Look upon me, and have mercy upon me, according to the judgment of them that love thy name.

The Arimathæan took thee from the tree, and having wrapped thee in a winding-sheet, buried thee in a grave.

Order my steps in thy word, and so shall no wickedness have dominion over me.

The myrrh-bearing women came, O my Christ, wisely bringing to thee the myrrh.

O deliver me from the wrongful dealings of men, and so shall I keep thy commandments.

O come, all creatures, and let us bring to the Creator the funeral songs.

Glory.

O Trinity, my God, Father, Son, and Holy Ghost, have mercy on the world.

Both now.

Vouchsafe, O Virgin, that thy servants may see the Resurrection of thy Son.

And again the Little Ectenia, with the Exclamation, For thou art the King of peace, O Christ our God, and the Redeemer of our souls, and to thee we ascribe glory, with thine unbeginning Father, and thy most holy, and good, and life-creating Spirit, now and ever . . . .

And straightway the following Troparia in Tone 5.

Blessed art thou, O Lord: O teach me thy statutes.

The assembly of Angels were amazed.... *And the rest. Vide page 25.*

Then again the Little Ectenia, with the Exclamation, For blessed is thy name, and glorified is thy kingdom, of the Father . . . .

And we sing the following Kathismal Hymn in Tone 1.

JOSEPH wrapped in pure fine linen and annointed with divine sweet spices the sacred Body begged from Pilate, and placed it in a new sepulchre, whither coming early, cried the women bearing myrrh, Shew us, as thou before didst say, O Christ, the Resurrection. *Glory.*

Shew us, as thou before didst say, O Christ, the Resurrection. *Both now.*

The choirs of Angels were amazed, seeing the Immortal, who resteth in the Father's

23*

bosom, laid in a grave as dead. And him in hades with the dead, as Maker and as Lord, their hosts surround and glorify.

Then Psalm 50 (51). *And straightway we sing the Canon in Tone* 6, *the Irmi of which are as followeth,*

I. Thee, who of old didst hide the oppressor and persecutor under the waves of the sea, thee, the children of the saved have hidden under the earth. But we, as the maidens, sing unto the Lord; for he hath triumphed gloriously.

III. Creation, beholding thee hanging on the Cross, thee who dost firmly hang the earth upon the waters, was convulsed with great fear, and cried, There is none holy save thee, O Lord.

IV. Abbacum, forseeing thy divine exhaustion on the Cross, in terror cried, Thou hast cut short the power of the strong, O Blessed One, by entering into communion with them that are in hades.

V. O Christ, Esaias beholding the evenless light of thine Epiphany, which mercifully shone unto us, rising early in the night, exclaimed, The dead shall rise, and they that are in the graves shall come to life, and all the earth-born shall rejoice.

VI. Jonas was taken into the bowels of

the whale, but not retained; for, bearing thine image who sufferedst and wast buried, he came forth from the monster as from a palace. Yet they that are held down by vanities and falsehoods forget this mercy, and call the guards.

Condakion. Tone 2.

HE that shutteth up the depths is beheld dead, and swathed with myrrh in fine linen the Immortal is placed as mortal in a tomb. And the women come to anoint him, wailing bitterly and crying, This Sabbath is most blessed, on which Christ sleepeth, and on the third day shall rise again.

VII. O wondrous miracle! He that delivered the pious Youths in the fiery furnace is laid dead in a grave, and mute for the salvation of us who sing, O God our Redeemer, blessed art thou.

VIII. O quake with fear, ye heavens, and let the foundations of the earth be moved; for, lo! he that liveth above is numbered with the dead, and in a narrow grave is laid by strangers, whom bless, ye youths, extol, ye priests, ye people, set him up for ever.

Let us praise, let us bless, let us worship

the Lord, singing unto him, and setting him up for ever.

IX. Weep not for me, O Mother, beholding in the grave the Son whom thou didst bear, as Virgin, in thy womb; for I shall arise and be glorified, and, as God, shall ever gloriously raise all them that magnify thee in faith and love.

Then the Little Ectenia, with the Exclamation, For all the Hosts of heaven praise thee, and to thee we ascribe glory, to the Father . . . .

Then the Exapostilarion. Tone 2.
Holy is the Lord our God, *thrice.*

And the Psalms of Praise follow, with Stichera in Tone 2.

TO-DAY a grave holdeth him whose hands hold all creation, and a stone covereth him whose virtue covereth the heavens. The Life sleepeth, and hades trembleth, and Adam is freed from bonds. Glory to thy dispensation, through which, having accomplished all things, thou hast granted unto us an eternal Sabbath, even thy most holy Resurrection from the dead.

WHAT meaneth this sight we see? what this present rest? The King of eternity, through suffering, hath accomplished his dispensation, and keepeth sabbath in the grave,

granting us new sabbath rest. Let us then
cry to him, Arise, O God, and judge the
earth; for thou reignest for ever, and hast
mercy without measure.

COME, let us behold our Life, who lieth
in a grave that he may quicken them
who lie in graves. Come to-day, and, seeing
him of Juda sleeping, let us cry as did the
Prophet, Couching down, thou didst sleep as
a lion, who shall rouse thee, O King? But
arise of thine own will, thou who hast willingly given thyself for us.

Tone 6.

JOSEPH begged the Body of Jesus, and
placed it in his own new sepulchre; for
he desired him to come forth from the grave
as from a bridal chamber. Thou that hast
crushed the power of death, and opened
Paradise to men, glory to thee. *Glory.*

THE great Moses mystically foretold this
day when saying, And God blessed the
seventh day. For this is the blessed Sabbath,
this is the day of rest, on which the only-
begotten Son of God rested from all his
works, according to the dispensation concerning death, and kept sabbath in his flesh, in
the which to return again by the Resurrection, and to grant to us eternal life; for

he alone is good and the Lover of mankind. *Both now.*

Most blessed art thou, Virgin . . . . *Vide
page* 39.

And the Great Doxology.

*And the Priest, having put on all his vest-
ments, entereth with the holy Gospel. And
after they have sung the Trisagion, he saith,*
Let us attend. Peace to all. Wisdom! *And
we sing the Troparion,* The honourable
Joseph . . . . *Vide page* 350.

*And the Troparion of the Prophecy fol-
loweth, in Tone* 2.

O CHRIST, thou that holdest the utmost
borders of the earth, art seen held in a
grave, that thou mightest deliver mankind
from the depths of hades, and make us immortal, and quicken us, as God immortal.

Prokimenon. Tone 4.

ARISE, O Lord, help us and deliver us,
for the glory of thy name. *Verse.* O
God, we have heard with our ears, and our
fathers have told us the noble works thou
didst in their days, and in the old time before them.

The Lection from the Prophecy of Ezekiel.
The hand of the Lord . . . . *ending,* per-

formed it, saith the Lord. *Chap.* XXXVII.
I—I4.

Prokimenon. Tone 7.

ARISE, O Lord my God, let thine hand
be lifted up, forget not thy poor at the
last. *Verse.* I will praise thee, O God, with
my whole heart, I will shew forth all thy
marvellous works.

*The Lection from the First Epistle of
Paul to the Corinthians, and from his Epistle
to the Galatians.*

Brethren! A little leaven leaveneth ....
to, sincerity and truth. I. *Cor.* v. 6—8.
Christ hath redeemed us .... *to,* through
faith. *Gal.* III. 13—14.

Alleluia. *Tone* 5.

LET God arise, and let his enemies be
scattered, and let them that hate him
flee from before him. *Verse.* As smoke is
driven away, so drive them away, as wax
melteth at the presence of fire. *Verse.* So
let the sinners perish at the presence of God,
but let the righteous rejoice.

The Lection from the holy Evangelist Matthew.

On the morrow .... *ending,* the guard
being with them. *Chap.* XXVII. 62—66.

Then the Ectenias, Let us all .... *And,*

Let us accomplish our morning prayer .... *And the rest, as customary. And the Dismissal.*

AT VESPERS ON HOLY AND GREAT SATURDAY.

About the Ninth Hour of the Day, they ring for Vespers, and the Priest vesteth as customarily. And we begin the Prefatory Psalm, and the Ectenia of Peace followeth. Then we sing the Lord, I have cried *in Tone* I. *And at the place of* 8 *verses we begin the Stichera.*

Stichera of the Resurrection. Tone I.

ACCEPT our evening prayers, O holy Lord, and grant us forgiveness of our sins; for thou alone hast made manifest the Resurrection to the world.

GO ye round about Sion, O ye people, and encompass her, and in her midst ascribe ye glory for the Resurrection from the dead; for this is our God, who hath delivered us from our transgressions.

O COME, ye people, let us praise and worship Christ, and glorify his Resurrection from the dead; for he is our God, who hath redeemed the world from the adversary's wiles.

BY thy Passion, Christ, we have been freed from passions, and by thy Resurrection delivered from corruption. Glory to thee, O Lord.

Other Stichera of the Great Sabbath, in Tone 8.

TO-DAY doth hades groaning cry, Better for me it were might I receive not him whom Mary bore; for on me he cometh to break my power, to crush the brazen gates, and, being God, to raise the souls I erst have held. Glory to thy Cross, O Lord, and to thy Resurrection, *twice*.

TO-DAY doth hades groaning cry, My power is overcome. I took one dead, as one among the dead, yet over him I had no power at all, but perished by him, and with those I ruled. I had the dead from ages, but lo! this one raiseth all. Glory to thy Cross, O Lord, and to thy Resurrection.

TO-DAY doth hades groaning cry, My might is sacrificed. The Shepherd is crucified and Adam raised. Them that I ruled I have lost. Them I devoured in my power I have disgorged them all. The Crucified hath opened the graves, and the power of death hath no avail. Glory to thy Cross, O Lord, and to thy Resurrection. *Glory*.

THE great Moses in mystery foretold this present day and said, And God blessed the seventh day. For this is the blessed Sabbath, this is the day of rest, on which the only-begotten Son of God rested from all his works, according to the dispensation concerning death, and kept sabbath in his flesh, in the which to return again by the Resurrection, and to grant to us eternal life; for he alone is good and the Lover of mankind. *Both now.*

To the Virgin. Tone 1.

LET us extol the Virgin Mary, who sprang from man and bore the Lord. She is the heavenly gate, the glory of the world, the song of bodiless Hosts, and boast of all the faithful. She hath appeared like to heaven, and as the house of God. She hath cast down the middle wall of enmity, and given us peace instead, and opened heaven's kingdom. Then having her, the stronghold of the faith, we also have the Lord she bore for our Defender. Courage then, courage, ye people of God, for he himself, the Almighty One, warreth against the enemy.

After the Stichera they sing the Tranquil Light.

No Prokimenon is said, but straightway, Wisdom! *And the Reader beginneth the Lections.*

Lection I.   Genesis I. 1—13.

In the beginning .... *ending,* the third day.

Lection II.   Esaias LX. 1—16.

Shine, shine, O Jerusalem, for thy light is come . . . . *ending,* I am the Lord that saveth thee, and the God of Jacob that redeemeth thee.

Lection III.   Exodus XII. 1—11.

And the Lord spake . . . . *ending,* the Lord's passover.

Lection IV.   Jonas I. 1—IV. 11.

The word of the Lord . . . . *ending,* much cattle.

Lection V.   Joshua V. 10—15.

The children of Israel encamped . . . . *ending,* And Joshua did so.

Lection VI.   Exodus XIII. 20—XV. 1. And the children of Israel took their journey . . . . *ending,* Then sang Moses and the children of Israel this song unto the Lord and spake, saying, *The Reader saith,* Let us sing unto the Lord. *And they answer and sing in Tone* 5, For he is gloriously glorified. *And the Reader of each Choir saith the verses alternately.*

The horse and the rider he hath thrown into the sea. Let us sing unto the Lord.

And both Choirs sing, For he is gloriously glorified. *And so after every verse.*

A help and defence hath he become to me unto salvation. Let us sing unto the Lord.

He is my God and I will glorify him, my fathers' God, and I will exalt him. Let us sing unto the Lord.

The Lord hath shattered the enemy, the Lord is his name: the chariots of Pharao and his host he hath thrown into the sea. Let us sing unto the Lord.

The chosen captains of horsemen are drowned in the Red Sea. Let us sing unto the Lord.

With the deep hath he covered them, they sank to the bottom like a stone. Let us sing unto the Lord.

Thy right hand, O Lord, is glorified in strength. Let us sing unto the Lord.

Thy right hand, O Lord, hath shattered the enemy, and in the greatness of thy glory thou hast crushed the adversary. Let us sing unto the Lord.

Thou didst send forth thy wrath, and it devoured them as stubble, and with the breath of thy fury the water divided. Let us sing unto the Lord.

The waters were congealed together as a

wall, the waves were congealed in the heart of the sea. Let us sing unto the Lord,

The enemy said, I will pursue, I will overtake, I will divide the spoil, my soul shall be satisfied, I will slay with my sword, my hand shall prevail. Let us sing unto the Lord.

Thou didst send forth thy breath, the sea covered them, they sank as lead in the mighty water. Let us sing unto the Lord.

Who is like unto thee, O Lord, among the gods? who is like unto thee, glorious in the saints, fearful in praises, doing wonders? Let us sing unto the Lord.

Thou didst stretch forth thy right hand, the earth swallowed them. Thou didst lead in thy righteousness this thy people which thou hast redeemed. Let us sing unto the Lord.

Thou hast comforted them by thy strength in thy holy habitation. The nations heard and were angry, sorrow took hold on the inhabitants of Philistima. Let us sing unto the Lord.

Then were the dukes of Edom troubled, and trembling took hold upon the princes of Moab, all the inhabitants of Canaan melted away. Let us sing unto the Lord.

Fear and trembling fell upon them, by

the greatness of thine arm they shall be as still as a stone. Let us sing unto the Lord.

Until thy people pass over, O Lord, until this thy people pass over, which thou hast purchased. Let us sing unto the Lord.

Thou shalt bring them in and plant them in the mountain of thine inheritance, in thy prepared dwelling - place, which thou hast established, O Lord, thy sanctuary, which thy hands have prepared. Let us sing unto the Lord.

The Lord reigneth to ages, and to ages, and continually. When the horse of Pharao went with his chariots and his horsemen into the sea, the Lord brought in upon them the water of the sea. Let us sing unto the Lord.

But the children of Israel walked on dry land in the midst of the sea. Let us sing unto the Lord.

Glory. Let us sing unto the Lord.

Both now. Let us sing unto the Lord. *And the last Reader singeth,* For he is gloriously glorified.

Lection VII. Sophonius III. 8—15.

Thus saith the Lord, Wait ye upon me until the day . . . . *ending,* see evil any more.

Lection VIII. Third Kings XVII. 8—24.

And the word of the Lord . . . . *ending,* in thy mouth is truth.

Lection IX. Esaias LXI. 10—LXII. 5.

My soul shall rejoice in the Lord, for he hath clothed me . . . . *ending,* so shall the Lord rejoice over thee.

Lection X. Genesis XXII. 1—18.

And it came to pass that God did tempt.... *ending,* obeyed my voice.

Lection XI. Esaias LXI. 1—10.

The spirit of the Lord . . . . *ending,* the seed which the Lord hath blessed, and they shall greatly rejoice in the Lord.

Lection XII. Fourth Kings IV. 8—37.

And it fell on a day . . . . *ending,* and took up her son and went out.

Lection XIII. Esaias LXIII. 11—LXIV. 5.

Thus saith the Lord, Where is he that brought . . . . *ending,* remember thee in thy ways.

Lection XIV. Jeremias XXXVIII.* 31—34.

Thus saith the Lord, Behold the days come . . . . *ending,* remember their sin no more.

Lection XV. Daniel III. 1.

In the eighteenth year, Nabuchodonosor the king made an image . . . . *to verse* 23,

---

* In the English Authorized Version XXXI.

24

fell down bound into the midst of the burning fiery furnace,

And walked in the midst of the flame, singing praises unto God and blessing the Lord. And Azarias stood up with them praying, and he opened his mouth in the midst of the fire, and spake, saying, Blessed art thou, O Lord God of our fathers, and praised and glorified is thy name for ever. For righteous art thou concerning all things which thou hast done unto us, and all thy works are true, and thy ways righteous, and all thy judgments are true. And thou hast made a decree of truth concerning all things which thou hast brought upon us, and upon Jerusalem, the holy city of our fathers. For in truth and judgment hast thou brought all these things upon us on account of our sins. For we have sinned and transgressed through turning away from thee. And in all things we have sinned exceedingly, and thy commandments we have not kept, nor loved them, nor done that which thou hast commanded us, to the intent that it might be well with us. And all the things that thou hast done unto us, and all the things that thou hast brought upon us in true judgment have been wrought. And thou hast delivered us into the hands of sinful enemies and wicked adversaries, and into the hands of a king unrighteous and evil above all that are upon the earth. And now it is not permitted unto us to open our mouth, and shame and reproach are come upon thy servants, and upon them that honour thee. But reject us not until the end, for thy holy name's sake, neither annul thy testament, nor remove thy mercy from us, for the sake of Abraham thy well-beloved, and for Isaac thy servant, and Israel thy saint, to whom thou didst promise to multiply their seed as the stars of heaven, and as the sand that is upon the sea-shore. For, O Lord, we have become little above all the nations, and we are this day humbled in all the earth on account of our sins. And at this time there is no prince, nor prophet, nor leader, neither is there holocaust, nor sacrifice, nor offering, nor incense, nor place to sacrifice before thee and to find mercy. But let us be accepted in a contrite soul and humble spirit. As a holocaust of rams and bulls, and as thousands of fat lambs, so let our sacrifice come before thee this day, and let it be perfected by thee, for there is no shame for them that put their trust in thee. And now we follow after thee with our whole heart, and we fear thee, and we seek thy face. Put us not to shame, but deal with us according to thy loving-kindness, and according to the plenitude of thy mercy. And deliver us according to thy wonders, and give glory to thy holy name, O Lord. And let them that do evil unto thy servants be confounded, and let them be put to shame by every power, and let their might be crushed. And let them know that thou art the Lord, the only God, and glorious above all the earth.

And the flame extended above the furnace about forty and nine cubits. And it passed through and consumed those of the Chaldæans that were found round about the furnace. But the Angel of the Lord came down unto them that were with Azarias in the furnace, and turned the flame of fire out of the furnace, and made the midst of the furnace as of a rushing wind of dew, and the fire in nowise touched them, nor distressed them, nor tormented them. Then the three, as with one mouth sang praises, and blessed and glorified God in the furnace, saying, Blessed art thou, O Lord God of our fathers, and to be praised and set up above all for ever. And blessed is the holy name of thy glory, and to be praised and set up above all for ever. Blessed art thou in the temple of thy holy glory, and to be praised and set up above all for ever. Blessed art thou that lookest upon the depths, that sittest upon the Cherubim, and to be praised and set up above all for ever. Blessed art thou upon the throne of glory of thy kingdom, and to be praised and set up above all for ever. Blessed art thou in the firmament of heaven, and to be praised and set up above all for ever.

We stop here, and sing, Praise ye the Lord, and set him up for ever, and for evermore.

And the Reader saith the verses.

ALL ye works of the Lord, speak well of the Lord. *And we,*
Praise him, and set him up for ever.

O ye Angels of the Lord, O ye heavens of the Lord, speak well of the Lord,
Praise him, and set him up for ever.

O all ye waters that are above the heavens, O all ye powers of the Lord, speak well of the Lord,
Praise him, and set him up for ever.

O ye sun and moon, O ye stars of heaven, speak well of the Lord,
Praise him, and set him up for ever.

O every shower and dew, O all ye winds, speak well of the Lord,
Praise him, and set him up for ever.

O ye fire and heat, O ye winter and summer, speak well of the Lord,
Praise him, and set him up for ever.

O ye dews and frosts, O ye ice and cold, speak well of the Lord,

Praise him, and set him up for ever.

O ye hoar-frosts and snows, O ye nights and days, speak well of the Lord,

Praise him, and set him up for ever.

O ye light and darkness, O ye lightnings and clouds, speak well of the Lord,

Praise him, and set him up for ever.

O thou earth, ye mountains and ye hills, and all things growing thereupon, speak well of the Lord,

Praise him, and set him up for ever.

O ye wells, O ye seas and floods, O ye whales and all that move in the waters, speak well of the Lord,

Praise him, and set him up for ever.

O all ye fowls of the air, O all ye beasts and cattle, speak well of the Lord,

Praise him, and set him up for ever.

O ye children of men, O let Israel speak well of the Lord,

Praise him, and set him up for ever.

O ye priests of the Lord, O ye servants of the Lord, speak well of the Lord,

Praise him, and set him up for ever.

O ye spirits and souls of the righteous, O ye holy and humble men of heart, speak well of the Lord,

Praise him, and set him up for ever.

O Ananias, Azarias and Misael, speak well of the Lord,

Praise him, and set him up for ever.

Let us bless the Father, the Son, and the Holy Ghost, let us praise him, and set him up for ever.

Both now and ever, and to ages of ages. Amen.

Praise ye the Lord, and set him up for ever.

Let us praise, let us bless, let us worship the Lord, singing unto him, and setting him up above all for ever, and for evermore.

Then followeth the Little Ectenia. And instead of the Trisagion, we sing,

As many as have been baptized into Christ . . . .

Then the Prokimenon in Tone 5.

LET all the earth worship thee and praise thee, let it sing praises to thy name, O Most High.

Verse. Cry aloud unto the Lord, all the earth, O sing praises unto his name.

The Lection from the Epistle of Paul to the Romans. Chap. VI. 3—11.

Brethren! As many of us as were baptized . . . . *ending*, Jesus Christ our Lord.

The Alleluia *is not sung, but after the*

Priest hath said, Peace to thee, *the Reader straightway saith in Tone* 7.

ARISE, O God, and judge the earth, for thou hast obtained an inheritance among all the nations. *And the Singers repeat the verse.*

Then the Reader.

Verse. God standeth in the congregation of the gods, and judgeth gods in the midst thereof. *Singers.* Arise, O God . . . .

Verse. How long will ye judge unrighteously, and accept the face of sinners? *Singers.* Arise, O God . . . .

Verse. Avenge ye the orphans and the needy, and right the humble and the poor. *Singers.* Arise, O God . . . .

Verse. Take ye the poor and needy, and deliver them out of the hand of the wicked. *Singers.* Arise, O God . . . .

Verse. For they have not known, neither have they understood, but have gone on in darkness. *Singers.* Arise, O God . . . .

Verse. Be ye shaken, O ye foundations of the earth. I have spoken, ye shall be gods, and all of ye the children of the Most High, but ye shall die as men, and as one of the princes ye shall fall. *And again,* Arise, O God, and judge the earth, for thou hast obtained an inheritance among all the nations.

The Gospel according to Matthew. Chap. XXVIII. I—20. In the end of the Sabbath.... *ending,* the end of the world. Amen.

And the Liturgy of S. Basil.

And instead of the Cherubic Hymn they sing,

LET all flesh of man be silent, and let it stand in fear and awe, and think of nothing earthly to itself. For the King of kings and the Lord of lords cometh to be slain, and to be given as food to the faithful. Him do precede the angelic Hosts with all their Principalities and Powers, the many-eyed Cherubim and the six-winged Seraphim, covering their faces and singing the song, Alleluia, alleluia, alleluia.

Communion Hymn.

THE Lord hath awakened as one that slept, and hath arisen and saved us. Alleluia, alleluia, alleluia.

XXI. EXTRACTS FROM THE FERIAL TRIODION, OR PENTECOSTARION.

THE MATINS
ON THE HOLY AND GREAT SUNDAY OF
PASCHA,
COMMONLY CALLED,
EASTER DAY.

As soon as the day beginneth, the bells are rung, and the Warden lighteth all the candles and lamps in the Church, and placeth two vessels holding burning charcoal, one in the Altar and the other in the middle of the Church, and casteth into them much incense, that the Church may be filled with sweet perfume. And the Western Gates of the Church are shut. And the Priest and Deacon put on their brightest vestments, and tapers are distributed. And the Priest taketh the honourable Cross, and the Deacon the censer, and, with lamps borne before them and accompanied by the Choir, they go into the Porch, singing the Sticheron in Tone 7.

THY Resurrection, O Saviour Christ, Angels sing in heaven. Vouchsafe to us also upon earth to extol thee with pure heart.

And the Priest, taking the censer from the Deacon in his right hand, and holding the honourable Cross in his left, censeth as customarily, and all stand around with burning tapers.

And the Priest exclaimeth,

GLORY to the holy, consubstantial, life-giving and undivided Trinity, always, now and ever, and to ages of ages.

Choir. Amen.

Then the Priest intoneth the Troparion in Tone 5.

CHRIST is risen from the dead, death by death down doth he tread, and on those within the tombs he bestoweth life.

And we repeat the same with melody. And thrice is it thus sung by the Priest and by us. Then the Priest intoneth these verses.

LET God arise, and let his enemies be scattered, and let them that hate him flee from before him.

As smoke is driven away, so drive them away, as *wax* melteth at the presence of fire,

So let the sinners perish at the presence of God, but let the righteous rejoice.

This is the day which the Lord hath made, let us rejoice and be glad therein.

Glory. Both now.

And after every verse we sing the Troparion, Christ is risen . . . .

Then the Priest loudly singeth,

CHRIST is risen from the dead, death by death down doth he tread.

And the Gates are opened, and he entereth, carrying the honourable Cross and accompanied by the Deacon, with lamps borne before them, and by the Choir singing,

AND on those within the tombs he bestoweth life.

And the Priest entereth the Altar, and the Deacon, standing on the Ambo, saith the Ectenia of Peace.

In peace let us pray to the Lord. *And the rest. Vide page 2.*

Then followeth the Canon in Tone i.

Ode I. Irmos.

IT is the day of Resurrection. O people, let us be enlightened. It is the Pascha, *the Lord's Pascha. For, from death to life, and from earth to heaven Christ our God hath brought us over, singing the hymn of victory.*

Refrain. Christ is risen . . . .

Let us cleanse our senses, and we shall behold Christ shining in the inaccessible light of the Resurrection, and shall clearly hear him saying, Hail! to us, singing the hymn of victory.

Let the heavens, as is meet, be glad, and let the earth rejoice, and let the world, visible and invisible, keep festival; for Christ hath risen, everlasting Joy.

Then again the Irmos. It is the day of Resurrection . . . .

And the Little Ectenia is said.

NOTE:—*This followeth all the Odes.*

Ode III. Irmos.

O COME, let us drink the new drink, not miraculously drawn from the barren rock, but the fountain of immortality, which is poured from the grave by Christ, in whom we are established.

Now all things are filled with light, heaven, and earth, and things beneath the earth. Then let all creation keep festival for Christ's arising, in which it is established.

Yesterday, O Christ, with thee I was entombed. To-day, with thee arising, I arise. Yesterday I was crucified with thee : glorify me together with thyself, O Saviour, in thy kingdom.

And again the Irmos. O come, let us drink . . . .

Hypacoë. *Tone* 4.

THEY who came with Mary, preventing the dawn, and finding the stone rolled away from the sepulchre, heard from the Angel, Why seek ye as a man among the dead him that dwelleth in everlasting light? Behold ye not the sheets of death? Hasten, and tell the world that the Lord hath risen, hath been the death of death, and that he is the Son of God that saveth the race of men.

Ode IV. *Irmos.*

UPON the sacred watch-tower, mayest thou stand with us, O divinely-speaking Abbacum, and shew us the light-bearing Angel unceasingly proclaiming, To-day is salvation to the world; for Christ, as Almighty, hath arisen.

Christ hath appeared as a male, opening the Virgin's womb. As our food he is called a Lamb, and undefiled; as free from stain, our Pascha; and, as true God, he is named, Perfect.

As a yearling lamb, Christ, our blessed crown, of his own will, as cleansing Pascha, was sacrificed for all; and again to us from the grave hath shone, as the glorious Sun of righteousness.

Before the foreshadowing ark David, Forefather of God, leaped and danced. And let us, God's holy people, seeing the types' fulfilment, be divinely glad; for Christ, as Almighty, hath arisen.

And again the Irmos. Upon the sacred watch-tower . . . .

Ode V. Irmos.

LET us in the deep dawn arise, and, instead of myrrh, let us bring the Lord a song, and we shall see Christ, the Sun of righteousness, shining life to all.

They that were held by hades' chains, when they beheld thy gentle pity, Christ, hurried onward to the light, praising with joyful feet the eternal Pascha.

Let us approach with lamps in hand to Christ, who, as a bridegroom, cometh from the tomb. And let us, with the festal-loving ranks, together celebrate the saving Pascha of our God.

And again the Irmos. Let us in the deep dawn . . . .

Ode VI. Irmos.

THOU didst descend into earth's lowest parts, O Christ, and didst break the eternal bars which held the captives; and on the third day, as Jonas from the whale, didst from the grave arise.

Keeping the seals unbroken, thou, O Christ, didst from the grave arise, who, in thy birth, didst not destroy the Virgin bars; and thou hast opened unto us the gates of Paradise.

My Saviour, who as God didst to the Father bring, of thine own will, thyself a living and unsacrificed victim, rising from the grave, hast raised with thyself Adam and all his race.

And again the Irmos. Thou didst descend . . . .

Condakion. Tone 8.

IF into the tomb thou didst descend, Immortal One, yet didst thou overthrow the might of hades, and as victor rise, O Christ, saying, Hail! to the women bearing myrrh, granting peace to thine Apostles, and resurrection to the fallen.

Icos. (Stanza.)

SEEKING as those that seek the day, very early in the morning came the maidens bearing myrrh to that Sun before the sun, that now had set within a grave; and they cried to one another, O Friends! Come, let us anoint with spices the quickening buried Body, the Flesh that raiseth fallen Adam, lying in the tomb. Let us go on, hastening like the Magi, and let us worship and bring the myrrh as gift to him, no longer wrapped in swaddling-clothes, but in fine linen, and let us weep and cry, Arise, O Lord, who givest resurrection to the fallen.

Then we sing,

Having seen the Resurrection of Christ.... *thrice. Vide page* 28.

Then,

JESUS hath risen from the grave, as he foretold, granting us eternal life and great mercy, *thrice.*

Ode VII. Irmos.

HE that delivered the Children from the furnace became man, and suffered as mortal, and, by his suffering, endued the mortal with the beauty of immortality, he, the God of our fathers, who alone is blessed and most glorious.

The women, wise of God, came after thee with myrrh; but him whom they sought with tears as mortal they worshipped with joy as living God, and told, O Christ, to thy Disciples the glad tidings of the mystic Pascha.

25

We celebrate the death of death, the over-throw of hades, the first-fruits of another endless life, and sing exultingly the Cause, him, the God of our fathers, who alone is blessed and most glorious.

And again the Irmos. He that delivered ....

Ode VIII. Irmos.

THIS is the chosen and holy Day, the King and Lord of Sabbaths, the Feast of feasts, the Triumph of triumphs, on which we bless Christ for ever.

Come, let us partake of the Vine's new fruit, of joy divine, in the glorious day of the Resurrection and Kingdom of Christ, singing to him as God for ever.

Lift up thine eyes, O Sion, round about and see; for, lo! thy children come to thee, as lights by God illumined, from the west and from the north, from the sea and from the east, in thee blessing Christ for ever.

Father almighty, and Word, and Spirit, united Nature in three Persons, Superessential, God most high, baptized in thee, we bless thee evermore.

Refrain preceding Ode IX.

An Angel cried to the one full of grace, Hail! Virgin pure. And again I say, Hail! for thy Son, after three days, hath risen from

the grave and raised the dead. Rejoice, ye
people.

Ode IX. Irmos.

*SHINE, shine, O new Jerusalem ; for the
glory of the Lord hath shone on thee.
Rejoice and exult, O Sion. And thou, pure
Mother of God, be glad for the Resurrection
of thy Son.*

O divine, O dear, O sweetest voice of
thine! For thou hast promised of a truth,
O Christ, to be with us until the world doth
end. Having this steadfast hope, we, thy
faithful ones, rejoice.

O Christ, thou great, most sacred Pascha,
Wisdom, and Word, and Power of God!
grant us more perfectly to partake of thee
in that thy kingdom's day that hath no evening.

And again the Irmos. Shine, shine, O
new Jerusalem . . . .

Exapostilarion.

ASLEEP in flesh as mortal, O King and
Lord, thou didst arise on the third day,
and raise Adam from corruption and abolish
death, O Pascha of immortality, Salvation of
the world.

*The Psalms of Praise with Stichera in
Tone* 1.

LET everything that hath breath praise
the Lord. O praise God in his Saints,

25*

praise him according to the greatness of his majesty.

Sticheron. We hymn, O Christ, thy saving Passion, and glorify thy Resurrection.

Praise him with the sound of the trumpet, praise him with psaltery and harp.

Sticheron. O Lord, who didst endure the Cross, and didst abolish death, and rise again from the dead; give us peace in our life, who alone art almighty.

Praise him with timbrel and choir, praise him with stringed instruments and organ.

Sticheron. O Christ, who didst spoil hades and raise man by thy Resurrection; vouchsafe that, with pure heart, we may hymn and glorify thee.

Praise him with well-tuned cymbals, praise him with loud cymbals. Let everything that hath breath praise the Lord.

Sticheron. We glorify thy Godlike condescension, and sing to thee, O Christ. Thou wast born of the Virgin and wast inseparably with the Father. Thou didst suffer as man, and didst, of thine own will, endure the Cross. Thou didst arise from the tomb, going out thence as from a bridal chamber to save the world. Glory to thee, O Lord.

Then the Stichera of Pascha in Tone 5.

Verse. Let God arise, and let his ene-

mies be scattered, and let them that hate
him flee from before him.

O-DAY the sacred Pascha is made
manifest to us, the new and holy
Pascha, the mystic Pascha, the all-
honourable Pascha, the Pascha which is
Christ the Redeemer, the spotless Pascha,
the mighty Pascha, the Pascha of the faithful, the Pascha that openeth unto us the
gates of Paradise, the Pascha that halloweth
all the faithful.

Verse. As smoke is driven away, so drive
them away, as wax melteth at the presence
of fire.

COME from that spectacle, ye women,
proclaimers of glad tidings, and say
unto Sion, Receive from us glad tidings of
joy of the Resurrection of Christ. Rejoice,
dance and be glad, O Jerusalem, beholding
Christ the King coming forth as a bridegroom from the tomb.

Verse. So let the sinners perish at the
presence of God, but let the righteous rejoice.

THE myrrh-bearing women going very
early in the morning to the tomb of the
Giver of life, saw an Angel sitting on the
stone, who spake to them and said, Why
seek ye the Living among the dead? Why
bewail ye the Immortal in the place of cor-

ruption? Go, and tell ye these things to his Disciples.

Verse. This is the day which the Lord hath made, let us rejoice and be glad therein.

THE Pascha of delight, Pascha, the Pascha of the Lord, the all-honourable Pascha hath shone on us. O Pascha, let us in joy embrace each other! O Pascha, our deliverance from sorrow! For to-day Christ, shining from the tomb as from a bridal chamber, filled the hearts of the women with joy by his words, Go ye, and tell the Apostles. *Glory. Both now.*

IT is the day of Resurrection, let us be enlightened by the Triumph, and let us embrace each other. Let us say, Brethren! even to them that hate us. Let us forgive all offences at the Resurrection, and thus let us exclaim,

CHRIST is risen from the dead, death by death down doth he tread, and on those within the tombs he bestoweth life.

And we sing, Christ is risen .... *many times, while the Salutation of Peace is given.*

Then, while all stand, is read

The Catechetical Discourse of our Father in the Saints, John, Archbishop of Constantinople, the Chrysostom, for the holy and

light-bearing Day of the most glorious and saving Resurrection of Christ our God.

HE that is pious and God-loving, let him enjoy this good and bright triumphal Feast. He that is a wise and prudent servant, let the same joyfully enter into the joy of his Master. He that hath laboured in fasting, let him now receive his denarius. He that hath worked from the first hour, let him to-day receive his just award. He that came at the end of the third hour, let him keep the Feast with thanksgiving. He that came only at the sixth hour, let him have no doubt, for he is in nowise rejected. He that missed even the ninth hour, let him approach, nothing doubting, nothing fearing. He that arrived even at the eleventh hour, let him not fear on account of his delay. For the Lord, being condescending, accepteth the last comer as the first, he resteth him that cometh at the eleventh hour as he resteth him that worked from the first hour, and he hath mercy on the last and sheweth favour to the first, and on this one bestoweth and to that one granteth, and he welcometh the deeds and kisseth the intentions, respecteth the work and approveth the purpose. Then come ye all into the joy of your Lord. Ye

first and ye last, ye rich and ye poor, rejoice together. Ye temperate and ye slothful,
honour the day. Ye that have fasted and
ye that have not fasted, rejoice this day.
The table is full, enjoy it all of you. The
calf is a fattened one, let no one depart a
hungred. Enjoy ye all the Feast of faith.
Receive ye all the riches of grace. Let no
one bewail his unworthiness, for the kingdom of all hath come. Let no one lament
over his sins, for pardon hath shone like a
light from the tomb. Let no one fear death,
for our Saviour's death hath liberated us.
He who was bound by it hath extinguished
it. Descending into hades, he made hades
captive, and he moved it that had tasted of
his flesh. Foreseeing this same, Esaias exclaimed, Hades, saith he, from beneath is
moved, for it is cast away by thee. It is
moved, for it is crushed. It is moved, for it
is slain. It is moved, for it is overthrown.
It is moved, for it is made captive. It took
the flesh, and discovered God. It took the
clay, and met heaven. It took what it saw,
and fell into what it did not see. Where is
thy sting, O death? Where is thy victory,
O hades? Christ hath arisen, and thou art
overthrown. Christ hath arisen, and the
demons have fallen. Christ hath arisen, and
the Angels rejoice. Christ hath arisen, and

life reigneth. Christ hath arisen, and not one dead resteth in the grave. For Christ, having arisen from the dead, became the first-fruits of them that slept. To him be glory and majesty to ages of ages. Amen.

And the Troparion to the Saint in Tone 8.

THE grace of thy mouth, shining forth like fire, hath enlightened the universe, hath offered the world treasures of liberality, and hath shewed to us the height of humility. And, as thou instructest us by thy words, Father John Chrysostom, pray Christ, the Word, to save our souls.

Then the Deacon saith the Great Ectenia.
Have mercy upon us . . . . *Vide page* 10.

And that of Supplication.
Let us accomplish our morning prayer . . . .
Vide page 12.
And after the Exclamation concluding the latter, Wisdom! *And we*, Give the blessing.
Priest. Blessed be Christ our God . . . .
Choir. Amen. Stablish, O God . . . .
Priest, holding the honourable Cross, Christ is risen . . . .
Choir. And on those within the tombs. . . .

And the Priest saith the Dismissal.

HE that arose from the dead, and trampled down death by death, and bestowed life

to them that were in the graves, Christ our
true God . . . .
Then, raising the Cross, he saith,
Christ is risen! *thrice.*
And we answer,
He is risen indeed! *thrice.*
And we sing in conclusion,
Christ is risen from the dead . . . . *thrice,*
adding,

TO us also hath he granted life everlasting.
Let us then bow down to his Resurrec-
tion on the third day.
And we kiss the honourable Cross.

THE HOURS ON HOLY PASCHA, AND THROUGHOUT THE BRIGHT WEEK.

The Priest beginneth, Blessed be our God,
always, now and ever, and to ages of ages.
And we answer, Amen.
And sing,
Christ is risen from the dead . . . . *thrice.*
Also we sing in Tone 7.
Having seen the Resurrection of Christ....
Vide page 28.
And the Hypacoë in Tone 4.
They who came with Mary . . . . *Vide
page* 382.

And the Condakion in Tone 8.

If into the tomb thou didst descend . . . .

Vide page 384.

Also these Troparia.

IN the tomb bodily, in hades with thy soul as God, in Paradise with the thief, and on the throne with the Father and the Spirit, wast thou, O Christ, unspeakably fulfilling all things.

Glory.

AS the receptacle of life, more beautiful than Paradise, and truly brighter than any kingly palace did thy tomb appear, O Christ, being the source of our Resurrection.

Both now. To the Virgin.

HAIL! sacred and divine abode of the Most High. For through thee, O Mother of God, joy is given to them that cry, Blessed art thou among women, O Lady most pure.

Then, Lord, have mercy, *forty times.*

Glory. Both now.

The more honourable than the Cherubim . . . .

In the name of the Lord, father, give the blessing.

Priest. Through the prayers of our holy Fathers . . . . *And we*, Amen.

And again we sing, Christ is risen . . . . *thrice.*

Glory. Both now. Lord, have mercy, *thrice.* Give the blessing.

And the Dismissal of the First Hour.

And on this wise are sung the Third, Sixth, and Ninth Hours ; also the Compline, and the Nocturns.

And if there should be no celebration of the Liturgy,

Instead of, Bless the Lord, O my soul .... *Vide page* 127, Christ is risen . . . . *thrice.* Having seen the Resurrection of Christ .... *once.*

Then, They who came with Mary . . . .

Glory. The Condakion, If into the tomb.... *Both now.*

Only-begotten Son . . . . *Vide page* 127.

And, with the Beatitudes, verses from the Paschal Canon.

The Lection from the Acts of the Apostles. Section 1.

THE former treatise have I made, O Theophilus, of all that Jesus began both to do and to teach, until the day in which he was taken up, after that he through the Holy Ghost had given commandments unto the Apostles whom he had chosen. To whom also he shewed himself alive after his passion by many infallible proofs, being seen of them forty days, and speaking of the things pertaining to the kingdom of God. And, being assembled together with them, commanded them that they should not depart from Jerusalem, but wait for the promise of the Father, which, saith he, ye have heard of me. For John truly baptized with water; but ye shall be baptized with the Holy Ghost not many days hence. When they therefore were come together, they asked of him, saying, Lord, wilt thou at this time restore again the kingdom to Israel? And he said unto them, It is not for you to know the times or the seasons, which the Father hath put in his own power. But ye shall receive power, after that the Holy Ghost is come upon you, and ye shall be witnesses unto me both in Jerusalem, and in all Judæa, and in Samaria, and unto the uttermost parts of the earth.

The Lection from the holy Evangelist John. Section I.

IN the beginning was the Word, and the Word was with God, and the Word was God. The same was in the beginning with God. All things were made by him; and without him was not anything made that was made. In him was life, and the life was the light of men. And the light shineth in darkness, and the darkness comprehended it not. There was a man sent from God, whose name was John. The same came for a witness, to bear witness of the Light, that all men through him might believe. He was not that Light, but was sent to bear witness of that Light. That was the true Light, which lighteth every man that cometh into the world. He was in the world, and the world was made by him, and the world knew him not. He came unto his own, and his own received him not. But as many as received him, to them gave he power to become the sons of God, even to them that believe on his name, which were born, not of blood, nor of the will of the flesh, nor of the will of man, but of God. And the Word was made flesh, and dwelt among us, and we beheld his glory, the glory as of the only-begotten of the Father, full of grace and truth. John bare witness of him, and cried, saying, This was he of whom I spake, He that cometh after me is preferred before me; for he was before me. And of his fulness have we all received, and grace for grace. For the law was given by Moses, but grace and truth came by Jesus Christ.

Then, Remember us, O Lord . . . . *And*, The heavenly Choir . . . . *The Confession*

of Faith. O God, remit and pardon . . . .
After Our Father . . . . *The Condakion,* If
into the tomb . . . . Lord, have mercy, *forty
times.*

Then, One holy, one Lord Jesus Christ,
to the glory of God the Father. Amen. *And,
instead of* Blessed be the name of the
Lord . . . . Christ is risen . . . . *thrice.*

And Psalm 33 (34).

I will bless the Lord at all times . . . .
ending, shall not want any good thing.

And the Dismissal.

AT VESPERS ON HOLY PASCHA.

The Priest beginneth, Glory to the holy,
consubstantial . . . . *And we answer,* Amen.

And sing as at Matins.

Thy Resurrection, O Saviour Christ . . . .

Also, Christ is risen . . . . *with the verses.*

*Then followeth the Ectenia of Peace, after
which we sing in Tone* 2.

LORD, I have cried unto thee, hear
me. Hear me, O Lord.
            Lord, 1 have cried unto thee, hear
me : attend to the voice of my prayer when
I cry unto thee. Hear me, O Lord.

Let my prayer be set forth before thee as

incense, the lifting up of my hands as the evening sacrifice. Hear me, O Lord.

Stichera on the Resurrection.

COME, let us worship God the Word incarnate of the Virgin Mary, who was begotten of the Father from eternity; for of his own will he bore the Cross, and was committed to the grave, and, having risen from the dead, hath saved me, an erring man.

Verse. For thy name's sake have I waited for thee, O Lord: my soul hath waited for thy word, my soul hath trusted in the Lord.

OUR Saviour Christ, nailed on the Cross, hath blotted out the handwriting against us, and destroyed the might of death. Let us then bow down to his Resurrection on the third day.

Verse. From the morning watch until night, from the morning watch let Israel trust in the Lord.

WITH Angels let us sing Christ's Resurrection, for he is our Redeemer and the Saviour of our souls. And he shall come again in fearful glory and resistless power to judge the world which he hath made.

Verse. For with the Lord is mercy, and with him is plenteous redemption, and he shall redeem Israel from all his transgressions.

O LORD, an Angel told thine incarnation and thy burial, and said unto the women, Come, see ye where the Lord was laid, but, as Almighty, he is risen, according as he said. Therefore we worship him who only is immortal. O Christ, Giver of life, have mercy on us.

Verse. Praise the Lord, all ye nations, praise him, all ye peoples.

BY thy Cross thou hast done away the curse of the tree, by thy Burial thou hast slain the might of death, and by thy Resurrection hast enlightened men. Therefore we cry to thee, O bountiful Christ our God, glory to thee.

Verse. For his mercy is confirmed upon us, and the truth of the Lord remaineth for ever.

O LORD, the gates of death opened unto thee with fear, and the warders of hades seeing thee were terrified; for thou didst shatter the gates of brass and break the iron bars, and lead us out of darkness and the shades of death, and burst our bonds in sunder. *Glory.*

LET us tune our lips to sing the hymn of our salvation. Come, let us all fall

26

down in the house of the Lord and say, Thou that wast crucified upon the tree, hast risen from the dead, and art in the bosom of the Father, be gracious to us sinners.

Both now. To the Virgin.

THE shadow of the law is passed away and grace hath come. For as the burning bush was not consumed, so the Virgin hath brought forth and Virgin doth remain. Instead of the fiery pillar ariseth the Sun of righteousness, instead of Moses, Christ, the Salvation of our souls.

Then the Tranquil Light.

And the Prokimenon in Tone 7.

WHO is so great a God as our God? Thou art the God that alone doest wonders.

Verse. Thou hast made known thy power among the people.

Verse. And I said, Now am I subdued: this is the change wrought by the right hand of the Most High.

Verse. I have remembered the works of the Lord, and called to mind thy wonders of old time.

The Lection from the holy Evangelist John.

When therefore it was evening .... *ending*, I will not believe. *Chap.* xx. 19—25.

Then the Ectenia, Let us all say with our whole soul . . . . *Vide page* 10.

The Prayer.

Vouchsafe, O Lord . . . . *Vide page* 11.

And the Ectenia, Let us accomplish our evening prayer . . . . *Vide page* 12.

And after the Exclamation concluding the latter we sing in Tone 2.

THY Resurrection, O Saviour Christ, hath enlightened all the world, and restored it to its first estate. O Lord almighty, glory to thee.

Then the Stichera of Pascha as at Matins. Vide page 388.

Then the Prayer of S. Simeon.

Lord, now lettest thou thy servant depart . . . . *And the rest, concluding Vespers as indicated at page* 44.

ON THE SUNDAY OF THE APOSTLE THOMAS.

Troparion.   Tone 7.

THOUGH the tomb was sealed, yet didst thou shine as life from the grave, O Christ our God. And, though the doors were closed, thou, the Redeemer of all, didst appear unto thy Disciples, and, through them, according to thy great mercy, renewest the right spirit in us.

Condakion. *Tone* 8.

WITH curious hand Thomas reached unto thy life-giving side, O Christ our God; yet, when through closed doors thou didst pass, the same, with the other Apostles, cried unto thee, Thou art my Lord and God.

Magnifying.

WE magnify thee, O Christ, Giver of life, who for our sake wentest down into hades, and with thyself didst raise all things.

ON THE SUNDAY OF THE MYRRH-BEARING WOMEN.

The Troparion on the Resurrection in Tone 2.

Glory. The honourable Joseph, taking down thy most pure Body from the tree, wrapped it in pure fine linen with sweet spices, and placed and closed it in a new tomb, but on the third day thou didst arise, O Lord, granting great mercy to the world.

Both now.

The Angel, appearing before the myrrh-bearing women at the sepulchre, cried, Myrrh is fitting for the dead, but Christ hath appeared free from corruption. But say ye,

The Lord is risen, granting great mercy to the world.

Condakion. Tone 2.

O CHRIST our God, thou didst command the myrrh - bearing women to rejoice, thou didst quench the wail of our mother Eve by thy Resurrection, and didst command thine Apostles to preach, The Saviour is risen from the tomb.

ON THE SUNDAY OF THE PARALYTIC.

The Troparion on the Resurrection in Tone 3, with its Verse to the Virgin.

Condakion. Tone 3.

O LORD, by thy divine presence, raise my soul grievously paralyzed by all kinds of sin and improper deeds, as of old thou didst raise the Paralytic, that, being saved, I may cry unto thee, O bountiful Christ, glory to thy might.

ON THE WEDNESDAY OF MID-PENTECOST.

Troparion. Tone 8.

THE Mid-feast having come, O Saviour, do thou nourish my thirsty soul with the waters of piety; for unto all thou hast said, Let him that thirsteth come unto me and drink. O Christ our God, the Fountain of life, glory to thee.

Condakion. Tone 4.

O CHRIST our God, about the middle of the feast of the law, thou, the Creator and Lord of all, didst say to them that stood around thee, Come, and draw the water of immortality. Therefore do we fall down before thee and faithfully exclaim, Grant thy bounties unto us, for thou art the Fountain of life.

ON THE SUNDAY OF THE SAMARITAN WOMAN.

The Troparion on the Resurrection in Tone 4, *and that of Mid-Pentecost.*

Condakion. Tone 8.

COMING in faith to the well, the woman of Samaria beheld thee, the Water of wisdom, of which having plentifully quaffed, she inherited eternally the kingdom above, ever being glorified.

ON THE SUNDAY OF THE BLIND MAN.

The Troparion on the Resurrection in Tone 5 *with its Verse to the Virgin.*

Condakion. Tone 4.

WITH blinded spiritual eyes I come to thee, O Christ, as the one blind from birth, and penitentially I cry to thee, Thou art the most bright Light of them that are in darkness.

ON THE WEDNESDAY BEFORE THE ASCENSION.

NOTE:—*To-day Holy Pascha endeth.*

Troparion. Ye faithful, come . . . .

To the Virgin. Hail! impassable gate . . . .

Condakion. With blinded spiritual eyes . . . .
As on the preceding Sunday.

And the Condakion of Holy Pascha. If into the tomb thou didst descend . . . . *Vide page* 384.

ON THE THURSDAY OF THE ASCENSION OF OUR LORD JESUS CHRIST.

Troparion. Tone 4.

THOU hast ascended in glory, O Christ our God, having made thy Disciples joyful by the promise of the Holy Ghost, they being informed thereof by the blessing; for thou art the Son of God, the Redeemer of the world.

Condakion. Tone 6.

HAVING accomplished thy dispensation for us, and united things on earth with those in heaven, thou didst ascend in glory, O Christ our God, in nowise forsaking them that love thee, but always abiding with them, and saying unto them, I am with you, and no one is against you.

Magnifying,

WE magnify thee, O Christ, Giver of life, and reverence thy divine Ascension into heaven with thy most pure Flesh.

Antiphons at Liturgy.

I. O clap your hands together, all ye nations, shout unto God with the voice of melody.

God is gone up with a merry noise, the Lord with the sound of the trumpet.

Glory. Both now.

And, after each verse, Through the prayers of the Mother of God, O Saviour, save us.

II. Great is the Lord, and exceeding great his praise, in the city of our God, in his holy mountain.

Beautiful for situation, the joy of the whole earth is Mount Sion, on the side of the north lieth the city of the great King.

And, after each verse,

O Son of God, who in glory didst ascend into heaven for us, save us who sing to thee, Alleluia.

Glory. Both now.

Only-begotten Son • . . . *Vide page* 127.

III. O hear ye this, all ye people; ponder it with your ears, all ye that dwell in the world.

I will incline mine ear to a parable, I will utter dark sayings upon the psaltery.

And, after each verse the Troparion, Thou hast ascended . . . .

Introit.

GOD is gone up with a merry noise, the Lord with the sound of the trumpet. O Son of God, who in glory didst ascend into heaven for us, save us who sing to thee, Alleluia.

Prokimenon.

BE thou exalted, O God, above the heavens, and thy glory over all the earth.

Verse. O God, my heart is ready, my heart is ready, I will give praise and sing in my glory.

Irmos of Ode 9, with Refrain.

MAGNIFY, my soul, the Ascension from earth to heaven of Christ, the Giver of life.

Thee, that above understanding and word art the Mother of God, and didst unspeakably bring forth in time the Timeless One, with one accord we faithful magnify.

Communion Hymn.

GOD is gone up with a merry noise, the Lord with the sound of the trumpet. Alleluia, alleluia, alleluia.

ON THE SIXTH SUNDAY AFTER PASCHA,

We sing the Office of the 318 *God-bearing Fathers of the First Ecumenical Synod of Nicæa.*

The Troparion on the Resurrection in Tone 6, *and that for the Fathers in the same Tone.*

OST glorified art thou, O Christ our God, who didst establish our Fathers as lights upon the earth, and by them hast guided us all in the true faith. O most Merciful One, glory to thee.

And the Troparion on the Ascension.

Thou hast ascended in glory . . . .

Condakion. Tone 8.

THE preaching of the Apostles and the doctrines of the Fathers have sealed the one faith of the Church, which, wearing the vestment of truth woven of divinity from above, regulateth and glorifieth the great mystery of piety.

NOTE : — *The Friday before Pentecost is the Octave of the Ascension, and the Office of this Festival is sung.*

ON THE SATURDAY BEFORE PENTECOST.

We celebrate the memory of our fathers and brethren who in time past have fallen asleep.

The Troparion &c. is as on the Saturday of Meat Fare. Vide page 261.

ON THE SUNDAY OF HOLY PENTECOST.

Stichera at the Great Vespers with the Lord, I have cried *in Tone* I.

WE celebrate the Pentecost, and the coming of the Spirit, the accomplishment of promise, and the fulfilment of our hope, and the mystery as great as it is reverend; and therefore cry to thee, Creator of all things, glory to thee, O Lord.

Glory. Both now.

COME, ye people, and let us worship the Godhead in three Persons, the Son in the Father, with the Holy Ghost. For the Father before all time begat the Son, co-eternal and co-throned, and the Holy Ghost was in the Father, glorified with the Son, one Might, one Substance, one Divinity, adoring which we all exclaim, Holy God art thou, who madest all things by the Son, through the co-operation of the Holy Ghost. Holy and mighty thou, through whom we know the Father and the Holy Spirit sojourned in the world. Holy and immortal thou, O Spirit Paraclete, proceeding from the Father and resting in the Son. O holy Trinity, glory to thee.

Troparion. Tone 8.

BLESSED art thou, O Christ our God, who madest the fishers wise, sending the Holy Ghost on them, and by them netting all the world. Glory to thee, O Lover of mankind.

Magnifying.

WE magnify thee, O Christ, Giver of life, and honour thy most holy Spirit, whom from the Father thou didst send unto thy divine Disciples.

Irmi of the Canon. Tone 7.

I. He that smiteth the enemies with uplifted hand covered Pharao and his chariots with the sea. Let us therefore sing to him, for he hath been glorified.

III. Thou saidst, O Christ, to thy Disciples, Abide ye in Jerusalem until ye be endued with power from on high; and I will send to you another Paraclete, like to myself, mine and my Father's Spirit, in whom ye shall be stablished.]

Kathisma. Tone 8.

THE lovers of the Saviour were filled with joy, and they who erst were cowards became bold, when to-day the Holy Ghost descended from on high upon the house of the Disciples, and they spake each to the nations in his several wise. For the tongues were divided in likeness as of fire, and them they burned not, but rather did bedew.

IV. Foreseeing thine advent from afar, O Christ, the Prophet cried, I have heard the greatness of thy might, O Lord; for thou hast come to save all thine anointed ones.

V. The spirit of salvation, conceived in fear, O Lord, within the Prophets, and brought to birth on earth, stablisheth the Apostles' hearts, and in the faithful straight-way is renewed; for light and peace are thy commands.

VI. Sick with the surge of worldly cares and sinking in the waves of sin, cast to the soul-destroying beast, like Jonas, Christ, I cry to thee, O save me from the depth that bringeth death.

Condakion. Tone 8.

WHEN the Highest descending confounded the tongues, then did he scatter the nations; and when he distributed the fiery tongues, then did he call all men to unity, and we glorify in harmony the most holy Spirit.

VII. Flung into the fiery furnace, the holy Children changed the flame to dew with hymns as thus they sang, Blessed art thou, O Lord, the God of our fathers.

VIII. The unburnt bush in Sinai shewed God to Moses, the slow of speech and harsh of tongue; and divine fervour made the Children three invincible singers in the furnace. O all ye works of the Lord, sing ye the Lord, and set him up for ever.

IX. Hail! thou, O Queen, most glorious Virgin Mother. For no well-speaking eloquent lips can worthily extol thee, and every mind is at a loss to understand thy bringing forth. Wherefore with one accord we glorify thee.

Stichera with the Psalms of Praise.

Tone 4.

TO-DAY all nations beheld wondrous things in David's city, when the Holy Ghost came down in fiery tongues, as the divinely speaking Luke relateth. For he saith, When Christ's Disciples were assembled, there came a sound as of a mighty rushing wind, and filled the house where they were sitting, and all began to speak, in strange tongues, doctrines strange and teachings strange of the holy Trinity.

Glory. Both now. Tone 6.

O HEAVENLY King, O Paraclete, the Spirit of truth, that art everywhere present and that fillest all things, that art the Treasury of blessings and the Giver of life;

come, and make thine abode in us, and
cleanse us from every defilement, and save
our souls, O Blessed One.

ON THE SUNDAY OF ALL SAINTS.

*The Troparion on the Resurrection in Tone 8,
and that for the Saints in Tone 4.*

THY Church adorned with the blood
of thy Martyrs in all the world as
with purple and fine linen, through
them crieth unto thee, O Christ our God,
Send down thy bounties upon thy people,
grant peace to thine estate, and great mercy
to our souls.

To the Virgin. Tone 4.

THE mystery hidden from eternity and unknown to the Angels is made manifest
through thee, O Mother of God, to them that
are on earth; for God, leaving not the Unity,
was incarnate, and suffered on the Cross for
our sake of his own goodwill, and thereby
raising the first-created man, delivered our
souls from death.

Condakion. Tone 6.

TO thee, O Lord, the Author of creation,
the world bringeth the God bearing Martyrs as the first-fruits of nature. At their
intercessions, through the Mother of God,

preserve, O most Merciful One, thy Church and thine estate in perfect peace.

NOTE:—*After to-day beginneth the Fast of the Apostles, which continueth until June* 29, *even until the Commemoration of the Apostles Peter and Paul.*

XXII. TROPARIA ETC. ON THE RE-SURRECTION IN THE EIGHT TONES FOR SUNDAYS.

———◦———

NOTE:— *These Troparia &c. are sung successively on Sundays, beginning on the Sunday following that of All Saints.*

TONE I.

Troparion.

THOUGH the stone was sealed by the Jews and the soldiers guarded thy precious Body, yet didst thou arise on the third day, O Saviour, granting life unto the world. Therefore did the heavenly Hosts cry unto thee, the Life-giver, Glory to thy Resurrection, O Christ! Glory

27

to thy Kingdom! Glory to thy Dispensation, thou who alone lovest mankind.

To the Virgin.

WHEN Gabriel bade thee, Virgin, Hail! then was the Lord of all incarnate made in thee, as in a sacred ark, according to the words of righteous David; and wider than the heavens didst thou become when bearing thy Creator. Glory to him who dwelt in thee! Glory to him who came from thee! Glory to him who by his birth delivered us from bondage.

Hypacoë.

THE penitence of the thief opened Paradise, the lamentation of the myrrh-bearing women announced joy; for Christ God is risen, granting great mercy to the world.

Condakion.

O GOD, thou didst arise from the grave in glory, and didst raise the world with thee. Then doth human nature extol thee as God, and death hath vanished, and Adam, O Lord, rejoiceth, while Eve, freed from her bonds, is exceeding glad and crieth, Thou art the Christ, who givest resurrection unto all.

TONE 2.

Troparion.

WHEN thou, the Living, the Immortal, didst condescend unto death, then didst thou slay hades by the light of thy Godhead. And when thou didst raise the dead from the lowermost parts of the earth, all the heavenly Hosts cried, O Christ, Giver of life, our God, glory to thee.

To the Virgin.

MOST glorious and above understanding are thy mysteries, O Mother of God; for, spotless and virgin, thou art acknowledged a true Mother, who didst bear the true God. Pray unto him to save our souls.

Hypacoë.

AFTER thy Passion the women went to the tomb to anoint thy Body, O Christ our God, and they saw Angels in the grave and were amazed; for they heard these say, The Lord is risen, granting great mercy to the world.

Condakion.

THOU didst arise from the grave, O all-powerful Saviour, and hades, beholding the miracle, quaked, and the dead rose again. Creation, seeing this, rejoiceth with thee, and Adam is exceeding glad, and the world extolleth thee, my Saviour, for ever.

27*

TONE 3.

Troparion.

LET the heavens rejoice and let the earth be glad; for the Lord hath stablished his power by his arm, having trampled down death by death and become the First-born from the dead, delivering us from the depths of hades, and granting great mercy to the world.

To the Virgin.

WE hymn thee, O Virgin Mother of God, who dost advocate the salvation of our race; for in the flesh taken from thee thy Son and our God suffered passion on the Cross, and, as Lover of mankind, delivered us from death.

Hypacoë.

OF vision amazing, but of gentle words as dew, the shining Angel saith to the myrrh - bearing women, Why seek ye the Living in the tombs? He is risen and hath emptied the tombs. The Unchangeable hath changed corruption. Then say unto God, How fearful are thy works; for thou hast saved the race of men.

Condakion.

TO-DAY, O Bountiful One, thou didst arise from the grave and lead us away from

the gates of death. To-day Adam rejoiceth
and Eve is exceeding glad, and all the Prophets and Patriarchs unceasingly extol the
divine might of thy kingdom.

TONE 4.

Troparion.

THE women-disciples of the Lord, having received from the Angel the joyful gospel of the resurrection, and
cast away the curse of the forefathers, cried
to the Apostles, Death is overthrown, and
Christ God hath risen, who giveth great
mercy to the world.

To the Virgin.

THE mystery hidden from eternity and unknown to Angels is made manifest through
thee, O Mother of God, to them that are
on earth; for God, leaving not the Unity,
was incarnate, and suffered on the Cross for
our sake of his own goodwill, and thereby
raising the first-created man, delivered our
souls from death.

Hypacoë.

HAVING first tidings of thy most glorious
Resurrection, the myrrh-bearing women,
O Christ, tell the Apostles that thou art
risen as God, and grantest great mercy to
the world.

Condakion.

MY Saviour and Redeemer, as God, hath delivered the earth-born from their bonds, and overthrown the gates of hades, and risen again, as Lord, on the third day.

TONE 5.
Troparion.

YE faithful, come, and hymn, and worship the Word, co-eternal with the Father and the Spirit, who was born of the Virgin for our salvation; for he willed to ascend the Cross in flesh, and to suffer death, and to raise the dead by his glorious Resurrection.

To the Virgin.

HAIL! impassable gate of the Lord. Hail! bulwark and protection of them that flee unto thee. Hail! untroubled haven, Mother Virgin, who didst bear thy God and Maker in flesh. Cease not to pray for them that hymn and reverence thy child-bearing.

Hypacoë.

AWED in mind at the angelic vision, and their souls enlightened by the divine Resurrection, the myrrh-bearing women told the Apostles the glad tidings, saying, Proclaim to the gentiles the Resurrection of the

Lord, who doeth wonders, and granteth great mercy unto us.

Condakion.

THOU didst go down to hades, O Saviour, and overthrow the gates by thy great power. Thou didst, as Creator, raise the dead and destroy the sting of death, and Adam is saved from the curse, O Lover of mankind. Wherefore we cry unto thee, Save us, O Lord.

TONE 6.

Troparion.

ANGELIC powers are at thy tomb, and the guards are deadened, and Mary standeth at the grave seeking thy most pure Body. Thou madest hades captive, not being tempted by it. Thou didst meet the Virgin, and grantest life. O risen Lord, glory to thee.

To the Virgin.

THOU, who didst call thy Mother blessed, of thine own will camest to suffer, and shining on the Cross that thou mightest bring back Adam, telledst the Angels, Rejoice with me, for the lost drachma is found. O God, who in wisdom hast made all things, glory to thee.

Hypacoë.

O CHRIST, by thy voluntary and life-effecting death, thou didst, as God, overthrow the gates of hades, and open unto us the ancient Paradise, and, risen from the dead, hast saved our life from corruption.

Condakion.

CHRIST God, the Giver of life, hath raised the dead from the dark abodes by his quickening hand, and granted resurrection to the human race; for he is the Saviour, Resurrection, Life, and God of all.

TONE 7.

Troparion.

THOU hast destroyed death by thy Cross, thou hast opened Paradise to the thief, thou hast stopped the lamentation of the myrrh-bearing women, and commanded thine Apostles to preach; for thou hast risen, Christ our God, granting great mercy to the world.

To the Virgin.

AS the treasury of our Resurrection, do thou, O all-hymned Virgin, raise us out of the pit and depth of sin; for thou hast saved them that were under the curse of sin, having borne our salvation, thou who before bearing wast Virgin, and in bearing wast Virgin, and after bearing ever abidest Virgin.

Hypacoë.

THOU that didst take upon thyself the form of man, and in thy Body didst endure the Cross, save me by thy Resurrection, O Christ our God, the Lover of mankind.

Condakion.

NO longer may the might of death hold man, for Christ hath come, destroying and scattering its powers Hades is held bound, the Prophets joyfully with one accord exclaim, The Saviour of the faithful hath appeared: come ye then to the Resurrection.

TONE 8.

Troparion.

THOU didst descend from on high, O Bountiful One, thou didst submit to the three days' burial that thou mightest deliver us from passions. O Life and Resurrection, Lord, glory to thee.

To the Virgin.

O THOU good Lord, who, for our sake, wast born of the Virgin, didst suffer crucifixion, overcome death by death, and rise again as God; reject not us, the work of thine hands: shew thy loving-kindness unto us, O Merciful One; hearken unto thy holy Mother praying for us, and save, O Saviour, thy despairing people.

Hypacoë.

THE myrrh-bearing women stood at the grave of the Life-giver, seeking the immortal Lord among the dead, and receiving from the Angel the glad tidings of joy, they proclaimed to the Apostles that Christ God is risen, giving great mercy to the world.

Condakion.

HAVING risen from the tomb, thou didst raise the dead and lift up Adam, and Eve rejoiceth in thy Resurrection, and the ends of the earth celebrate thine Arising, O most Merciful One.

XXIII. TROPARIA ETC. FOR WEEK DAYS.

Troparion. Tone 4.

WE unworthy ones pray you, O Leaders of the heavenly Hosts, by your prayers to cover us with the protection of the wings of your immaterial glory, preserving us who come to you and earnestly exclaim, Deliver us from sorrows, ye Principals of the Powers above.

To the Virgin.

TO her who was brought up in the Temple for the Holy of holies, to her who was endued with faith, wisdom and perpetual virginity, the Archangel Gabriel brought from heaven greeting and hail. Hail! blessed one. Hail! most glorified one. The Lord is with thee.

Condakion. Tone 2.

O ARCHANGELS of God, Ministers of
divine glory, Princes among the Angels
and Instructors of men; ask for what is
profitable for us, and for much mercy, ye
Leaders of the immaterial Hosts.

ON TUESDAYS. TO THE FORERUNNER.

Troparion. Tone 2.

THE memory of the just is blessed,
but for thee, O Baptist, the Lord's
testimony sufficeth; for thou hast appeared to be verily the most honourable of
the Prophets, in that thou wast blessed to
baptize in the waters him whom thou didst
preach. And, having joyfully suffered for
the truth, thou didst announce, even to them
in hades, God manifest in flesh, who taketh
away the sins of the world and granteth
great mercy unto us.

To the Virgin.

WE have been made partakers of the divine nature through thee, O ever-virgin
Mother of God; for thou didst bring forth
for us incarnate God. Therefore, as is meet,
with reverence we magnify thee.

Condakion. Tone 3.

SHE that afore was barren to-day beareth
Christ's Forerunner, and in him doth end

all prophecy; for, having in the Jordan laid
his hands on him whom Prophets preached
of old, he is revealed of God the Word the
Prophet, Preacher, and Forerunner.

ON WEDNESDAYS. TO THE MOTHER OF GOD AT THE CROSS.

Troparion. Tone 1.

O Lord, save thy people and bless thine
inheritance . . . . *Vide page* 52.

To the Virgin at the Cross.

HAVING thy mediation, most pure one,
and delivered by thy prayers from dangers, and preserved in all things by the
Cross of thy Son, with reverence, as is meet,
we all do magnify thee.

Condakion. Tone 4.

Thou that wast of thy own will raised
upon the Cross . . . . *Vide page* 52.

ON THURSDAYS. TO THE APOSTLES, AND TO NICOLAS THE WONDERWORKER.

Troparion to the Apostles. Tone 3.

 HOLY Apostles, pray unto the merciful God that he may grant our souls
remission of sins.

Troparion to Nicolas.   Tone 4.

THE Truth hath made thee a standard of
faith, a pattern of meekness, and a
teacher of temperance to thy flock. Thus
didst thou, O holy priestly Father Nicolas,
by humiliation acquire greatness, by thy
poverty, riches. Pray Christ our God to save
our souls.

To the Virgin.

THE Word of the Father, Christ our God,
we acknowledge was made flesh of thee,
O Virgin Mother of God, who alone art
pure, alone art blessed. Therefore without
ceasing we sing and magnify thee.

Condakion to the Apostles.   Tone 2.

O LORD, thou hast received those steadfast and divinely inspired Preachers, the
chiefest of Apostles, into the enjoyment of
thy blessings and rest; for thou hast accepted
their sufferings and death as more than
any sacrifice, thou that alone knowest the
hearts.

Condakion to Nicolas.   Tone 3.

O HOLY Nicolas, thou didst appear in
Myra as a wonderworker; for, having
fulfilled the gospel of Christ, thou didst lay
down thy life for thy people, and didst save
the innocent from death. Therefore art thou

sanctified as a great treasury of the grace of God.

ON FRIDAYS. TO THE HOLY CROSS.

Troparion &c. as on Wednesdays.

ON SATURDAYS. TO ALL SAINTS, AND FOR THE DEPARTED.

Troparion to All Saints. Tone 2.

APOSTLES, Martyrs, Prophets, Divines, Venerables and Just, who have done a good work, kept the faith, and have daring with the Saviour; pray for us to him, the Blessed One, to save our souls.

Troparion for the Departed. Tone 8.

REMEMBER, O Lord, for thou art good, all thy servants, and forgive them all their sins throughout life; for there is none sinless save thee, who art able to give rest unto the departed.

To the Virgin.

O HOLY Mother of the unapproachable Light, with angelic hymns we honour thee, and reverently we magnify thee.

Condakion for the Departed. Tone 8.

O CHRIST, rest the souls of thy servants with the Saints, where there is no sickness, nor sorrow, nor lamentation, but life everlasting.

Condakion to All Saints.   Tone 8.

TO thee, O Lord, the Author of creation, the world bringeth the God-bearing Martyrs, as the first-fruits of nature. At their intercessions, through the Mother of God, preserve, O most Merciful One, thy Church and thine estate in perfect peace.

XXIV. TROPARIA ETC. FOR THE FESTIVALS OF THE LORD AND OF THE HOLY MOTHER OF GOD, AND FOR SOME OTHERS THROUGHOUT THE YEAR.

SEP. 8, THE NATIVITY OF OUR MOST HOLY LADY, THE MOTHER OF GOD AND EVER-VIRGIN MARY.

Troparion. Tone 4.

THY Nativity, O Virgin Mother of God, hath brought gladness to the whole universe; for from thee Christ our God, the Sun of righteousness, hath shone, who, having destroyed the curse, giveth us blessings, and, having put away death, giveth us life everlasting.

Condakion. Tone 4.

BY thy holy Nativity, O most pure one, Joakim and Anna were freed from the reproach of barrenness and Eve from deadly corruption. Thy people also celebrate the same, being thereby delivered from the punishment of sin, and cry to thee, The barren parents bear the Mother of God, the nourisher of our life.

Magnifying.

WE magnify thee, most holy Virgin, and honour thy holy Parents, and glorify thy most glorious Nativity.

Prokimenon as on Wednesdays. Vide page 145.

Irmos of Ode 9, *with Refrain.*

MAGNIFY, my soul, the most glorious Birth of the Mother of God.

Wonderful is a virgin-mother, and strange a maiden giving birth; but yet in thee, O Mother of God, were both fulfilled. Therefore we all of earthly race cease not to magnify thee.

Communion Hymn as on Wednesdays. Vide page 159.

SEP. 14. THE EXALTATION OF THE HON-
OURABLE AND LIFE-EFFECTING CROSS.

*Troparion and Condakion as on Wednes-
days. Vide page* 429.

Magnifying.

WE magnify thee, O Christ, Giver of life,
and honour thy holy Cross, by the
which thou hast saved us from the yoke of
the enemy.

Antiphons at Liturgy.

I. O God, my God, look upon me: why
hast thou forsaken me?

But thou dwellest in the holy place: thou
art the praise of Israel.

*Glory. Both now.
And, after each verse,*

Through the prayers of the Mother of
God, O Saviour, save us.

II. O God, why hast thou cast us off for
ever? why doth thine anger smoke against
the sheep of thy pasture?

But God is our King from ages, who hath
wrought salvation in the midst of the earth.

And, after each verse,

O Son of God, who in the flesh wast
crucified, save us who sing to thee, Alleluia.

Glory. Both now.

Only-begotten Son .... *Vide page* 127.

28*

III. The Lord reigneth, let the people tremble.

Bow yourselves before the Lord in his holy courts.

And, after each verse, the Troparion,

O Lord, save thy people, and bless . . . .

Introit.

EXALT ye the Lord our God, and worship at his footstool, for he is holy. O Son of God, who in the flesh wast crucified, save us who sing to thee, Alleluia.

Prokimenon. Exalt ye the Lord our God . . . . *as above. Verse.* The Lord reigneth, let the people tremble.

Irmos of Ode 9, with Refrain.

MAGNIFY, my soul, the Lord's most precious Cross.

O Mother of God, thou art the mystical Paradise, which, untilled, produced Christ, through whom on earth is planted that life-bearing tree, the Cross. Therefore this now exalted we adore, and thee we magnify.

Communion Hymn.

THE light of thy countenance hath been signed upon us, O Lord. Alleluia, alleluia, alleluia.

Dismissal.

CHRIST our true God, through the prayers of his all-pure Mother, through the might of his honourable and life-effecting Cross, through the intercessions of the holy, glorious, and all-praised Apostles . . . .

SEP. 26. THE DECEASE OF THE HOLY APOSTLE AND EVANGELIST, JOHN THE DIVINE.

Troparion. Tone 2.

APOSTLE beloved of Christ God, hasten to deliver a people that are without defence. He that accepted thee to rest upon his breast, accepteth thy falling down before him. Then pray him, O Divine, to disperse the gathering throng of heathen, and ask for us peace and great mercy.

Condakion. Tone 2.

WHO can tell thy mightiness, O virgin one? For thou art full of wonders, and pourest forth healings, and prayest for our souls, O Divine and Friend of Christ.

Magnifying.

WE magnify thee, O Apostle and Evangelist of Christ, John the Divine, and honour thine afflictions and toils, in the which thou didst labour for the gospel of Christ.

OCT. 1. THE PROTECTION OF OUR MOST
HOLY LADY, THE MOTHER OF GOD AND
EVER-VIRGIN MARY.

Troparion. Tone 4.

TO-DAY we faithful hold a joyful feast, being shadowed by thy presence, O Mother of God, and, looking on thy most pure icon, humbly say, Cover us with thine honourable protection, and deliver us from all evil, praying thy Son, Christ our God, to save our souls.

Condakion. Tone 3.

TO-DAY the Virgin is present in the Church, and with the companies of Saints invisibly prayeth unto God for us. Angels with Archbishops bow down, Apostles and Prophets exceedingly rejoice; for the Mother of God now supplicateth the eternal God for us.

NOV. 8. THE COUNCIL OF THE ARCH-
ANGEL MICHAEL, AND THE OTHER
HEAVENLY BODILESS HOSTS.

*Troparion and Condakion as on Mondays.
Vide pages* 427 *and* 428.|

Magnifyings.

WE magnify you, O ye Archangels and Angels, and all ye Hosts, ye Cherubim and ye Seraphim, glorifying the Lord.

We magnify you, O ye Archangels, ye Angels, ye Principalities, ye Virtues, ye Thrones, ye Dominations, ye Powers, ye Cherubim, and ye fearful Seraphim, praising the Lord.

NOV. 13. OUR FATHER IN THE SAINTS, JOHN CHRYSOSTOM, ARCHBISHOP OF CONSTANTINOPLE.

Troparion. Tone 8.

THE grace of thy mouth, shining forth like fire, hath enlightened the universe, hath offered the world treasures of liberality, and hath shewed to us the height of humility. And, as thou instructest us by thy words, Father John Chrysostom, pray Christ, the Word of God, to save our souls.

Condakion. Tone 6.

THOU didst receive divine grace from heaven, and by thy lips didst teach all men to worship one God in Trinity. O most blessed and venerable John Chrysostom, we praise thee who art worthy; for thou art our instructor, and explainest divine things.

Magnifying.

WE magnify thee, O divine Father John Chrysostom, and honour thine honourable memory; for thou prayest for us unto Christ our God.

NOV. 21. THE PRESENTATION IN THE
TEMPLE OF OUR MOST HOLY LADY, THE
MOTHER OF GOD AND EVER-VIRGIN
MARY.

Troparion. Tone 4.

T O-DAY is the foreshadowing of God's
goodwill, and the preaching of the
salvation of men; for the Virgin is
clearly seen in the Temple, and announceth
Christ unto all. Then let us cry aloud to
her, Hail! thou fulfilment of the Creator's
dispensation.

Condakion. Tone 4.

THE spotless dwelling of the Saviour, the
precious palace and Virgin, the sacred
treasury of God's glory is this day brought
into the house of the Lord, carrying there-
into with herself grace which is in the divine
Spirit, she, whom the Angels of God sing,
This is the heavenly abode.

Magnifying.

WE magnify thee, O most holy Virgin,
the God-chosen Maiden, and honour
thy Presentation in the Temple of the Lord.

*Prokimenon and Communion Hymn as on
Sep. 8th.*

Irmos of Ode 9, *with Refrain.*

MAGNIFY, my soul, her who is more honourable than the Hosts above, the most pure Virgin Mother of God.

Let hands defiled in nowise touch the spiritual ark of God; but let believing lips, ceaselessly singing the Angel's words, cry to the Mother of God with joy, Thou truly art higher than all things, Virgin pure.

NOV. 24. THE GREAT MARTYR KATHARINE.

Troparion. Tone 4.

WISE one, thou with virtues, as with rays of the sun, hast shone on them that had not faith, and, as a most bright moon, hast driven away darkness from them that walk in the night of unbelief; and thou, God-chosen Virgin, blessed Katharine, art assured of royalty and invested with martyrdom. Thou, with desire, art risen unto Christ, thy glorious Spouse, into the heavenly bridechamber, and by him art crowned with a royal crown; and with Angels thou standest before him, praying for us who keep thine honoured memory.

Condakion. Tone 2.

YE honourable choir that love the Martyrs, arouse ye now divinely to extol the all-wise Katharine; for in the arena she proclaimed Christ, treading the serpent down, and overcame the reasonings of the Orators.

Magnifying.

WE magnify thee, O holy and great Martyr Katharine, and honour thine honourable sufferings which thou hast borne for Christ's sake.

NOV. 30. THE APOSTLE ANDREW, THE FIRST-CALLED.

Troparion. Tone 4.

O ANDREW, First-called of the Apostles, and own brother of their Leader, pray the Lord of all to give peace to the world and great mercy to our souls.

Condakion. Tone 2.

WE extol him, called of God, whose name signifieth, Manly one, the first of the coming Church, Peter's near kinsman. For as in ancient time to this his brother, so now to us he saith, Come, we have found even him whom we desire.

Magnifying.

WE magnify thee, O First-called Apostle of Christ, Andrew, and honour thine afflictions and toils, in the which thou didst labour for the gospel of Christ.

DEC. 6. OUR FATHER IN THE SAINTS, NICOLAS, ARCHBISHOP OF MYRA.

Troparion and Condakion as on Thursdays. Vide page 430.

Magnifying.

WE magnify thee, O divine Father Nicolas, and honour thine honourable memory; for thou prayest for us unto Christ our God.

DEC. 25. THE NATIVITY OF OUR LORD, GOD, AND SAVIOUR JESUS CHRIST, COMMONLY CALLED, CHRISTMAS DAY.

Troparion. Tone 4.

O CHRIST our God, upon the world thy birth hath shined the light of knowledge; for at it they that served the stars were taught by a star to worship thee, the Sun of righteousness, and to know thee, the Dayspring from on high. Glory to thee, O Lord.

Magnifying.

WE magnify thee, O Christ, Giver of life, who now wast born in flesh for our sake of the unmarried and most pure Virgin Mary.

Sticheron in Tone 6 *at Matins after the Gospel.*

GLORY be to God on high, and on earth be peace. To-day doth Bethlehem re-

ceive him that sitteth ever with the Father.
To-day the Angels glorify, as God, the In-
fant born. Glory be to God on high, and
on earth be peace, goodwill to men.

Irmi of the Canon. Tone I.

I. Christ is born, him glorify. Christ from
heaven, go to greet him. Christ on earth,
be lifted up. Sing to the Lord, all the
whole earth, and in gladness praise him, O
ye nations; for he hath been glorified.

III. To the Son of the Father unspeakably begotten before the worlds, and of the
Virgin without seed incarnate late in time,
to Christ our God let us exclaim, Thou
who hast lifted up our horn, holy art thou,
O Lord.

Hypacoë. Tone 8.

O BABE, in manger lying, the heavens
brought to thee the first-fruits of the
gentiles, calling the Magi by a star. Not a
sceptre, nor a throne struck them with
astonishment, but thine utter poverty. For
what is humbler than a cave? What is
meaner than a swathe? And yet in these
the riches of thy Godhead clearly shone.
Glory to thee, O Lord.

IV. Rod of the root of Jesse, and flower
thereof, O Christ, thou from the Virgin hast
bloomed forth; and thou, the Praised One,

hast come from the thick shady mount, incarnate of a maid, O immaterial God. Glory to thy might, O Lord.

V. God of peace, Father of bounties, the Angel of thy great counsel thou hast sent, bringing us peace. And so we, led into divine wisdom's light, after night rising betimes, magnify thee, O Lover of mankind.

VI. As the sea-monster vomited from its entrails their contents, Jonas, as it took him in, so the Word, dwelling in the Virgin and assuming flesh from her, kept her unchanged as he passed through; for from that to which he was not subject he held her that bore him free.

Condakion. Tone 3.

TO-DAY the Virgin beareth him above all essence, and earth offereth the Inaccessible a cave. Angels with Shepherds glorify, and the Magi journey with the star. For our sake he hath been born a little Child he, God before the worlds.

VII. The Children reared in piety, the impious command despising, feared not the threat of fire; but, standing in the midst of flame, they sang, God of our fathers, blessed art thou.

VIII. The furnace shedding dew portrayed a type of wondrous portent, for it burned not the Youths whom it received. So too the fire of Godhead doth not burn that virgin womb which it hath entered. Therefore let us chant in song, Let all creation bless the Lord, and set him up for evermore.

IX. A mystery strange and wondrous I behold. The cave is heaven, the Virgin is the throne of Cherubim, the manger is the place where the Incomprehensible is laid, Christ our God, whom singing, we magnify.

Irmos of the Second Canon.

Content as free from risk, through awe
We easier silent be. But, Virgin, for the
    love of thee,
Urged on to weave harmonious songs,
Our task is hard. Then, Mother, strength,
Such as we need, bestow, and give the strain.

Stichera with the Psalms of Praise.

Tone 4.

BE glad, ye just; ye heavens, rejoice; ye mountains, leap; for Christ is born. The Virgin sitteth like the Cherubim, and beareth in her bosom God the Word made flesh. The Shepherds glorify the Child, the Magi bring the Lord their gifts, and Angels sing, Glory to thee, O uncontained God.

Glory. Both now.

Tone 2.

TO-DAY in Bethlehem of the Virgin Christ is born. To-day beginneth the Unbeginning, and the Word becometh flesh. The Hosts of heaven rejoice, and earth with men is glad. The Magi bring their gifts, the wonder Shepherds tell, and we unceasingly exclaim, Glory to God on high, and peace on earth, goodwill to men.

JAN. I. THE CIRCUMCISION OF OUR LORD JESUS CHRIST.

Troparion. Tone 1.

JESUS, thou that sittest on high on the light-bearing throne with thine unbeginning Father and thy divine Spirit, didst condescend to be born on earth of a Virgin, thy husbandless Mother, and wast accordingly circumcised as man on the eighth day. Glory then to thy good counsel! Glory to thy dispensation! Glory to thy condescension, thou that alone lovest mankind.

Condakion. Tone 3.

THE Lord of all submitteth to circumcision, and, in his goodness, circumciseth also the sins of men, and this day giveth salvation to the world. Then doth Basil, the Hierarch of the Creator and light-bearing Minister of Christ, rejoice on high.

Prokimenon at Liturgy as on a Sunday of Tone 6.

Communion Hymn as on Sundays.

JAN. 6. THE DIVINE MANIFESTATION OF OUR LORD, GOD, AND SAVIOUR, JESUS CHRIST, COMMONLY CALLED, THE EPIPHANY.

Troparion. Tone 1.

IN Jordan when thou wast baptized, O Lord, the worship of the Trinity was manifested. For the voice of the Father bare witness unto thee, calling thee the beloved Son, and the Spirit, in appearance as a dove, confirmed the truth of the words. Thou who wast manifested, Christ our God, and enlightenedst the world, glory to thee.

Hypacoë after Ode III. Tone 2.

WHEN all things thou enlightenedst by thine Epiphany, then fled the sea of unbelief, and Jordan turned back its streams, raising us to heaven. Then, through the intercessions of the Mother of God, preserve us on the wave of thy divine commandments, O Christ our God, and save us.

Condakion. *Tone* 4.

TO-DAY, O Lord, thou didst manifest thyself to all the world, and thy light hath come upon us who in understanding sing to thee, Thou didst come, thou didst appear, O Light inaccessible.

Magnifying.

WE magnify thee, O Christ, Giver of life, who now hast been baptized in flesh by John in the waters of Jordan for our sake.

JAN. 30. OUR FATHERS IN THE SAINTS, THE THREE DIVINES, BASIL THE GREAT, GREGORY THE DIVINE, AND JOHN CHRYSOSTOM.

Troparion. *Tone* 1.

AS equals of the Apostles, and Teachers of the universe, pray the Lord of all to grant peace to the world and great mercy to our souls.

Condakion. *Tone* 2.

O LORD, thou hast received those priestly and divinely inspired Preachers, the chiefest of Teachers, into the enjoyment of thy blessings and rest; for thou hast accepted their sufferings and death as more than any sacrifice, thou that art glorified in the Saints.

FEB. 2.   THE   PRESENTATION   IN   THE
TEMPLE   OF   OUR   LORD   JESUS   CHRIST.

Troparion.   Tone I.

HAIL! Virgin Mother of God, full of
grace.   For from thee the Sun of
righteousness, Christ our God, hath
risen, enlightening them that are in darkness.
Rejoice thou also, O righteous Elder, who
didst receive in thine arms the Deliverer of
our souls, him that giveth resurrection
unto us.

Condakion.   Tone I.

THOU, O Christ our God, who by thy
birth didst sanctify the Virgin, and
blessedst, as was meet, the hands of Simeon,
didst purpose our salvation, and hast now
accomplished this.   Do thou, O Lover of
mankind, preserve thine estate from wars,
and strengthen the princes who have found
favour before thee.

Magnifying.

WE magnify thee, O Christ, Giver of life,
and honour thy most pure Mother, who
bringeth thee, according to the law, into the
Temple of the Lord.

Introit.

THE Lord hath declared his salvation: his
righteousness hath he openly shewed in

the sight of the heathen. O Son of God, who wast carried in the arms of righteous Simeon, save us who sing to thee, Alleluia.

Prokimenon and Communion Hymn as on Sep. 8th.

Irmos of Ode 9, with Refrain.

O GOD-BEARING Virgin, the hope of Christians, protect, watch, and save them that put their trust in thee.

In the law, in shadows, and in scripture we faithful see an image. Every male that openeth the womb is holy unto God. Therefore we magnify the first-begotten Word of the unbeginning Father, who is the first-begotten Son of the Mother unknown of man.

Dismissal.

HE that for our salvation vouchsafed to be carried in the arms of righteous Simeon, Christ our true God . . . .

MARCH 25. THE ANNUNCIATION OF OUR MOST HOLY LADY, THE MOTHER OF GOD.

Troparion. Tone 4.

TO-DAY is the crowning of our salvation, and the manifestation of the mystery which was from eternity. The Son of God becometh the Son of the Virgin, and Gabriel giveth the good tidings of grace. Then with him let us cry to the Mother of God, Hail! full of grace, the Lord is with thee.

Condakion. Tone 8.

TO thee, O Virgin, the chosen guide, thy servants sing a triumphal song, ascribing thanks to thee for the deliverance from evils, and since thou hast an invincible might, deliver us, we beseech thee, from every ill, that we may cry unto thee, Hail! O unmarried Bride.

Magnifying.

WE sing the Archangel's song to thee, O pure one, Hail! full of grace, the Lord is with thee.

Prokimenon.

PROCLAIM ye from day to day the salvation of our God. *Verse.* O sing unto the Lord a new song, sing unto the Lord, all the whole earth.

Irmos of Ode 9, with Refrain.

We sing the Archangel's . . . . *As above.*
Let hands defiled . . . . *Vide page* 441.

Communion Hymn.

The Lord hath elected Sion, he hath

chosen her as an habitation for himself.
Alleluia, alleluia, alleluia.

APRIL 23. THE GREAT MARTYR AND VICTORIOUS WONDERWORKER, GEORGE.

Troparion. Tone 2.

DELIVERER of captives, defender of the poor, physician of the sick, and champion of kings, O victorious and great Martyr George, pray Christ our God to save our souls.

Condakion. Tone 4.

HUSBANDED by God, thou hast appeared an honourable husbandman of piety, and hast gathered for thyself sheaves of virtues. Thou sowedst in tears and reapest in joy. Athlete, thou, through blood, art garnered unto Christ, and, by thy prayers, O Saint, gainest for all men forgiveness of sins.

Magnifying.

WE magnify thee, O holy and victorious great Martyr George, and honour thine honourable sufferings which thou hast borne for Christ's sake.

MAY 8. THE GLORIOUS AND ALL-PRAISED APOSTLE AND EVANGELIST, JOHN THE DIVINE.

Troparion, Condakion and Magnifying as on September 26. *Vide page* 437.

JUNE 24. THE NATIVITY OF THE HONOURABLE GLORIOUS PROPHET, FORERUNNER, AND BAPTIST JOHN.

Troparion. Tone 4.

PROPHET and Forerunner of the advent of Christ, we, lovingly honouring thee, are insufficient worthily to extol thee; for the barren bore thee, and a dumb father spake at thy glorious and honourable Birth, which declared to the world the incarnation of the Son of God.

Condakion. Tone 3.

SHE that afore was barren to-day beareth Christ's Forerunner, and in him doth end all prophecy; for having in the Jordan laid his hands on him whom Prophets preached of old, he is revealed of God the Word the Prophet, Preacher, and Forerunner.

Magnifying.

WE magnify thee, O John, Forerunner of the Saviour, and honour thy most glorious birth from a barren mother.

JUNE 29. THE GLORIOUS AND ALL-PRAISED LEADERS OF THE APOSTLES, PETER AND PAUL.

Troparion. Tone 4.

YE first-throned of the Apostles and Teachers of the universe, pray the Lord of all to grant peace to the world and great mercy to our souls.

Condakion. Tone 2.

O LORD, thou hast received those steadfast and divinely inspired Preachers, the chiefest of Apostles, into the enjoyment of thy blessings and rest; for thou hast accepted their sufferings and death as more than any sacrifice, thou that alone knowest the hearts.

Magnifying.

WE magnify you, O ye Apostles of Christ, who have enlightened all the world with your teachings, and have led all the ends of the earth unto Christ.

JULY 20. THE GLORIOUS PROPHET ELIAS.

Troparion. Tone 4.

THE incarnate Angel, the first of the Prophets and second Forerunner of the advent of Christ, even the glorious Elias, sent down from above grace upon

Elissæus, dispersed diseases and cleansed lepers. Therefore to them that honour him he is a fount of healing.

Condakion. Tone 2.

PROPHET and Foreseer of the mighty works of God, O famous Elias, whose voice forbade the clouds discharge the rain, entreat for us the only Lover of mankind.

AUG. 6. THE TRANSFIGURATION OF THE LORD.

Troparion. Tone 6.

THOU wast transfigured on the mountain, O Christ God, thereby shewing thy glory to thy Disciples as much as they could bear. O may thine everlasting light shine also upon us sinners, through the intercessions of the Mother of God. O Giver of light, glory to thee.

Condakion. Tone 6.

THOU wast transfigured on the mountain, O Christ God, and thy Disciples, as much as they could bear, beheld thy glory, that when they should see thee crucified, they might understand thy voluntary Passion, and preach to the world that thou art verily the Light of the Father.

Magnifying.

WE magnify thee, O Christ, Giver of life, and reverence the most glorious Transfiguration of thy most pure Flesh.

Antiphons at Liturgy.

I. Cry aloud unto the Lord, all the earth, sing unto his name, give glory to his praise.

Thou art invested with honour and majesty, who dost cloth thyself with light as with a garment.

Glory. Both now.

And, after each verse,

Through the prayers of the Mother of God, O Saviour, save us.

II. Beautiful for situation, the joy of the whole earth is mount Sion, on the side of the north lieth the city of the great King.

The hill of Sion which he loveth, and hath built, as an unicorn, for his sanctuary.

And, after each verse,

O Son of God, who wast transfigured on the mountain, save us who sing to thee, Alleluia.

Glory. Both now.

Only-begotten Son . . . . *Vide page* 127.

III. They that put their trust in the Lord shall be as mount Sion: they shall be immovable for ever who dwell at Jerusalem.

Who shall ascend into the hill of Sion?
or who shall stand in his holy place.

And, after each verse the Troparion,
Thou wast transfigured . . . .

Introit.

O LORD, send forth thy light and thy
truth: these shall lead me, and bring me
unto thy holy mountain. O Son of God,
who wast transfigured on mount Thabor,
save us who sing to thee, Alleluia.

Prokimenon.

HOW great are thy works, O Lord: in
wisdom hast thou made them all. *Verse.*
Bless the Lord, O my soul: O Lord my
God, thou art very great.

Irmos of Ode 9, with Refrain.

MAGNIFY, my soul, the Transfiguration
of the Lord on Thabor.
Thy giving-birth appeareth without stain.
God came forth from thee incarnate, appeared
on earth, and dwelt with men. Therefore,
O Mother of God, we magnify thee all.

Communion Hymn.

O LORD, in the light of thy countenance
shall we go forth, and in thy name rejoice for ever. Alleluia, alleluia, alleluia.

Dismissal.

HE that was transfigured in glory on mount Thabor before his holy Disciples and Apostles, Christ our true God . . . .

AUG. 15. THE REPOSE OF OUR MOST HOLY LADY, THE MOTHER OF GOD AND EVER-VIRGIN MARY.

Troparion. Tone 1.

O MOTHER of God, in thy child-birth thou didst retain thy virginity, in thy Repose thou didst not forsake the world. Thou hast passed away unto life, thyself being the Mother of Life, and, by thine intercessions, deliverest our souls from death.

Condakion. Tone 2.

THE grave and death could not retain the Mother of God, who is unceasing in prayers, and a strong trust in intercessions; for he who dwelt in the Ever-virgin hath taken away to life her who was the Mother of Life.

Magnifying.

WE magnify thee, O most spotless Mother of Christ our God, and glorify thy most glorious Repose.

Prokimenon and Communion Hymn as on Sep. 8th.

Irmos of Ode 9, with Refrain.

WHEN the Angels beheld the Repose of the all-pure one, they marvelled as virginity went up from earth to heaven.

The bounds of nature were overpast in thee, O pure Virgin; for virginity remained in child-bearing, and death was conjoined with life. After giving birth thou continuedst virgin, and after death continuest to live, ever saving, O Mother of God, them that are thine heritage.

AUG. 29. THE BEHEADING OF THE HON-
OURABLE GLORIOUS PROPHET, FORE-
RUNNER, AND BAPTIST JOHN.

Troparion as on Tuesdays. Vide page 428.

Condakion. Tone 5.

THE Beheading of the glorious Forerunner was the divine dispensation that he might preach to those in hades the advent of the Saviour. Lament then, Herodias, because thou askedst the unlawful murder; for thou didst not love, neither the law of God, neither eternal life, but only time's deceitfulness.

Magnifying.

WE magnify thee, O John, Baptist of the Saviour, and reverence thine honourable Beheading.

XXV. TROPARIA AND CONDAKIA COMMON FOR THE SAINTS.

FOR PROPHETS.

Troparion. *Tone* 2.

 LORD, celebrating the memory of thy Prophet *N.*, we, through him, beseech thee, Save our souls.

Condakion. *Tone* 4.

THY pure heart, enlightened by the Spirit, became the receptacle of the brightest prophecy; for thou seest the future as though it were present. Therefore do we reverence thee, blessed and glorious Prophet *N.*

FOR AN APOSTLE.

Troparion. *Tone* 3.

 HOLY Apostle *N.*, pray the merciful God to grant our souls remission of sins.

Condakion. *Tone* 4.

THE Church hath gained thee, O Apostle *N.*, as a shining star, being everywhere enlightened by thy numerous miracles. Then do we cry unto Christ, O Merciful One, save them that in faith honour the memory of thine Apostle.

FOR APOSTLES.

Troparion. *Tone* 3.

HOLY Apostles, pray the merciful God to grant our souls remission of sins.

Condakion. *Tone* 4.

O YE prudent Apostles of the Lord, ye have appeared as vines in the vineyard of Christ, bearing in virtues clusters that produce for us wine of salvation, of which having partaken, we are filled with gladness, and celebrate your honourable memory. Then pray that we may be granted mercy, and the forgiveness of sins.

FOR A DIVINE.

Troparion. *Tone* 4.

The truth hath made thee .... *Vide* *page* 430.

Condakion. *Tone* 2.

THOU thunder Divine, a spiritual trumpet, a planter of faith and cutter down of heresy, welcome to the Trinity. O great Divine *N.*, ever standing with the Angels, pray without ceasing for us.

FOR DIVINES.

Troparion. Tone 4.

GOD of our Fathers, who ever dealest with us according to thy clemency; remove not thy mercy from us, but, through their intercessions, direct our life in peace.

Condakion. Tone 8.

O YE invincible teachers of virtue and ornaments of the priesthood, the Church in song glorifieth you. Then, by your prayers, gain for them that lovingly honour you perfection of virtues and deliverance from temptations.

FOR A VENERABLE.

Troparion. Tone 8.

In thee, O Father, is a pattern of certain salvation . . . . *Vide page* 270.

Condakion. Tone 2.

WITH pure sincerity divinely armed, and wielding the strong lance of ceaseless prayers, thou hast pierced through the demon hosts. Then Father *N.*, pray always for us all.

FOR VENERABLES.

Troparion. Tone 4.

O God of our Fathers .... *Vide page* 463.

Condakion. Tone 2.

O YE Venerables divinely wise, having passed unwetted through many waves, ye have sunk the bodiless enemies in the streams of your tears; and, having received the gift of miracles, ye pray unceasingly for us all.

FOR A MARTYR.

Troparion. Tone 4.

THY Martyr *N.*, O Lord, by his sufferings, hath obtained an incorruptible crown from thee, our God; for, having thy strength to help him, he overcame his persecutors, and the vain efforts of the demons. O save our souls through his prayers.

Condakion. Tone 6.

O HOLY Martyr *N.*, thou hast appeared as a bright star undimmed by the world, announcing by its dawn the Sun of righteousness, and hast extinguished all vanity, giving light unto us. O pray unceasingly for us.

FOR MARTYRS.

Troparion. Tone 4.

THY Martyrs, O Lord, by their sufferings, have obtained incorruptible crowns from thee, our God; for, having thy strength to help them, they overcame their persecutors and the vain efforts of the demons. O save our souls through their prayers.

Another, in Tone 1.

THROUGH the afflictions of thy Saints, which they suffered for thee, be entreated, O Lord, and heal all our afflictions, we beseech thee, O Lover of men.

Condakion. Tone 2.

O DIVINE Martyrs, appearing as bright lamps, ye have illuminated every creature with the shining of miracles, allaying sickness, and dispersing darkness, and praying Christ God without ceasing for us all.

FOR A PRIEST-MARTYR

Troparion. Tone 4.

BECOME sharer in the lot and successor in a throne of the Apostles, O divinely inspired one, thou hast found the work of an ambassador. Wherefore, rightly dividing the word of truth,

30

thou hast suffered for the faith even unto blood. O Priest-martyr *N.*, pray Christ our God to save our souls.

Condakion. Tone 4.

O THOU divinely wise one, who didst live piously in the priesthood and walk in the way of martyrdom, thou didst quench the sacrifices of idols and become a defender of thy flock. Therefore we reverence thee, and mystically cry to thee, Ever deliver us from evils by thy prayers, O Father *N.*

FOR PRIEST-MARTYRS.

Troparion. Tone 3.

O God of our Fathers . . . . *Vide page* 463.

Condakion. Tone 3.

WE assemble to-day and praise you with songs, O ye Priest-martyrs, as unsetting lights of the Sun of wisdom; for ye have shined unto them that were in the darkness of folly, and bidden all to the height of piety. Therefore we cry to you, Hail! ye supporters of abstinents.

FOR A VENERABLE MARTYR.

Troparion. Tone 8.

In thee, O Father . . . . *As for a Venerable.*

Condakion. Tone 2.

AS a pious and tried abstinent, and an honourable willing athlete, and a model of the ascetic life, let us with songs worthily extol *N.*, the ever-praised, for he hath trodden down the serpent.

FOR VENERABLE MARTYRS.

Troparion. Tone 4.

O God of our Fathers . . . . *Vide page 463.*

Condakion. Tone 2.

O ye Venerables . . . . *Vide page 464.*

FOR A WOMAN MARTYR.

Troparion. Tone 4.

THY lamb, O Jesus, *N.*, crieth aloud unto thee, I love thee, my Bridegroom, and, seeking for thee, I endure sufferings, crucify myself with thee, and am buried in thy baptism, and suffer for thy sake that I may reign with thee, and I die for thee that I may live with thee. Accept me then as a pure sacrifice which I lovingly bring to thee. Through her prayers, O Merciful One, save our souls.

Condakion. Tone 2.

HAVING found thy most honourable dwelling as a cure for our souls, we faithful

30*

cry to thee, O Virgin Martyr *N.*, illustrious in name, pray Christ our God unceasingly for us.

FOR WOMEN MARTYRS.

Troparion.   Tone 1.

YE admirable ones, called lambs of the Lamb and Shepherd, ye were conducted through martyrdom unto Christ, and have finished your course, and kept the faith.   Therefore to‑day, magnifying Christ in the joy of our souls, we keep your holy memory.

Condakion.   Tone 4.

WE celebrate the memory of the Martyrs of Christ, in faith asking them for help to deliver us all from every affliction, and cry, Our God is with us, who in his goodwill glorified them.

FOR A VENERABLE WOMAN.

Troparion.   Tone 8.

In thee, O Mother, is a pattern . . . . *Vide page* 270.

Condakion.   Tone 2.

FOR the love of the Lord, O venerable one, thou hast hated a life of ease, enlightening thy soul by abstinence, and hast mightily prevailed against demons.   Then, by thy prayers, make naught the assaults of our enemies.

FOR VENERABLE WOMEN.

Troparion. Tone 2.

YE glorious ones of Christ, beautiful in soul and exceeding rich, supporters of nuns and their guides, renouncing the companionship of a worldly betrothal, ye were espoused with true desire unto him, and have risen to the heights of immortality. Then pray for us unceasingly, who lovingly celebrate your memory.

Condakion. Tone 2.

WASTING your bodies with fasting, and beseeching the Creator with vigilant prayers to obtain perfect pardon for your sins, ye have gained divine forgiveness and the kingdom of heaven. O pray for us to Christ our God.

FOR A VENERABLE WOMAN MARTYR.

Troparion. Tone 4.

Thy lamb, O Jesus . . . . *Vide page* 467.

Condakion. Tone 4.

THY divine memory, O *N.*, shining to-day, telleth of thy life, and appeareth to the world as a sun; for thou, through continence, hast put down the uprisings of the flesh, and, through the blood of suffering, wast espoused unto Christ. Therefore deliver them that praise thee from every ill, that we may cry unto thee, Hail! O venerable Mother.

FOR A CONFESSOR.

Troparion. Tone 8.

NSTRUCTOR of orthodoxy, teacher of piety and purity, light of the world, divinely inspired ornament of high priests, O most prudent *N.*, thou spiritual trumpet, who hast enlightened all men by thy teachings; pray Christ our God to save our souls.

Condakion. Tone 2.

O DIVINELY wise and sacred Father *N.*, thou hast purified thyself by continence, quelling the desires of the flesh and increasing in faith, and thou appearest as a tree of life that hath flourished in Paradise.

FOR THE UNMERCENARY.

Troparion. Tone 8.

HOLY and unmercenary Wonderworkers, visit our infirmities; for freely have ye received, so freely give.

Condakion. Tone 2.

HAVING received the grace of healing, O Physicians and glorious Wonderworkers, ye extend health to those in want. Come then, and, by your presence, drive away the daring of adversaries, and heal the world by your miracles.

———◦◦◦———

XXVI. DIPTYCHS,
OR REMEMBRANCER.

EMEMBER, O Lord Jesus Christ, our God, thine eternal mercies and bounties, according to which thou didst become man, and didst condescend to suffer crucifixion and death for them that rightly believe in thee, and didst **rise from** the dead, ascend into heaven, and sit on the right hand of God the Father, and lookest down on the humble prayers of them that call upon thee from all their heart. Bend down thine ear, and hearken unto the humble supplication of me, thine unworthy servant, which I offer unto thee as a sweet-smelling, spiritual perfume for all thy people. And firstly, remember thy holy Church, catholic and apostolical, which thou hast saved by thine honourable Blood, and confirm and strengthen her, extend and multiply her, and pacify her, and preserve her for ever unprevailed by the gates of hell. Quiet the dissensions of churches, quench the rage of the heathen, and quickly destroy and uproot the risings of heresies, and turn them into naught by the power of thy Holy Ghost.

Genuflection.

SAVE, O Lord, and have mercy upon our Sovereign. (*Here shall mention be made of the Reigning House, and of all the Authorities.*) Surround their government with peace, and subdue under their feet all enemies and adversaries, and speak peaceful and good things in their hearts in favour of thy holy Church and of all thy people, that we, in their peace, may also lead a peaceful and quiet life, in the true Faith and in all godliness and honesty. *Genuflection.*

SAVE, O Lord, and have mercy upon the most holy Governing Synod, and upon the most holy ecumenical Patriarchs, and all the most reverend orthodox Metropolitans, Archbishops and Bishops, the Priesthood and Diaconate, and all church Officers whom thou hast appointed to feed thy spiritual flock, and, by their prayers, have mercy upon me, and save me, a sinner.

Genuflection.

SAVE, O Lord, and have mercy upon my spiritual Father *N.*, and, by his holy prayers, forgive my transgressions.

Genuflection.

SAVE, O Lord, and have mercy upon my parents, brothers, and sisters, *NN.*, and my kinsmen in flesh, and all the neighbours of my family, and my friends; and grant thy blessings unto them in this world, and in the world to come. *Genuflection.*

SAVE, O Lord, and have mercy upon the aged and the young, upon the poor, upon the orphans and widows, and upon them thy servants that are in sickness, sorrow, misfortune and grief, in privations and captivity, in prison and in exile, and more especially upon them that, for thy sake and their orthodox Faith, are being persecuted by ungodly nations, by apostates, and by heretics; and remember them, visit them, strengthen and comfort them, and quickly, by thy power, grant unto them remission, freedom and deliverance. *Genuflection.*

SAVE, O Lord, and have mercy upon those of our fathers and brethren that are sent on service, or are journeying, and upon all orthodox Christians. *Genuflection.*

SAVE, O Lord, and have mercy upon them that hate and injure me, and do evil unto me, and let them not perish on account of me, a sinner. *Genuflection.*

ENLIGHTEN with the light of thy knowledge all them that have seceded from the orthodox Faith, and are blinded by perilous heresies, and unite them to thy holy, apostolical, and catholic Church. *Genuflection.*

FOR THE DEPARTED.

REMEMBER, O Lord, all them that have departed this life, all orthodox Kings and Queens, pious Dukes and Duchesses, the most holy Patriarchs, Metropolitans, Archbishops and Bishops, and them that have served thee in priestly Orders, or in church Offices, or in monastic Orders, and rest them with the Saints in thine eternal habitations. *Genuflection.*

REMEMBER, O Lord, the souls of thy departed servants, my parents, *NN.*, and all my kinsmen in flesh; and forgive them all their sins, voluntary and involuntary, granting unto them the kingdom and communion of thine eternal blessings, and the enjoyment of thine everlasting, infinite, and blissful life. *Genuflection.*

REMEMBER also, O Lord, all our fathers, brethren and sisters, who have fallen asleep in the hope of resurrection and life eternal, and all orthodox Christians, here or elsewhere lying, and make them dwell with thy Saints where the light of thy countenance shineth, and have mercy upon us; for thou art good and lovest mankind. Amen.

Genuflection.

GRANT, O Lord, remission of sins to all our fathers, brethren and sisters, who have before departed in faith and in the hope of resurrection, and render unto them, Everlasting remembrance, *thrice.*

And, in conclusion,

It is very meet .... *Vide page* 61.

Glory. Both now.

Lord, have mercy, *thrice.*

O LORD Jesus Christ, Son of God, for the sake of the prayers of thy most holy Mother, of our venerable and God-bearing Fathers, and of all the Saints, have mercy upon us. Amen.

XXVII. OF THE RECITATION OF THE PSALTER.

The Psalter is divided into 20 *Kathisms, and each of these is subdivided into* 3 *parts, called Stases, according to Table I.*

And the Kathisms are recited in the Daily Office according to Table II.

NOTE:—*At the conclusion of every Stasis the Reader saith,*

Glory to the Father . . . .

And the Choir singeth,

Both now, and ever . . . .

Alleluia, alleluia, alleluia, glory to thee, O God, *thrice.*

Lord, have mercy, *thrice.*

Glory to the Father . . . .

Then the Reader saith,

Both now, and ever . . . .

And continueth reading, beginning the next Stasis.

TABLE I.

KATHISMS.	STASES.		
	1	2	3
	Psalms.	Psalms.	Psalms.
I.	1—3.	4—6.	7, 8.
II.	9, 10(11).	11(12)—13(14).	14(15)—16(17).
III.	17(18).	18(19)—20(21).	21(22)—23(24).
IV.	24(25)—26(27).	27(28)—29(30).	30(31), 31(32).
V.	32(33), 33(34).	34(35), 35(36).	36(37).
VI.	37(38)—39(40).	40(41)—42(43).	43(44)—45(46).
VII.	46(47)—48(49).	49(50), 50(51).	51(52)—54(55).
VIII.	55(56)—57(58).	58(59)—60(61).	61(62)—63(64).
IX.	64(65)—66(67).	67(68).	68(69), 69(70).
X.	70(71), 71(72).	72(73), 73(74).	74(75)—76(77).
XI.	77(78).	78(79)—80(81).	81(82)—84(85).
XII.	85(86)—87(88).	88(89).	89(90), 90(91).
XIII.	91(92)—93(94).	94(95)—96(97).	97(98)—100(101).
XIV.	101(102), 102(103).	103(104).	104(105).
XV.	105(106).	106(107).	107(108), 108(109).
XVI.	109(110)—111(112).	112(113)—114(116 v.9).	115(116 v.10)—117(118).
XVII.	118(119) v.1—72.	v.73—131.	v.132—176.
XVIII.	119(120)—123(124).	124(125)—128(129).	129(130)—133(134).
XIX.	134(135)—136(137).	137(138)—139(140).	140(141)—142(143).
XX.	143(144), 144(145).	145(146)—147.	148—150.

NOTE:—The numbers of the Psalms given in brackets are those according to the English Authorized Version.

TABLE II.

Days of the Week.	Name of the Office.	A. From the Monday of S. Thomas until the Octave of Exaltation, i.e., until Sept. 21.	B. From Sept. 22 until Dec. 20, and from Jan. 15 until the Saturday before the Sunday of the Prodigal Son.	C. In the 1st, 2nd, 3rd, 4th, and 6th. Weeks of the Fast.	D. In the 5th. Week of the Fast.	E. In Holy Passion Week.
Sunday	At Great Vespers.	Kathism 1.	1.	1.	1.	1.
	At Matins.	2, 3, 17.	2, 3.	2, 3, 17.	2, 3, 17.	2, 3.
		Kathism 17 is omitted on Sundays when they sing the Many mercies.				
Monday	At Nocturns.	*On this and the next four days Kathism 17, but on Saturdays Kathism 9.*				
	At Matins.	4, 5. *(from Dec. Fare.)*	Mat. 4, 5, 6. Vespers. 18.	Matins. 4, 5, 6. Hours. 7, 8, 9. Vespers. 18.	4, 5, 6. 7, 8, 9. 10.	4, 5, 6. 7, 8. 18.
	At Vespers.	6.				

Day						
Tuesday	At Matins. 7, 8. At Vespers. 9.	Mat. 7, 8, 9. Vespers. 18.	Matins. 10, 11, 12. Hours. 13, 14, 15, 16. Vespers. 18.	11, 12, 13. 14, 15, 16. 19.	9, 10, 11. 12, 13. 18.
Wednesd.	At Matins. 10, 11. At Vespers. 12.	Mat. 10, 11, 12. Vespers. 18.	Matins. 19, 20, 1. Hours. 2, 3, 4, 5. Vespers. 18.	20, 1, 2. 3, 4, 5, 6. 7.	14, 15, 16. 19, 20. 18.
Thursday	At Matins. 13, 14. At Vespers. 15.	Mat. 13, 14, 15. Vespers. 18.	Matins. 6, 7, 8. Hours. 9, 10, 11, 12. Vespers. 18.	8. 9, 10, 11. 12.	
Friday	At Matins. 19, 20. At Vespers. 18.	Mat. 19. 20. Vespers. 18.	Matins. 13, 14, 15. Hours. 19. 20. Vespers. 18.	13, 14, 15. 19, 20. 18.	
Saturday	At Nocturns. 9. At Matins. 16, 17.	Nocturns. 9. Mat. 16. 17.	9. 16, 17.	9. 16, 17.	17 *with Verses.*

According to this order also are read the Kathisms 20 to Jan. 15, and in the Weeks of Meat and Cheese

When there are only three Kathisms at Hours they are said at Terce, Sext, and None; and when only two, at Terce and Sext.

XXVIII. TABLE OF EPISTLE AND GOSPEL LESSONS.

AT LITURGY.

Lessons for Sundays &c.

Easter Sun.	Acts I. 1-8.	John I. 1-17.
Easter Mon.	Acts I. 12-17, 21-26.	John I. 18-28.
Easter Tues.	Acts II. 14-21.	Luke XXV. 12-35.
Easter Wed.	Acts II. 22-36.	John I. 35-51.
Easter Thurs.	Acts II. 38-43.	John III. 1-15.
Easter Fri.	Acts III. 1-8.	John II. 12-22.
Easter Sat.	Acts III. 11-16.	John III.22-33.
Sun. of Thomas.	Acts V. 12-20.	John XX.19-31.
Sun. of Myrrh-bearers.	Acts VI. 1-7.	Mark XV. 43-XVI. 8.
Sun. of Paralytic.	Acts IX.23-42.	John V. 1-15.
Sun. of Samaritan.	Acts XI. 19-26, 29-30.	John IV. 5-42.

Sun. of Blind Man.	Acts XVI. 16-34.	John IX. 1-38.
Ascension.	Acts I. 1-12.	Luke XXIV. 36-53.
Sun. of Holy Fathers.	Acts XX. 16-18, 28-36.	John XVII. 1-13.
Pentecost Sun.	Acts II. 1-11.	John VII. 37-52, VIII. 12.
Sunday of All Saints.	Heb. XI. 22-XII. 2.	Matt. X. 32-33, 37-38, XIX. 27-30.
Sun. 2 aft. Pent.	Rom. II. 10-16.	Matt. IV. 18-23.
Sun. 3 aft. Pent.	Rom. V. 1-10.	Matt. VI. 22-33.
Sun. 4 aft. Pent.	Rom. VI. 18-23.	Matt. VIII. 5-13.
Sun. 5 aft. Pent.	Rom. X. 1-10.	Matt. VIII. 28-IX. 1.
Sun. 6 aft. Pent.	Rom. XII. 6-14.	Matt. IX. 1-8.
Sun. 7 aft. Pent.	Rom. XV. 1-7.	Matt. IX. 27-35.
Sun. 8 aft. Pent.	1 Cor. I. 10-18.	Matt. XIV. 14-22.
Sun. 9 aft. Pent.	1 Cor. III. 9-17.	Matt. XIV. 22-34.
Sun. 10 aft. Pent.	1 Cor. IV. 9-16.	Matt. XVII. 14-23.
Sun. 11 aft. Pent.	1 Cor. IX. 2-12.	Matt. XVIII. 23-35.
Sun. 12 aft. Pent.	1 Cor. XV. 1-11.	Matt. XIX. 16-26.
Sun. 13 aft. Pent.	1 Cor. XVI. 13-24.	Matt. XXI. 33-42.
Sun. 14 aft. Pent.	2 Cor. I. 21-II. 4.	Matt. XXII. 1-14.
Sun. 15 aft. Pent.	2 Cor. IV. 6-15.	Matt. XXII. 35-46.

Sun. 16 aft. Pent. 2 Cor. VI. 1-10. Matt. XXV. 14-30.

Sun. 17 aft. Pent. 2 Cor. VI. 16-VII. 1. Matt. XV. 21-28.

Sun. 18 aft. Pent. 2 Cor. IX. 6-11. Luke V. 1-11.

Sun. 19 aft. Pent. 2 Cor. XI. 31-XII. 9. Luke VI. 31-36.

Sun. 20 aft. Pent. Gal. I. 11-19. Luke VII. 11-16.

Sun. 21 aft. Pent. Gal. II. 16-20. Luke VIII. 5-15.

Sun. 22 aft. Pent. Gal. VI. 11-18. Luke XVI. 19-31.

Sun. 23 aft. Pent. Eph. II. 4-10. Luke VIII. 26-39.

Sun. 24 aft. Pent. Eph. II. 14-22. Luke VIII. 41-56.

Sun. 25 aft. Pent. Eph. IV. 1-6. Luke X. 25-37.

Sun. 26 aft. Pent. Eph. V. 9-19. Luke XII. 16-21.

Snn. 27 aft. Pent. Eph. VI. 10-17. Luke XIII. 10-17.

Sun. 28 aft. Pent. Col. I. 12-18. Luke XIV. 16-24.

Sun. 29 aft. Pent. Col. III. 4-11. Luke XVII. 12-19.

Sun. 30 aft. Pent. Col. III. 12-16. Luke XVIII. 18-27.

Sun. 31 aft. Pent. 1 Tim. I. 15-17. Luke XVII. 35-43.

Sun. 32 aft. Pent. 1 Tim. IV. 9-15. Luke XIX. 1-10.

Sun. of Publican. 2 Tim. III. 10-15. Luke XVIII. 10-14.

Sun. of Prodigal. 1 Cor. VI. 12-20. Luke XV. 11-32.

Sat. of Meat Fare. 1 Thess. IV. 13-17. John V. 24-30.

Sun. of Meat Fare. 1 Cor. VIII. 8-IX. 2. Matt. XXV. 31-46.

Sat. of Cheese Fare.   Gal. v. 22-vi. 2. Matt. xi. 27-30.

Sun. of Cheese Fare.   Rom. xiii. 11-xiv. 4. Matt. vi. 14-21.

Sat. 1 of Fast.   2 Tim. ii. 1-10. John xv. 17-xvi. 2.

Sun. 1 of Fast.   Heb. xi. 24-26, 32-xii. 2. John i. 43-51.

Sun. 2 of Fast.   Heb. i. 10-ii. 2. Mark ii. 1-12.

Sun. 3 of Fast.   Heb. iv. 14-v. 6. Mark viii. 34-ix. 1.

Sun. 4 of Fast.   Heb. vi. 13-20. Mark ix. 17-31.

Sat. 5 of Fast.   Heb. ix. 1-7. Luke x. 38-42, xi. 27-28.

Sun. 5 of Fast.   Heb. ix. 11-14. Mark x. 32-45.

Sat. of Lazarus.   Heb. xii. 28-xiii. 8. John xi. 1-45.

Palm Sunday.   Philip. iv. 4-9. John xii. 1-18.

Holy and Gt. Monday.   Matt. xxiv. 3-35.

Holy and Gt. Tuesday.   Matt. xxiv. 36-xxvi. 2.

Holy and Gt. Wednesday.   Matt. xxvi. 6-16.

Holy and Gt. Thursday.   1 Cor. xi. 23-32. Matt. xxvi. 1-20. John xiii. 3-17. Matt. xxvi. 21-39. Luke xxii. 43-45. Matt. xxvi. 40-xxvii. 2.

31*

Holy and Gt. Rom. VI. 3-11. Matt. XXVIII. 1-
Saturday. 20.

Lessons for Festivals.

Sep. 8. Nativity Philip. II. 5-11. Luke X. 38-42,
of the Mother XI. 27, 28.
of God.

Sep. 14. Exalta- 1 Cor. I. 18-24. John XIX. 6-20,
tion. 25-27, 30-35.

Sep. 26 Decease 1 John IV. 12- John XIX. 25-27,
of John the 19. XXI. 24, 25.
Divine.

Oct. 1. Protec- Epis. and Gos. as on Sep. 8.
tion of the
Mother of
God.

Nov. 8. S. Mi- Heb. II. 2-10. Luke X. 16-21.
chael and All
Angels.

Nov. 13. S. Chrys- Heb. VII. 26- John X. 9-16.
ostom. VIII. 2.

Nov. 21. Present- Heb. IX. 1-7. As on Sep. 8.
ation of the
Mother of
God.

Nov. 24. S. Kath- Gal. III. 23- Mark V. 24-34.
arine. IV. 5.

Nov. 30. S. An- 1 Cor. IV. 9-16. John I. 35-51.
drew.

Dec. 6. S. Nicolas. Heb. XIII. 17-21. Luke VI. 17-23.

Dec. 24. Christ- Heb. I. 1-11. 3. Luke II. 1-20.
mas Eve.
If falling on Gal. III. 15-22. Matt. XIII. 31-36.
Sat. or Sun.
Dec. 25. Christ- Gal. IV. 4-7. Matt. II. 1-12.
mas Day.
Jan. 1. Circum- Col. II. 8-12. Luke II. 20, 21,
cision. 40-52.
Jan. 6. Epi- Titus II. 11-14, Matt. III. 13-17.
phany. III. 4-7.
Jan. 30. The Heb. XIII. 7-16. Matt. V. 13-19.
ThreeDivines.
Feb. 2. Present- Heb. VII. 7-17. Luke II. 22-40.
ation of the
Lord.
Mch. 25. Annun- Heb. II. 11-18. Luke I. 24-38.
ciation.
Apl. 23. S. Acts XII. 1-11. John XV. 17-
George. XVI. 2.
May 8. John Epis. and Gos. as on Sept. 26.
the Divine.
June 24. Nativ- Rom. XIII. 11- Luke I. 1-25, 57-
ity of the XIV. 4. 68, 76, 80.
Forerunner.
June 29. SS. Pe- 2 Cor. XI. 21- Matt. XVI. 13-19.
ter and Paul. XII. 9.
July 20. S. Elias. James V. 10- Luke IV. 22-30.
20.
Aug. 6. Trans- 2 Pet. I. 10-19. Matt. XVII. 1-9.
figuration.

Aug. 15. As-   Epis. and Gos. as on Sep. 8.
sumption.
  29. Behead- Acts XIII. 25- Mark VI. 14-30.
ing of the   33.
Forerunner.

Lessons common for the Saints.

For the Mother Philip. II. 5-11, Luke x. 38-42,
of God.   Or, Heb. IX.   XI. 27-28.
              1-7.
On Fest. of the I Cor. I. 18-24. John XII. 28-36.
Cross.
For the Angels. Heb. II. 2-10. Luke x. 16-21,
                                  Or, Matt. XIII.
                                  24-30, 36-43.
For the Fore- Acts XIII. 25- Matt. XI. 2-15.
runner.   32.
For Prophets.   I Cor. XIV. 20- Matt. XXIII. 29-
                25, Or, Heb.   39, Or, Luke
                VI. 13-20.   XI. 47-54.
                Or, James
                V. 10-20.
For an Apostle. I Cor. IV. 9-16. Matt. IX. 36-38,
                                   x. 5-8.
For Apostles.   I Cor. IV. 9-16. Luke x. 1-15, Or,
                                  Luke x. 16-21.
For a Divine.   Heb. VII. 26- John x. 9-16.
                VIII. 2.

For Divines. Heb. XIII. 17- Matt. v. 14-19,
22. *Or*, John x.
9-16.

For Venerables. Gal. v. 22-VI. 2. Matt. XI. 27-30,
Or, Luke VI.
17-23.

For a Martyr. 2 Tim. II. 1-10. Luke XII. 2-12,
Or, Joh : xv.
17-XVI. 2,

For Martyrs. Rom. VIII. 28- Matt. x. 15-22,
39, *Or*, Heb. *Or*, Luke XXI.
XI. 33-40. 12-19.

For a Priest- Heb. XIII. 7-16. Luke XII. 32-40.
martyr.

For Priest-mar- Heb. v. 4-10, Luke VI. 17-23,
tyrs. *Or*, Philip. *Or*, Luke x.
III. 20-IV. 3. 22-24, *Or*,
Luke XIV. 25-
35.

For a Ven. 2 Tim. I. 8-18, Mark VIII. 34-38.
Martyr. *Or*, Rom.
VIII. 28-39.

For Ven. Mar- 2 Tim. I. 8-18, Matt. x. 32-33,
tyrs. *Or*, Rom. 37-38, *Or*,
VIII. 28-39. Matt. XIX. 27-
30, *Or*, Luke
XII. 8-12.

For Martyrs 2 Cor. VI. 1-10, Matt. xv. 21-28,
(women). *Or*, Gal. III. *Or*, Mark v.
23-29. 24-34.

For Venerables Gal. III. 23-29. Matt. XXV. 1-13,
(women).   *Or*, Luke VII.
36-50.

For Confessors. Eph. VI. 10-17. Luke XII. 8-12.
For the Un-   1 Cor. XII. 27- Matt. X. 1, 5-8.
mercenary.   XIII. 8.

AT MATINS.

The XI Gospels on the Resurrection read successively on Sundays beginning on the Sunday of All Saints.

I. Matt. XXVIII. 16-20.	VI. Luke XXIV. 36-53.
II. Mark XVI. 1-8.	VII. John XX. 1-10.
III. Mark XVI. 9-20.	VIII. John XX. 11-18.
IV. Luke XXIV. 1-12.	IX. John XX. 19-31.
V. Luke XXIV. 12-35.	X. John XXI. 1-14.
	XI. John XXI. 15-25.

NOTE:— *On the Sunday of S. Thomas No. I is read; on that of the Myrrh-bearing Women, No. III; on that of the Paralytic, No. IV; on that of the Samaritan Woman, No. VII; on that of the Blind Man, No. VIII, and on the Sixth Sunday after Pascha, No. X.*

Gospels for Festivals.

Palm Sunday.	Matt. XXI. 1-11, 15-17.
Ascension.	Mark XVI. 9-20.
Pentecost.	John XX. 19-23.

Exaltation.	John XII. 28-36.
Christmas.	Matt. I. 18-25.
Circumcision.	John X. 1-9.
Epiphany.	Mark I. 9-11.
Presentation.	Luke II. 25-32.
Transfiguration.	Luke IX. 28-36.
Common for the Mother of God.	Luke I. 39-49, 56.

XXIX. THE KALENDAR.

SEPTEMBER.

A. 1. *The Beginning of the Indict, i. e., of the New Year.* Our venerable Father Simeon the Stylite, A. D. 460. And his mother Martha. And the Council of the Mother of God at Miasinæ.

g. 2. The Martyr Mamas, A. D. 260. And our ven. Father, John the Faster, Patriarch of Constantinople, A. D. 619.

f. 3. The Priest-martyr Anthimus, Bp. of Nicomedia, A. D. 288. And our ven. Father Theoctistus, A. D. 451.

e. 4. The Priest-martyr Babylas, Archbp. of Antioch the Gt., and three young men, his disciples, A. D. 253. And the Prophet and Seer of God, Moses.

d. 5. *The Prophet Zacharias, father of the honourable John, the Forerunner. And the ven. Elizabeth.*

c. 6. *The Miracle wrought at Colosse in Chonæ by the Archangel Michael.*

b. 7. Vigil of the Nativity of the most holy Mother of God. The Martyr Sozon, A. D. 288.

A. 8. THE NATIVITY OF OUR MOST HOLY LADY, THE MOTHER OF GOD AND EVER-VIRGIN MARY.

g. 9. *The righteous Progenitors of God, Joakim and Anna.*

f. 10. The Martyrs Menodora, Metrodora, and Nymphodora, A. D. 304.

e. 11. Our venerable Mother Theodora of Alexandria, A. D. 472.

d. 12. The Priest-martyr Autonomus, A. D. 292.

> His Office is sung on the 11th., for to-day is the Octave of the Nativity of the Mother of God.

c. 13. The Memory of the Dedication of the Church of the Resurrection of Christ our God.* Vigil of the Exaltation of the honourable and life-effecting Cross. The Priest-martyr Cornelius the Centurion.

b. 14. THE EXALTATION OF THE HONOURABLE AND LIFE-EFFECTING CROSS.

> Festival commemorative of the finding of the Lord's Cross at Jerusalem, A. D. 325.

---

* At Jerusalem, A. D. 330.

A. 15. The Gt. Martyr Nicetas, burnt at Gotha, A. D. 370.

g. 16. The Gt. Martyr Euphemia, the all-praised, who suffered, A. D. 288.

f. 17. The Martyr Sophia, and her three daughters, Faith, Hope and Charity, A. D. 122.

e. 18. Our ven. Father Eumenius, Bp. and Wonderworker of Gortyna.

d. 19. The Martyrs Trophimus, Sabbatius and Dorymedon, who suffered at Antioch, A. D. 281.

c. 20. The Gt. Martyr Eustace, and his wife Tatiana, and their children, Agapius and Theopistus, A. D. 100.

b. 21. The Apostle Cordatus.
> His Office is sung on the 22nd., for to-day is the Octave of Exaltation.

A. 22. The Priest-martyr Phocas, A. D. 102.

g. 23. *The Conception of the honourable, glorious Prophet, Forerunner, and Baptist of the Lord, John.*

f. 24. The Proto-martyr and equal of the Apostles, Thecla.

e. 25. Our ven. Mother Euphrosyne, A. D. 430. *And the Decease of our ven. Father, Sergius the Wonderworker, Abbot of the Monastery of the life-originating Trinity, which is at Macovst, A. D.* 1392.

d. 26. THE DECEASE OF THE APOSTLE AND EVANGELIST, JOHN THE DIVINE.

c. 27. The Martyr Callistratus and his companions, A. D. 288.

b. 28. *Our ven. Father Chariton, Confessor, who suffered A. D. 276.*

A. 29. Our ven. Father Cyriacus, Anchoret, A. D. 401.

g. 30. The Priest-martyr Gregory, Bp. of Gt. Armenia, A. D. 290. *And Michael, First Metropolitan of Kiev.*

OCTOBER.

f. 1. THE PROTECTION OF OUR MOST HOLY LADY, THE MOTHER OF GOD AND EVER-VIRGIN MARY.

Festival instituted in the days of King Leo the Wise, A. D. 911.

And the Apostle Ananias, one of the 70. And our ven. Father Roman the Melodist, A. D. 496.

e. 2. The Priest-martyr Cyprian. And the Martyr Justina, A. D. 255.

d. 3. The Priest-martyr Dionysius the Areopagite.

c. 4. The Priest-martyr Hierotheus, Bp. of Athens.

b. 5. The Martyr Charitina, A. D. 290.

A. 6. *The glorious Apostle Thomas.*

g. 7. The Martyrs Sergius and Bacchus, A. D. 296.

f. 8. Our ven. Mother Pelagia.

e. 9. *The Apostle James, the son of Alphæus.* And our ven. Father Andronicus, and his wife Athanasia, A. D. 501.

d. 10. The Martyrs Eulampius and his sister Eulampia, who suffered A. D. 296.

c. 11. The Apostle Philip, one of the 7 Deacons. And our ven. Father Theophany, Confessor, Bp. of Nicæa, and composer of Canons, A. D. 808.

> Sunday of the 350 holy Fathers of the Seventh Synod, held at Nicæa, A. D. 787.

b. 12. The Martyrs Probus, Tarachus and Andronicus, A D. 296. And our ven. Father Cosmas of the Holy City, the composer of Canons.

A. 13. The Martyrs, Carpus, Bp. of the Church at Thyatira, and Papylas the Deacon, and with them Agathodora and Agathonica, the sisters of Papylas, who suffered A. D. 255.

g. 14. The Martyrs Nazarius, Gervase, Protasius and Celsus, who suffered A. D. 57. *And our ven. Mother Parasceva, whose Relics were translated to Tirnova, A. D.* 1201.

f. 15. Our ven. Father Euthymius the New. And the Ven. Martyr Lucian, Presbyter of Antioch the Gt., A. D. 290.

e. 16. The Martyr Longinus the Centurion.

d. 17. The Prophet Hosea. And the Ven. Martyr Andrew of Crete, who suffered A.D. 761.

c. 18. *The Apostle and Evangelist Luke.*

b. 19. The Prophet Joel. And the Martyr Varus, who suffered in Egypt, A. D. 304. And our ven. Father, John of Rilsk, A. D. 954. And the Priest-martyr Sadothus, A. D. 1280.

A. 20. The Gt. Martyr Artemius, A. D. 352.

g. 21. Our ven. Father Hilarion the Gt., A. D. 333.

f. 22. The equal of the Apostles, Abercius, Bp. of Hierapolis, A. D. 186. And the Seven Children of Ephesus, Maximilian, Exacustodianus, Iamblichus, Martinian, Dionysius, John and Constantine, who fell asleep in the reign of Decius and awoke in the time of Theodosius the Less.

e. 23. *The Apostle James, the Brother of God, First Bp. of Jerusalem, who wrote the Divine Liturgy, which was abbreviated by Basil the Gt., and still further by John Chrysostom.*

d. 24. The Martyr Arethas, and those with him, who suffered A. D. 542. And our Father in the Saints, Athanasius, Patriarch of Constantinople, A. D. 362.

c. 25. The Martyrs and Notaries, Marcian and Martyrius, A. D. 346.

b. 26. *The glorious Gt. Martyr, Demetrius the Myroblete, A. D. 296.* And the remembrance of the Great Earthquake at Constantinople, A. D. 758.

A. 27. The Martyr Nestor. And the Martyr Capitolina, and her slave Erotiata, A. D. 296.

g. 28. The Martyrs Terence and Neonilla, and their children. And our ven. Father Stephen the Sabbaite, the composer of Canons, A. D. 780. *And the Martyr Parasceva, A. D.* 290.

f. 29. The Ven. Martyr Anastasia of Rome, A. D. 256. And our ven. Father Abram the Recluse, A. D. 350.

e. 30. The Martyrs, Zenobius and his sister Zenobia, who suffered A. D. 290.

d. 31. The Apostles, Stachys, Amplius, Urban, Narcissus and Aristobulus. And the Martyr Epimachus, A. D. 251.

NOVEMBER.

c. 1. The wonderworking and unmercenary Cosmas and Damian of Asia, and their ven. mother Theodotia.

b. 2. The Martyrs, Acindynus, Pegasius, Aphthonius, Elpidiphorus and Anempodistus, who suffered in Persia, A. D. 320.

A. 3. The Martyrs, Acepsimas, Bp., Joseph, Presbyter, and Aethalas, Deacon, who suffered in Persia, A. D. 313. And the Dedication of the Church of the Gt. Martyr George at Lydda,* where his honourable body is laid.

---

* In the days of Constantine the Great.

g. 4. Our ven. Father Ioannicius the Gt., A. D. 758.

f. 5. The Martyrs Galaction and Episteme, A. D. 285.

e. 6. Our Father in the Saints, Paul, Archbp. of Constantinople, A. D. 351.

d. 7. The 33 Martyrs at Melite, A. D. 290. And our ven. Father, Lazarus the Wonderworker.

c. 8. THE COUNCIL OF THE ARCHANGEL MICHAEL, AND THE OTHER HEAVENLY BODILESS HOSTS.

b. 9. The Martyrs Onesiphorus and Porphyry, A. D. 290. And our ven. Mother Matrona, A. D. 466.

A. 10. The Apostles, Erastus, Olympus, Rhodion, Sosipater, Tertius and Quartus.

g. 11. The Martyrs, Menas, Victor and Vincent, A. D. 296. And our ven. Father and Confessor, Theodore of the Studium, A. D. 804.

f. 12. Our Father in the Saints, John the Almoner, Patriarch of Constantinople, A. D. 615. And our ven. Father Nilus of Egypt, A. D. 602.

e. 13. OUR FATHER IN THE SAINTS, JOHN, ARCHBISHOP OF CONSTANTINOPLE, A. D. 402.

d. 14. *The all-praised Apostle Philip.*

32

c. 15. The Martyrs and Confessors, Gurias, Samon and Abibus.

> NOTE: — To-day beginneth the Fast of the Nativity of the Lord.

b. 16. *The Apostle and Evangelist Matthew.*

A. 17. Our Father in the Saints, Gregory, Bp. and Wonderworker of Neocæsarea, A. D. 275.

g. 18. The Martyrs Plato and Roman, the former, A. D. 296, and the other, A. D. 305.

f. 19. The Prophet Obadias. And the Martyr Barlaam. And our ven. Fathers of Indian ascetic life, Barlaam and Prince Joasaph.

e. 20. Vigil of the Presentation of the Mother of God. And our ven. Father, Gregory of Decapolis, A. D. 837. And our Father in the Saints, Proclus, Archbp. of Constantinople, A. D. 441.

d. 21. THE PRESENTATION IN THE TEMPLE OF OUR MOST HOLY LADY, THE MOTHER OF GOD AND EVER-VIRGIN MARY.

c. 22. The Apostle Philemon, and those with him, who suffered A. D. 68.

b. 23. Our Fathers in the Saints, Amphilochius, Bp. of Iconium, and Gregory, Bp. of Acragas, the former, A. D. 374, and the other, A. D. 721.

A. 24. THE GT. MARTYR KATHARINE A. D. 304. And the Gt. Martyr Mercurius, A. D. 255.

g. 25. Our Fathers in the Saints, the Priest-martyrs, Clement, Pope of Rome, and Peter of Alexandria. Clement suffered A. D. 79, and Peter, A. D. 296. Octave of the Presentation of the Mother of God.

f. 26. Our ven. Father Alypius the Stylite, A. D. 608.

e. 27. The Gt. Martyr James the Persian, A. D. 396.

d. 28. The Ven. Martyr Stephen the New, A. D. 766.

c. 29. The Martyr Paramon, A. D. 255. And the Martyr Philumenus, A. D. 276.

b. 30. THE ALL-PRAISED APOSTLE ANDREW, THE FIRST-CALLED.

DECEMBER.

A. 1. The Prophet Nahum.

g. 2. The Prophet Abbacum.

f. 3. The Prophet Sophonius. And our ven. Father Theodulus.

e. 4. *The Gt. Martyr Barbara, A. D.* 290. And our ven. Father, John Damascene, A. D. 735.

d. 5. *Our ven. and God-bearing Father, Sabbas the Sanctified, A. D.* 524.

32*

c. 6. OUR FATHER IN THE SAINTS, NIC-OLAS, ARCHBP. OF MYRA IN LYCIA, THE WONDERWORKER.

b. 7. Our Father in the Saints, Ambrose, Bp. of Milan, A. D. 374.

A. 8. Our ven. Father Patapius.

g. 9. *The Conception of Anna, when she conceived the Mother of God.*

f. 10. The Martyrs, Menas, Hermogenes and Eugraphus, A. D. 304.

e. 11. Our ven. Father Daniel the Stylite, A. D. 467.

Sunday of holy Forefathers.

d. 12. Our ven. Father, Spyridon the Wonderworker, Bp. of Trimythus, A. D. 343.

c. 13. *The Martyrs, Eustratius, Auxence, Eugene, Mardarius and Orestes, A. D.* 296.

b. 14. The Martyrs, Thyrsus, Leucius, Philemon, Apollonius, Arian and Callinicus, A. D. 256 and A. D. 296.

A. 15. The Priest-martyr Eleutherius, A. D. 120. And our ven. Father, Paul of Latra, A. D. 882.

g. 16. The Prophet Aggeus.

f. 17. The Prophet Daniel. And the Three Children, Ananias, Azarias and Misael.

e. 18. The Martyr Sebastian, and his companions, who suffered A. D. 292.

Sunday before the Nativity of Christ, Of holy Fathers.

d. 19. The Martyr Boniface, A. D. 290.

c. 20. Preparation for the Nativity of our Lord, God, and Saviour, Jesus Christ. And the Priest-martyr, Ignatius Theophorus, A. D. 109.

b. 21. The Martyr Juliana, A. D. 299. *And the Decease of our Father in the Saints, Peter, Metropolitan of Kiev, A. D.* 1334.

A. 22. The Gt. Martyr Anastasia, A. D. 290.

g. 23. The 10 Martyrs of Crete, A. D. 252.

f. 24. The Ven. Martyr Eugenia, A. D. 270.

e. 25. THE NATIVITY OF OUR LORD, GOD, AND SAVIOUR, JESUS CHRIST.

d. 26. *The Council of the Mother of God.*

> Sunday after the Nativity of Christ, Of Joseph the Spouse, David the King, and James the Lord's Brother.

c. 27. *The Apostle, Proto-martyr, and Archdeacon, Stephen.* And our ven. Father and Confessor, Theodore the Scribe.

b. 28. The 2000 Martyrs burned in a Church in Nicomedia, A. D. 286.

A. 29. The Innocents massacred by Herod at Bethlehem. And our ven. Father, Marcel, Abbot of the Monastery of Vigilance, A. D. 459.

g. 30. The Martyr Anysia, A. D. 298.

f. 31. The Ven. Melania of Rome, A. D. 400.

> Her Office is sung on the 30th., for to-day is the Octave of the Nativity of the Lord.

JANUARY.

e. 1. THE CIRCUMCISION OF OUR LORD JESUS CHRIST.

And our Father in the Saints, Basil the Great, Archbp. of Cæsarea in Cappadocia, A. D. 353.

d. 2. Preparation for the Epiphany. And our Father in the Saints, Silvester, Pope of Rome, A. D. 332.

c. 3. The Prophet Malachias. And the Martyr Gordias, A. D. 320.

b. 4. The Council of the 70 Apostles. And our ven. Father Theoctistus, Abbot of Cucum in Sicily.

A. 5. The Martyrs Theopemptus and Theonas, who suffered A. D. 290.

g. 6. THE EPIPHANY, THAT IS, THE DIVINE MANIFESTATION OF OUR LORD, GOD, AND SAVIOUR, JESUS CHRIST.

f. 7. *The Council of the glorious Prophet, Forerunner and Baptist, John.*

e. 8. Our ven. Father George Chosevite. And Emilian, Confessor, A. D. 820.

d. 9. The Martyr Polyeuctus, A. D. 255.

c. 10. Our Father in the Saints, Gregory, Bp. of Nyssa, A. D. 374.

b. 11. *Our ven. Father Theodosius, Founder of Community Life, A. D. 485.*

A. 12. The Martyr Tatiana, the Deaconess, A. D. 208. And our Father in the Saints, Sabbas, Archbp. of Serbia.

g. 13. The Martyrs Hermylus and Stratonicus.

f. 14. Our ven. Fathers massacred at Sinai and Raitha, A. D. 296.

> Their Office is sung on the 13th., for to-day is the Octave of Epiphany.

e. 15. Our ven. Fathers Paul of Thebes and John the Cotter. Paul passed away A. D. 343, and John about A. D. 450.

d. 16. The Veneration of the Bonds of the Apostle Peter.

c. 17. *Our venerable and God-bearing Father, Antony the Great, A. D. 366.*

b. 18. *Our Fathers in the Saints, Athanasius and Cyril, Archbishops of Alexandria, the former, A. D. 318, and the latter, A. D. 415.*

A. 19. Our ven. Father, Macarius of Egypt, A. D. 373.

g. 20. *Our ven. and God-bearing Father, Euthymius the Great, A. D. 465.*

f. 21. Our ven. Father and Confessor, Maximus, A. D. 653. And the Martys, Eugene, Canidius, Valerian and Aquilas, burnt A. D. 292.

e. 22. The Apostle Timothy. And the Ven. Martyr Anastasius the Persian, A. D. 619.

d. 23. The Priest-martyr, Clement, Bp. of Ancyra.

c. 24. Our ven. Mother Xenia.

b. 25. *Our Father in the Saints, Gregory the Divine, Archbishop of Constantinople, A. D. 374.*

A. 26. Our ven. Father Xenophon, A.D. 520.

g. 27. *The Translation of the Relics of our Father in the Saints, John Chrysostom, A. D. 435.*

f. 28. Our ven. Father Ephrem the Syrian, A. D. 373.

e. 29. The Translation of the Relics of the Priest-martyr Ignatius Theophorus.

d. 30. The Priest-martyr Hippolyte, Pope of Rome, A. D. 261.

AND OUR FATHERS IN THE SAINTS, BASIL THE GT., GREGORY THE DIVINE, AND JOHN CHRYSOSTOM.

c. 31. The wonderworking and unmercenary, Cyrus and John, A. D. 292.

FEBRUARY.

b. 1. Vigil of the Presentation of our Lord, God, and Saviour, Jesus Christ. And the Martyr Tryphon, A. D. 256.

A. 2. THE PRESENTATION OF OUR LORD JESUS CHRIST.

g. 3. The righteous Simeon, the Receiver of God, and Anna the Prophetess.

f. 4. Our ven. Father Isidore of Pelusium, A. D. 415.

e. 5. The Martyr Agatha, A. D. 256.

d. 6. Our ven. Father Bucolus, Bp. of Smyrna.

c. 7. Our ven. Father Parthenius, Bp. of Lampsacus, A. D. 318. And our ven. Father Luke.

b. 8. The Gt. Martyr Theodore the General, A. D. 320.

A. 9. The Martyr Nicephor, A. D. 260.

To-day is the Octave of the Presentation of the Lord, and the Office of the Martyr is sung on the 10th.

g. 10. The Martyr Charalampes, A. D. 198.

f. 11. The Priest-martyr Blasius, A. D. 320.

e. 12. Our Father in the Saints, Meletius, Archbp. of Antioch the Gt., A. D. 375. *And our Father in the Saints, Alexis, Metropolitan and Wonderworker of All Russia, A. D. 1386.*

d. 13. Our ven. Father Martinian, A. D. 415. And our Father in the Saints, Simeon of Serbia, the new Myroblete.

c. 14. Our ven. Father Auxence, A. D. 440. And our Father in the Saints, Cyril, Bp. of Catana, A. D. 866.*

---

* Teacher of the Slavs and Bulgarians, and Inventor of their Alphabet.

b. 15. The Apostle Onesimus.

A. 16. The Martyrs, Pamphilus, Valentius, Paul, Seleucus, Porphyry, Julian and Theodulus. And 5 Egyptians, Elias, Jeremias, Esaias, Samuel and Daniel, who suffered A. D. 292.

g. 17. The Gt. Martyr Theodore Tyro, A. D. 297.

f. 18. Our Father in the Saints, Leo, Pope of Rome, A. D. 460.

e. 19. The Apostle Archippus.

d. 20. Our Father in the Saints, Leo, Bp. of Catana, A. D. 780.

c. 21. Our ven. Father Timothy of Symboli. And our Father in the Saints, Eustathius, Archbp. of Antioch, A. D. 368.

b. 22. The Invention of the Relics of the Martyrs of Eugenia, A. D. 384.

A. 23. The Priest-martyr Polycarp, Bp. of Smyrna, A. D. 143.

g. 24. *The First and Second Inventions of the honourable Head of the Forerunner.*

f. 25. Our Father in the Saints, Tarasius, Archbishop of Constantinople, A. D. 808.

e. 26. Our Father in the Saints, Porphyry, Archbp. of Gaza, A. D. 451.

d. 27. Our ven. Father and Confessor, Procopius of Decapolis.

c. 28. Our ven. Father and Confessor, Basil, co-ascetic with Procopius, A. D. 740.

d. 29. Our ven. Father, Cassian of Rome, A. D. 431.

MARCH.

c. 1. The Ven. Martyr Eudocia, A. D. 160.

b. 2. The Priest-martyr Theodotus, Bp. of Cyrene, A. D. 320.

A. 3. The Martyr Eutropius, and his companions, Cleonicus and Basiliscus, who suffered A. D. 296.

g. 4. Our ven. Father Gerasimus of Jordan, A. D. 450.

f. 5. The Martyr Conon, A. D. 256.

e. 6. The 42 Martyrs of Amorium, Theodore, Constantine, Callistus, Theophilus, and the rest, A. D. 849.

d. 7. The Priest-martyrs of Cherson, the Bps. Basil, Ephrem, Eugene, Ether, and the rest, A. D. 296.

c. 8. Our ven. Father and Confessor, Theophylact, Bp. of Nicomedia, A. D. 832.

b. 9. *The 40 Martyrs of Sebastia, A. D. 320.*

A. 10. The Martyr Cordatus, and his companions, Cyprian, Anectus, and Criscentus, who suffered A. D. 256.

g. 11. Our Father in the Saints, Sophronius, Patriarch of Jerusalem, A. D. 636. And Gregory, Pope of Rome, A. D. 644.

f. 12. Our ven. Father and Confessor, Theophany of Syngriana, A. D. 832.

e. 13. The Translation of the Relics of our Father in the Saints, Nicephor, Patriarch of Constantinople, A. D. 771.

d. 14. Our ven. Father Benedict, A. D. 433.

c. 15. The Martyr Agapius, and his six companions, who suffered A. D. 290.

b. 16. The Martyrs Sabinus and Papas, A. D. 292.

A. 17. Our ven. Father Alexis, the man of God, A. D. 406.

g. 18. Our Father in the Saints, Cyril, Archbishop of Jerusalem, A. D. 374.

f. 19. The Martyrs Chrysanthus and Daria, A. D. 284.

e. 20. Our ven. Fathers of the Monastery of S. Sabbas, murdered by the Saracens.

d. 21. Our Father in the Saints, James, Bp. and Confessor.

c. 22. The Priest-martyr Basil, Presbyter of the Church of Ancyra, A. D. 353.

b. 23. The Ven. Martyr Nicon, and his 200 disciples who suffered with him.

A. 24. Vigil of the Annunciation of the most holy Mother of God.

g. 25. THE ANNUNCIATION OF OUR MOST HOLY LADY, THE MOTHER OF GOD AND EVER-VIRGIN MARY.

f. 26. The Council of the Archangel Gabriel.

e. 27. The Martyr Matrona of Thessalonica.

d. 28. Our ven. Father Hilarion the New, and Stephen the Wonderworker, A. D. 832.

c. 29. Our ven. Father Mark, Bp. of Arethusa, and Cyril, Deacon, and those with them, who suffered A. D. 352.

b. 30. Our ven. Father John, writer of the work entitled, Climax of virtues, A. D. 570.

A. 31. The ven. and wonderworking Hypatius, Bp. of Gangra.

APRIL.

g. 1. Our ven. Mother Mary of Egypt, A. D. 520.

f. 2. Our ven. Father Titus the Wonderworker.

e. 3. Our ven. Father and Confessor, Nicetas, Abbot of the Monastery of Medicius, A. D. 821.

d. 4. Our ven. Fathers, Joseph the Hymnographist, and George of Malæum. Joseph was of A. D. 838.

c. 5. The Martyrs Theodulus and Agathapodus, and those with them, who suffered A. D. 300.

b. 6. Our Father in the Saints, Eutyches, Archbishop of Constantinople, A. D. 546.

A. 7. Our ven. Father George, Bp. of Melite, A. D. 850.

g. 8. The Apostles, Herodion, Agabus, Rufus, Asyncritus, Phlegon and Hermes, and those with them.

f. 9. The Martyr Eupsychius, A. D. 353.

e. 10. The Martyrs, Terence, Africanus, Maximus, Pompey, and 36 others, A. D. 255.

d. 11. The Priest-martyr Antypas, Bp. of Pergamus in Asia, A. D. 85.

c. 12. Our Father in the Saints, Basil, Bp. and Confessor of Parium, A. D. 736.

b. 13. The Priest-martyr Artemon, A. D. 290.

A. 14. Our Father in the Saints and Confessor, Martin, Pope of Rome, A. D. 645. And the Martyrs, Antony, John and Eustace of Vilna, A. D. 1342.

g. 15. The Apostles, Aristarchus, Pudens and Trophimus, who suffered A. D. 69.

f. 16. The Martyrs, Agapia, Irene and Chionia, A. D. 296.

e. 17. Our Father in the Saints, Simeon, Bp. of Persia, who suffered A. D. 343. And our Father in the Saints, Acacius, Bp. of Melite, A. D. 415.

d. 18. Our ven. Father John, disciple of Gregory of Decapolis, A. D. 849.

c. 19. Our ven. Father John of the Old Caves.

b. 20. Our ven. Father Theodore Trichinas.

A. 21. The Priest-martyr Januarius, Bp. and the Deacons, Proculus, Faustus, and the rest, who suffered A. D. 305. And the Priest-martyr Theodore of Pergia, A. D. 141.

g. 22. Our ven. Father Theodore Syceotes, A. D. 541.

f. 23. *The glorious Gt. Martyr and victorious Wonderworker George.*

e. 24. The Martyr Sabbas the General, A. D. 278.

d. 25. *The Ap. and Evangelist Mark, who suffered A. D. 64.*

c. 26. The Priest-martyr Basil, Bp. of Amasia, A. D. 320.

b. 27. The Priest-martyr Simeon, the Lord's kinsman, A. D. 109.

A. 28. The Apostles Jason and Sosipater.

g. 29. The 9 Martyrs of Cysicum.

f. 30. *The Apostle James, the brother of John the Divine.*

MAY.

e. 1. The Prophet Jeremias.

d. 2. Our Father in the Saints, Athanasius the Gt., Patriarch of Alexandria, A. D. 362.

c. 3. The Martyrs Timothy and Maura. *And the Decease of our ven. Father, Theodosius, Abbot of the Monastery of Pechersky and Founder of Community Life in the land of Russia, A. D. 1082.*

b. 4. The Martyr Pelagia, A. D. 288.

A. 5. The glorious Martyr Irene, A. D. 315.

g. 6. The righteous and much afflicted Job.

f. 7. The Commemoration of the apparition in the heavens of the sign of the honourable Cross at Jerusalem, A. D. 346.

e. 8. THE GLORIOUS AND ALL-PRAISED APOSTLE AND EVANGELIST, THE BELOVED VIRGIN, JOHN THE DIVINE.

d. 9. The Prophet Esaias. And the Martyr Christopher, A. D. 256. *And the Translation of the honourable Relics of our Father in the Saints Nicolas the Wonderworker from Myra to the city of Bari, A. D. 1096.*

c. 10. *The Apostle Simon Zelotes.*

b. 11. The Priest-martyr Mocius, A. D. 288.

A. 12. Our Fathers in the Saints, Epiphanius, Bp. of Cyprus, and Germanus, Patriarch of Constantinople. The former, A. D. 402, and the latter, A. D. 730.

g. 13. The Martyr Glyceria, A. D. 141.

f. 14. The Martyr Isidore of Chios, who suffered A. D. 251.

e. 15. Our ven. Father Pachomius the Great, A. D. 323.

d. 16. Our ven. Father Theodore the Sanctified, disciple of Pachomius.

c. 17. The Apostle Andronicus, and Junia, and those with them.

b. 18. The Martyr Theodotus of Ancyra. And the Martyrs, Peter, Dionysius, Andrew, Paul, Christina, Hercules, Paulinus and Benedimus. And the seven Virgins, Alexandra, Thecusa, Claudia, Phauna, Euphrasia, Matrona and Julia.

A. 19. The Priest-martyr Patrick, Bp. of Prusa, and his companions.

g. 20. The Martyr Thalaleus, and those with him, who suffered A. D. 284.

f. 21. *The great Sovereigns and equals of the Apostles, Constantine and Helen.*

e. 22. The Martyr Basiliscus, A. D. 307.

d. 23. Our Father in the Saints, Michael, Bp. and Confessor of Synnada, A. D. 833.

c. 24. Our ven. Father Simeon of the hill of marvels, A. D. 584.

b. 25. *The Third Invention of the Head of the Forerunner.*

A. 26. The Apostle Carpus, one of the Seventy.

g. 27. The Priest-martyr Therapontus, A. D. 259.

f. 28. Our ven. Father Nicetas, Bp. of Chalcedon, A. D. 836. The 318 holy Fathers of the 1st. Synod.

e. 29. The Ven. Martyr Theodosia, Virgin, who suffered A. D. 305.

d. 30. Our ven. Father Isaac, of the Monastery of Dalmatia, A. D. 374.

33

c. 31. The Apostle Hermes. And the Martyr Hermes, A. D. 141.

JUNE.

b. 1. The Martyr Justin the Philosopher, and another Martyr Justin, who suffered A. D. 142.

A. 2. Our Father in the Saints, Nicephor, Patriarch of Constantinople, A. D. 844. *And the Gt. Martyr, John of Belgrade, A. D. 1492.*

g. 3. The Martyr Lucillian, and those with him, Claudius, Hypatius, Paul and Dionysius, A. D. 278.

f. 4. Our Father in the Saints, Metrophanes, Patriarch of Constantinople, A. D. 307.

e. 5. The Priest-martyr Dorotheus, Bp. of Tyre, A. D. 352.

d. 6. Our ven. Father Besarion the Wonderworker, A. D. 466. And our ven. Father Hilarion the New, of the Monastery of Dalmatia, A. D. 864.

c. 7. The Priest-martyr Theodotus, Bp. of Ancyra.

b. 8. The Gt. Martyr Theodore the General.

A. 9. Our Father in the Saints, Cyril, Archbp. of Alexandria, A. D. 415.

g. 10. The Priest-martyr Timothy, Bp. of Prusa, A. D. 362.

f. 11. *The Apostles Bartholomew and Barnabas.*

e. 12. *Our ven. Father Onyphrius, A. D.* 345. And our ven. Father Peter of Athos.

d. 13. The Martyr Aquilina. And Triphyllius, Bp. of Cyprus.

c. 14. The Prophet Elissæus. And our Father in the Saints, Methodius, Patriarch of Constantinople, A. D. 865.

b. 15. The Prophet Amos.

A. 16. The wonderworking Tychon, Bp. of Amathus, A. D. 854.

g. 17. The Martyrs, Manuel, Sabel and Ismael of Persia, A. D. 362.

f. 18. The Martyr Leontius, A. D. 73.

e. 19. *The Apostle Jude, the Lord's Brother.*

d. 20. The Priest-martyr Methodius, Bp. of Patara, A. D. 275.

c. 21. The Martyr Julian of Tarsus.

b. 22. The Priest-martyr Eusebius, Bp. of Samosata, A. D. 360.

A. 23. The Martyr Agrippina, A. D. 275.

g. 24. THE NATIVITY OF THE HONOURABLE, GLORIOUS PROPHET, FORERUNNER, AND BAPTIST, JOHN.

f. 25. The Ven. Martyr Febronia, A. D. 286.

e. 26. Our ven. Father David of Thessalonica.

d. 27. Our ven. Father Sampson, the entertainer of strangers, A. D. 541.

c. 28. The Translation of the Relics of the unmercenary Wonderworkers, Cyrus and John, A. D. 400.

b. 29. THE GLORIOUS AND ALL-PRAISED LEADERS OF THE APOSTLES, PETER AND PAUL.

A. 30. *The Council of the glorious and all-praised 12 Apostles.*

JULY.

g. 1. The unmercenary Wonderworkers, Cosmas and Damian, who suffered A. D. 284.

f. 2. The Deposition of the honourable Robe of the Mother of God at Blachernæ, A. D. 454.

e. 3. The Martyr Hyacinth, A. D. 108.

d. 4. Our Father in the Saints, Andrew, Archbp. of Crete, the Jerusalemite, A. D. 686. And the ven. Martha, mother of S. Simeon of the hill of marvels.

c. 5. *Our ven. Father Athanasius of Athos, A. D. 988.*

b. 6. Our ven. Father Sisoes the Gt.

A. 7. Our ven. Fathers, Thomas of Maleum, and Acacius, who testified to the Climax.

g. 8. The Gt. Martyr Procopius.

f. 9. The Priest-martyr Pancratius, Bp. of Tauromenia.

e. 10. The 45 Martyrs of Nicopolis in

Armenia, who suffered A. D. 317. *And the Commemoration of our ven. Father, Antony of Pechersky, which is at Kiev, who became the Head of all Russian Monks.*

d. 11. The Martyr, the greatly esteemed Euphemia, called, The Landmark of the Fathers, who suffered A. D. 288. And the Decease of the blessed Olga, Princess of Russia, called in holy Baptism, Helen, A. D. 976.

c. 12. The Martyrs Proclus and Hilary, A. D. 106. And our ven. Father Michael Malenna, A. D. 931.

b. 13. *The Council of the Archangel Gabriel.* And our ven. Father Stephen the Sabbaite.
> Sunday of holy Fathers of the first Six Synods.

A. 14. The Apostle Aquilas, A. D. 65.

g. 15. The Martyrs Cyriacus and Julitta, who suffered A. D. 296. *And the equal of the Apostles, the Gt. Prince Vladimir, called in holy Baptism, Basil, who passed away A. D. 1015.*

f. 16. The Priest-martyr Athenogenes, and his 10 disciples, who suffered A. D. 296.

e. 17. The Gt. Martyr Marina, A. D. 270.

d. 18. The Martyr Hyacinth of Amastrida. And the Martyr Emilian, A. D. 351.

c. 19. Our ven. Mother Macrina, the sister of the great Basil, A. D. 380. And our ven. Father Dius, A. D. 384.

b. 20. *The glorious Prophet Elias.*

A. 21. Our ven. Father Simeon, for Christ's sake mad, and his co-ascetic, John, A. D. 508. And the Prophet Iezekiel.

g. 22. The Myrrh-bearer and equal of the Apostles, Mary Magdalene. And the Recovery of the Relics of the Priest-martyr Phocas.

f. 23. The Martyrs Trophimus and Theophilus, and those with them, A. D. 296.

e. 24. The Martyr Christina, A. D. 200. *And the Martyrs Boris and Gleb, called in holy Baptism, Roman and David.*

d. 25. *The Repose of Anna, the mother of the most holy Mother of God.*

c. 26. The Priest-martyr Hermolaus, and those with him, Hermippus and Hermocrates, who suffered A. D. 304.

b. 27. *The Gt. Martyr and Physician, Pantelimon*, A. D. 304.

A. 28. The Apostles and Deacons, Prochorus, Nicanor, Timon and Parmenas.

g. 29. The Martyr Callinicus, A. D. 290.

f. 30. The Apostles, Silus and Silvanus, Crescent, Epenetus and Andronicus.

e. 31. Vigil of the Procession of the honourable Cross. And Eudocimus the Just, A. D. 808.

AUGUST.

d. 1. *The Procession of the honourable and life-effecting Cross.* And the Memory of the 7 Martyrs Maccabees, and their mother Salomone, and their teacher Eleazar.

> On this day beginneth the Fast of the Mother of God, which continueth until the 15th. of the month, the Day of her Repose.

c. 2. *The Translation of the Relics of the Proto-martyr and Archdeacon Stephen from Jerusalem to Constantinople, A. D. 312.*

b. 3. Our ven. Fathers, Isaac, Dalmatus and Faustus.

A. 4. The 7 Children of Ephesus.

g. 5. The Vigil of the Transfiguration of the Lord. And the Martyr Eusignius, A.D. 361.

f. 6. THE TRANSFIGURATION OF OUR LORD, GOD, AND SAVIOUR JESUS CHRIST.

e. 7. The Ven. Martyr Dometius, A. D. 363.

d. 8. The Confessor Emilian, Bp. of Cyzicum, A. D. 836.

c. 9. *The Apostle Matthew.*

b. 10. The Martyr and Archdeacon Laurence, A. D. 285.

A. 11. The Martyr and Archdeacon Euplus, A. D. 296.

g. 12. The Martyrs Photius and Anicetus, who suffered A. D. 288.

f. 13. Our ven. Father and Confessor Maximus, A. D. 655.

His Office is sung on the 12th., to-day being the Octave of the Transfiguration of the Lord.

e. 14. Vigil of the Repose of the most holy Mother of God. And the Prophet Michæus. *And the Translation of the honourable Relics of our ven. Father Theodosius, Abbot of Pechersky, A. D.* 1091.

d. 15. THE REPOSE OF OUR MOST HOLY LADY, THE GOD-BEARING EVER-VIRGIN MARY.

c. 16. *The Translation from Edessa to Constantinople of the Image not made by hands of our Lord Jesus Christ, called, The Holy Kerchief, A. D.* 908.

b. 17. The Martyr Myron, A. D. 255.

A. 18. The Martyrs Florus and Laurus, A. D. 320.

g. 19. The Martyr Andrew the General. and with him 2593 others, A. D. 304.

f. 20. The Prophet Samuel.

e. 21. The Apostle Thaddæus. And the Martyr Bassa, and her children, Theognius, Agapius, and Pistus.

d. 22. The Martyr Agathonicus, and those with him, Zoticus, Theoprepius, Acindinus and Severian.

c. 23. The Martyr Luppus.

His Office is sung on the 22nd., for to-day is the Octave of the Festival of the Repose of the most holy Mother of God.

b. 24. The Priest-martyr Eutyches, disciple of John the Diyine. And the Translation of the honourable Relics of our Father in the Saints, Peter, Metropolitan of Kiev and Wonderworker of All Russia, A. D. 1471.

A. 25. The Recovery of the Relics of the Apostle Bartholomew. And the Memory of the Apostle Titus.

g. 26. The Martyrs Adrian and Natalia, A. D. 304.

f. 27. Our ven. Father Poemen, A. D. 415.

e. 28. Our ven. Father Moses the Ethiopian.

d. 29. THE BEHEADING OF THE HONOUR-ABLE, GLORIOUS PROPHET, FORERUNNER, AND BAPTIST, JOHN.

c. 30. Our Fathers in the Saints, the Patriarchs of Constantinople, Alexander, John and Paul.

b. 31. *The Deposition of the honourable Girdle of the most holy Mother of God at Constantinople*, A. D. 908.

XXX. AN ALMANACK FOR FIFTY YEARS,

FROM A. D. 1891 TO A. D. 1940.

A. M.	A. D.	Indict.	Cycle of the Sun.	Cycle of the Moon.	Dominical Letter.	The Triodion beginneth,	Pascha.
7399	1891	4	7	8	A	Feb. 10.	Apl. 21.
7400	1892	5	8	9	C	Jan. 26.	Apl. 5.
7401	1893	6	9	10	D	Jan. 17.	Mch. 28.
7402	1894	7	10	11	E	Feb. 6.	Apl. 17.
7403	1895	8	11	12	F	Jan. 22.	Apl. 2.
7404	1896	9	12	13	A	Jan. 14.	Mch. 24.
7405	1897	10	13	14	B	Feb. 2.	Apl. 13.
7406	1898	11	14	15	C	Jan. 25.	Apl. 5.
7407	1899	12	15	16	D	Feb. 7.	Apl. 18.
7408	1900	13	16	17	F	Jan. 30.	Apl. 9.
7409	1901	14	17	18	G	Jan. 21.	Apl. 1.

A. M.	A. D.	Indict.	Cycle of the Sun.	Cycle of the Moon.	Dominical Letter.	The Triodion beginneth,	Pascha.
7410	1902	15	18	19	A	Feb. 3.	Apl. 14.
7411	1903	1	19	1	B	Jan. 26.	Apl. 6.
7412	1904	2	20	2	D	Jan. 18.	Mch. 28.
7413	1905	3	21	3	E	Feb. 6.	Apl. 17.
7414	1906	4	22	4	F	Jan. 22.	Apl. 2.
7415	1907	5	23	5	G	Feb. 11.	Apl. 22.
7416	1908	6	24	6	B	Feb. 3.	Apl. 13.
7417	1909	7	25	7	C	Jan. 18.	Mch. 29.
7418	1910	8	26	8	D	Feb. 7.	Apl. 18.
7419	1911	9	27	9	E	Jan. 30.	Apl. 10.
7420	1912	10	28	10	G	Jan. 15.	Mch. 25.
7421	1913	11	1	11	A	Feb. 3.	Apl. 14.
7422	1914	12	2	12	B	Jan. 26	Apl. 6.
7423	1915	13	3	13	C	Jan. 11.	Mch. 22.
7424	1916	14	4	14	E	Jan. 31.	Apl. 10.
7425	1917	15	5	15	F	Jan. 22.	Apl. 2.
7426	1918	1	6	16	G	Feb. 11.	Apl. 22.
7427	1919	2	7	17	A	Jan. 27.	Apl. 7.
7428	1920	3	8	18	C	Jan. 19.	Mch. 29.
7429	1921	4	9	19	D	Feb. 7.	Apl. 18.
7430	1922	5	10	1	E	Jan. 23.	Apl. 3.
7431	1923	6	11	2	F	Jan. 15.	Mch. 26.
7432	1924	7	12	3	A	Feb. 4.	Apl. 14.
7433	1925	8	13	4	B	Jan. 26.	Apl. 6.
7434	1926	9	14	5	C	Feb. 8.	Apl. 19.

A. M.	A. D.	Indict.	Cycle of the Sun.	Cycle of the Moon.	Dominical Letter.	The Triodion beginneth,	Pascha.
7435	1927	10	15	6	D	Jan. 31.	Apl. 11.
7436	1928	11	16	7	F	Jan. 23.	Apl. 2.
7437	1929	12	17	8	G	Feb. 11.	Apl. 22.
7438	1930	13	18	9	A	Jan. 27.	Apl. 7.
7439	1931	14	19	10	B	Jan. 19.	Mch. 30.
7440	1932	15	20	11	D	Feb. 8.	Apl. 18.
7441	1933	1	21	12	E	Jan. 23.	Apl. 3.
7442	1934	2	22	13	F	Jan. 15.	Mch. 26.
7443	1935	3	23	14	G	Feb. 4.	Apl. 15.
7444	1936	4	24	15	B	Jan. 20.	Mch. 30.
7445	1937	5	25	16	C	Feb. 8.	Apl. 19.
7446	1938	6	26	17	D	Jan. 31.	Apl. 11.
7447	1939	7	27	18	E	Jan. 16.	Mch. 27.
7448	1940	8	28	19	G	Feb. 5.	Apl. 15.

FINIS.